IMAGES of America

CLINTON COUNTY

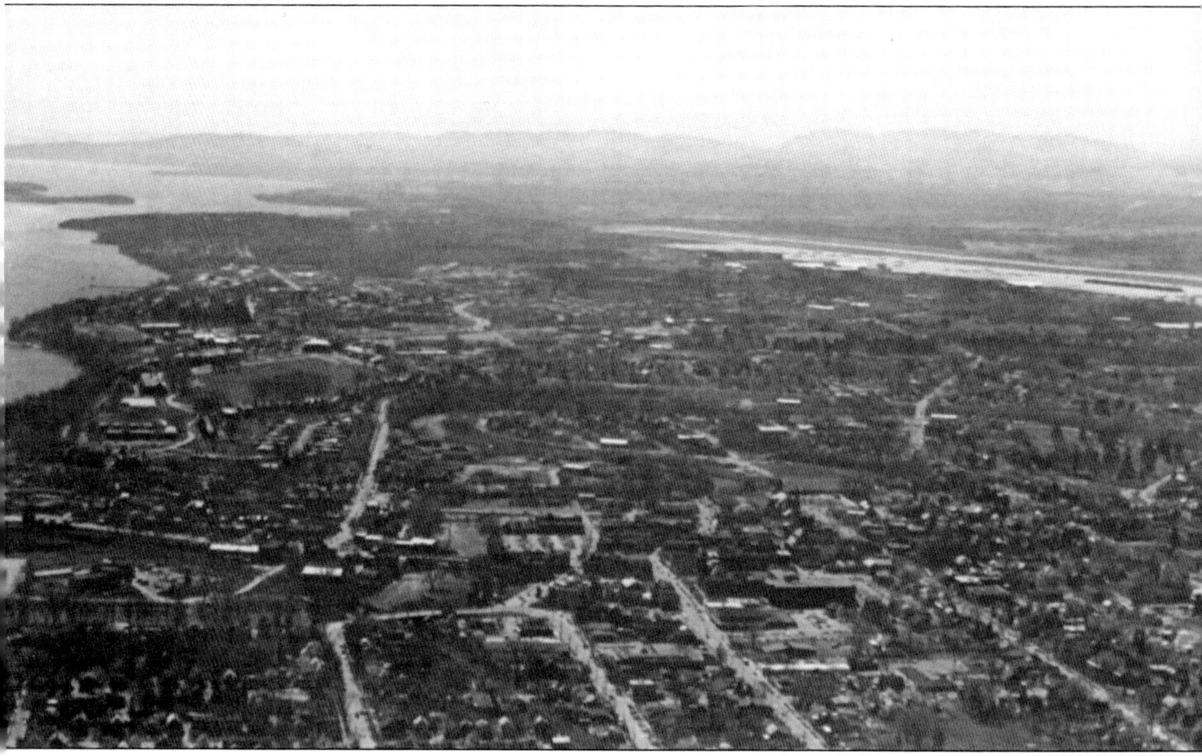

This 1981 aerial photograph of Plattsburgh looks to the south. Besides offering a vision of the city's layout, the image captures the proximity of Lake Champlain and the Adirondack Mountains. Both geographic features shaped life in Clinton County by offering transportation, protection from storms, natural resources, and opportunities for recreation. (Courtesy of the Clinton County Historian's Office.)

On the Cover: Every year, local farmers had to hire a crew or band together to thresh the grains grown on their farms. This image, taken at Samuel Howe's farm in Beekmantown, shows, from left to right, Bill Howe, Ed Stuvell, Sam Howe, ? McCaffery, Jim Graves, Chetty Geores, James Howe, and Ruth Howe, all standing in front of the barn. (Courtesy of the Clinton County Historian's Office.)

IMAGES
of America

CLINTON COUNTY

Anastasia L. Pratt

ARCADIA
PUBLISHING

ISBN 978-0-7385-7370-0

Published by Arcadia Publishing
Charleston, South Carolina

Printed in the United States of America

Library of Congress Control Number: 2010925881

For all general information, please contact Arcadia Publishing:
Telephone 843-853-2070
Fax 843-853-0044
E-mail sales@arcadiapublishing.com
For customer service and orders:
Toll-Free 1-888-313-2665

Visit us on the Internet at www.arcadiapublishing.com

To my family

Contents

ACKNOWLEDGMENTS

Clinton County's commitment to culture and history extends far beyond the four walls of my office and dates from long before my 2008 appointment as Clinton County historian. Though I cannot personally thank every person who has donated materials, volunteered to work in the archives, promoted historical events, or joined together to celebrate this region, I admire all of them. Thank you for recognizing the value of our history.

I am grateful to the people of Clinton County and the Clinton County legislature for entrusting me to do this job. The past continues to inform my life in a very real way, reinforced by the wealth of their archives. All images appear courtesy of the Clinton County Historian's Office.

Thank you, as well, to my family for their love and support.

INTRODUCTION

In 1609, Samuel de Champlain traveled along Lake Champlain in the area now known as Clinton County, New York. Over the course of his journeys, he noted the beauty of the lake to the east and the mountains to the south and cataloged a wide variety of animals, fish, and plants found in this region. Champlain's observations, already understood by the Algonkian Indians who used this region as a hunting ground, eventually led to the settlement of Clinton County, with French colonists moving in from the north and English colonists settling in the southern portion.

According to local legend, Jean Laframboise, a French farmer in Chazy, and William Gilliland, an English businessman in South Plattsburgh, were the first permanent settlers of the county. However, a host of others also helped to settle the county by moving here temporarily or permanently, helping to clear the land of trees and rocks and then working the land to establish an agricultural community. Due to their hard work, the county entered an industrial era, logging and manufacturing potash that could be used as fertilizer or as an ingredient in soap and glass.

By 1775, the county was a fairly active place, and Lake Champlain was a bustling trade corridor that attracted the attention of the British in Canada and the American colonists to the south and east. On October 11, 1776, Lake Champlain became the site of a significant naval battle waged over rights to the lake. Considered one birthplace of the U.S. Navy, the Battle of Valcour pitted Benedict Arnold and the American colonists against a much larger British fleet. Although the Americans did not technically win that battle, they managed to delay the British troops until they were forced to retreat to Canada for the winter. That delay allowed the Americans to rally their forces and eventually defeat the British. With victory, peace returned to Clinton County, though the long tradition of a military presence had begun.

The Revolutionary War also brought an official status to the region. In 1788, Clinton County was created by an act of the New York State Legislature. From that time, Plattsburgh has been the county seat. Over time, the boundaries of the county have changed, with portions of Essex and Franklin Counties being carved out of Clinton County; as a result, the county's current total land area is 1,118 square miles, of which 1,039 square miles are land.

In 1806, iron ore was discovered in the county, leading to the creation of several mining towns and the increased development of many existing towns. Keeseville, Au Sable, Au Sable Forks, Black Brook, Lyon Mountain, Dannemora, and Chateaugay all mined for iron ore. In some instances, the deposits were large enough that mining continued into the 1980s. Iron ore found in Clinton County was used in several major construction projects, including the Brooklyn and Golden Gate Bridges.

Even as iron ore was being mined, war was approaching Clinton County again. Pitting the British against the Americans, the War of 1812 brought a multitude of soldiers to the region. More famous for its battles around Washington, D.C., the war required control of Lake Champlain, the major highway between New York and northern New England and the rest of the colonies. The battles at Plattsburgh—one on land and one at sea—occurred on September 11, 1848, with minor skirmishes occuring before that day. In the battles, the American forces were able to defeat the British through a series of maneuvers that capitalized on knowledge of local topography. As a result of the actions in Plattsburgh, the Americans were able to win the War of 1812 and cement their freedom as an independent country.

With the war over, residents of Clinton County were able to return to their normal lives, in which agriculture figured prominently. Farms grew apples, potatoes, and corn—all of which thrive quite well in this region—and raised cows. Together, those farms helped to feed the people of the county, supplementing the personal gardens and small animal holdings of individual households. The farms could not continue without the industries of the area, however. Mining, logging, starch production, and other businesses helped to provide more solid financial ground for the people of the county. Today, in addition to farms, Clinton County is home to many manufacturing pursuits, including companies that make medicines (WyethAyerst and Akrimax), trains (Bombardier), buses (Nova Bus), chandeliers and other lights (Schonbek), and snowmobile tracks (Camoplast).

The 1844–1845 construction of Dannemora Prison (now Clinton Correctional Facility) created another economic boon for the region. Charged with building the third prison in New York State, Ransom Cook chose a spot that was near iron ore deposits and far removed from any major transportation routes or cities. "Little Siberia," perched on Dannemora Mountain, was virtually impossible to escape. Cook's plan to put inmates to work mining iron was quickly discovered to be unprofitable, but the prison remained open and became one of New York State's maximum security prisons and a major local employer.

Even while part of the local economy was forming around prisons, social justice movements were springing up in Clinton County. Residents of the county were active in the Underground Railroad and abolitionist movements, working to transport slaves to freedom long before the Civil War started. Spurred on by the Quaker community that had founded Peru (originally known as the Quaker Union), residents joined the abolition movement, building special barns, houses, and wagons to hide runaway slaves. Echoes of that commitment to social justice still reverberate through the county, both in remembrance of those activities and in community efforts to help refugees, provide shelter and food for the homeless, and protest injustice.

At times, those protests have run counter to the relatively constant local military presence, as was the case during the Vietnam War. Home to various manned forts and training facilities through World War I, the county welcomed the Plattsburgh Air Force Base, one of the strategic air command bases, in 1954. While it was open, the base flew FB111s, B52s, B24s, B47s, and KC135s. Although the base survived several realignment and closure committees, it was closed in 1995. The former runway is now home to the Clinton County International Airport.

Among the county's more famous citizens are: Captain De Chasy, a French soldier who fought at Isle la Motte, Vermont, and for whom Chazy is named; Zephaniah Platt and his brothers, who founded Plattsburgh; Benjamin Mooers, who founded the town of Mooers after being granted the land; the Keese family, who founded Keeseville and who were active members of the Quaker Union and the local abolitionist movement; Ransom Cook, who built Dannemora Prison; John Henry Hopkins Jr., a minister who wrote "We Three Kings," the Christmas carol; Jean Arthur, an actress in the 1930s and 1940s; Rockwell Blake, a tenor who has sung in operas throughout the world; John Lloyd Young, an actor and singer who won the 2006 Tony Award for his role in *Jersey Boys*; Michael Anderson, one of the astronauts who died in the *Columbia* disaster; Jesse Boulrice, a hockey player with the Philadelphia Flyers; Dave Annable, an actor who attended college at Plattsburgh State University; and Soovin Kim, a world-renowned violinist.

One

Family Life

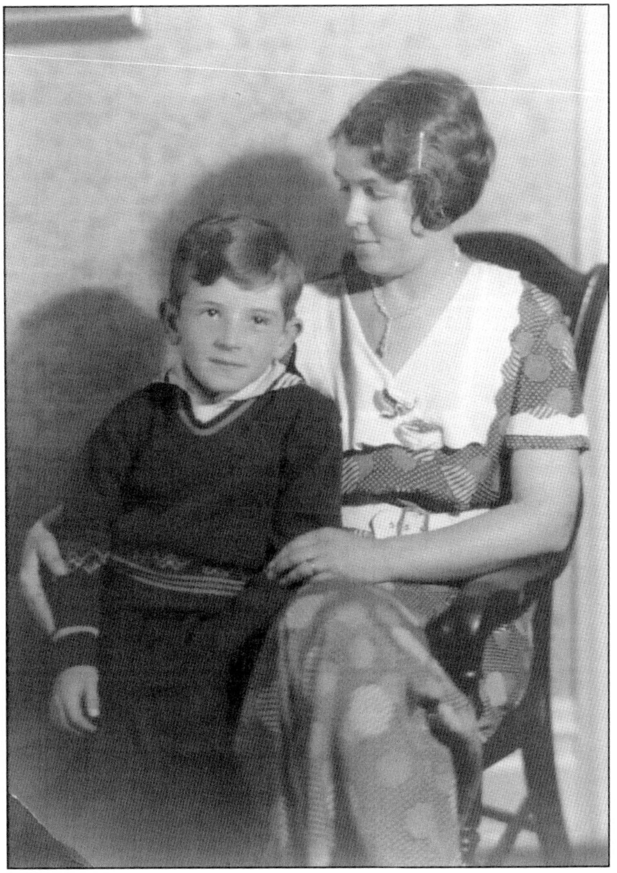

Winford Cheeseman stands in front of his mother, Maddie. The image captures the spirit of a loving relationship shared by this Ellenburg family, which also included father and husband Marshall Cheeseman. Like many other Clinton County families, the Cheesemans had a large extended family, complete with uncles, aunts, and cousins.

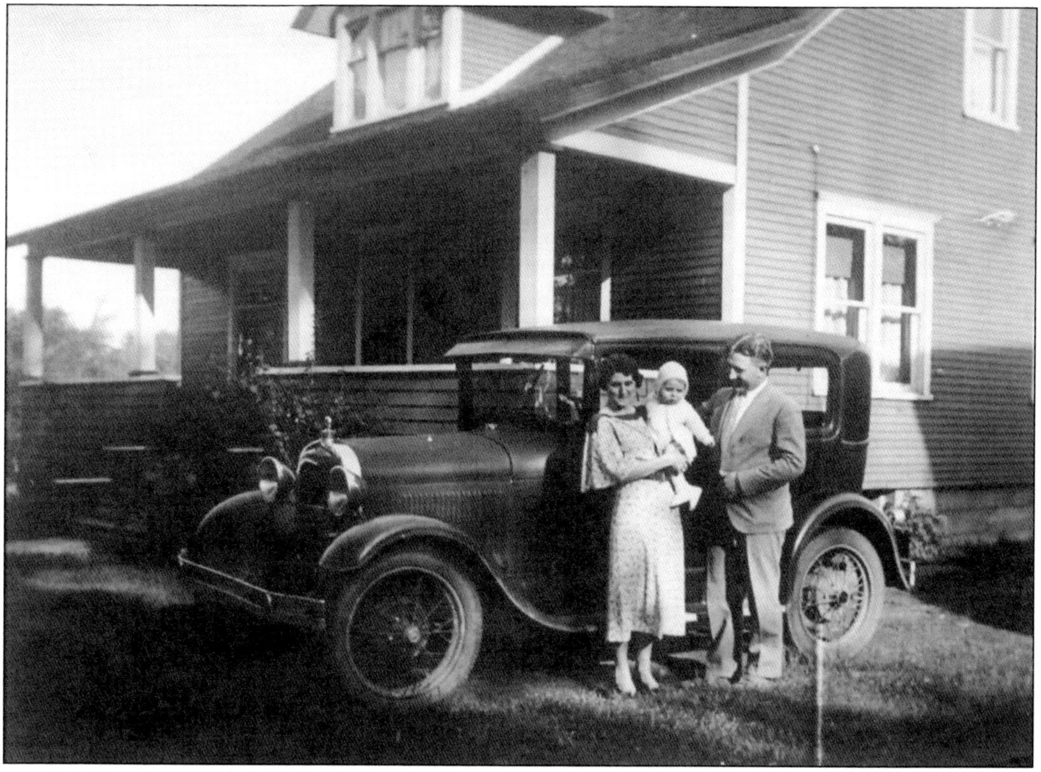

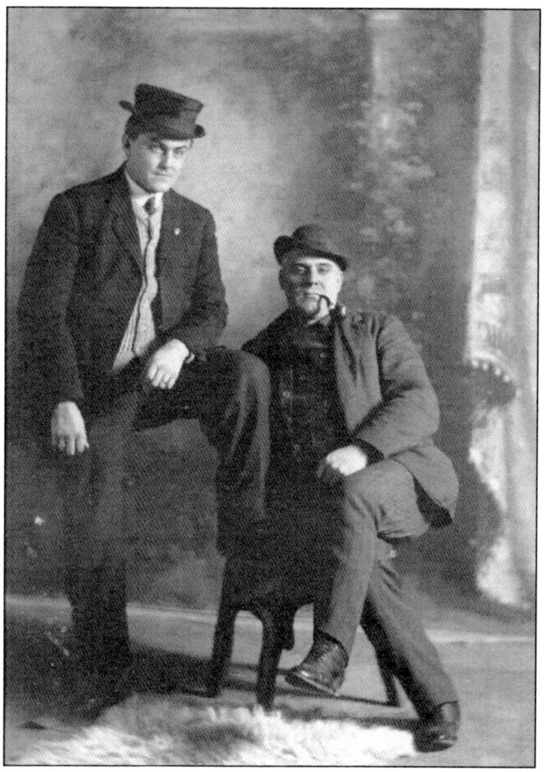

Dr. and Mrs. Harrold are shown here with their son, "Junior." While Mrs. Harrold looks directly toward the camera, Dr. Harrold looks on his family with pride. The Harrold family lived in Ellenburg.

Some surnames are incredibly common in Clinton County today and have been for the last 150 years. Trombley is one such name, though variations in spelling give rise to Trombly, Tromblee, Tremblay, Trembly, and Trembley families as well. This image of the Trombley brothers offers a whimsical pose that no doubt reflects the jaunty and hardworking nature of the two men.

Family portraits, such as this one, were produced throughout the county. In addition to displaying familial relationships, the portraits evidence the burgeoning importance of photography and the wide array of studios. Some of the studios in Clinton County were Bigelow's, Brush's, Howard and Co's, WFC LaMore's, and Savage's.

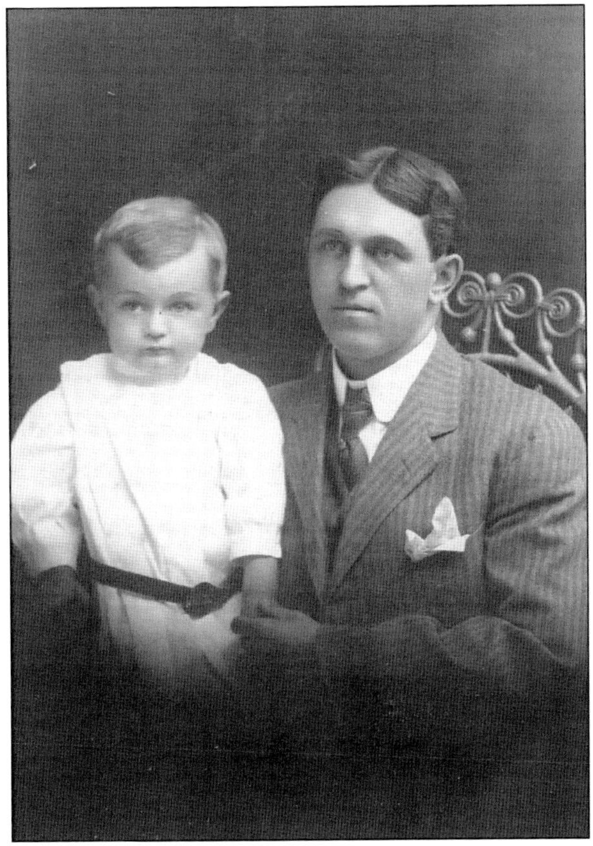

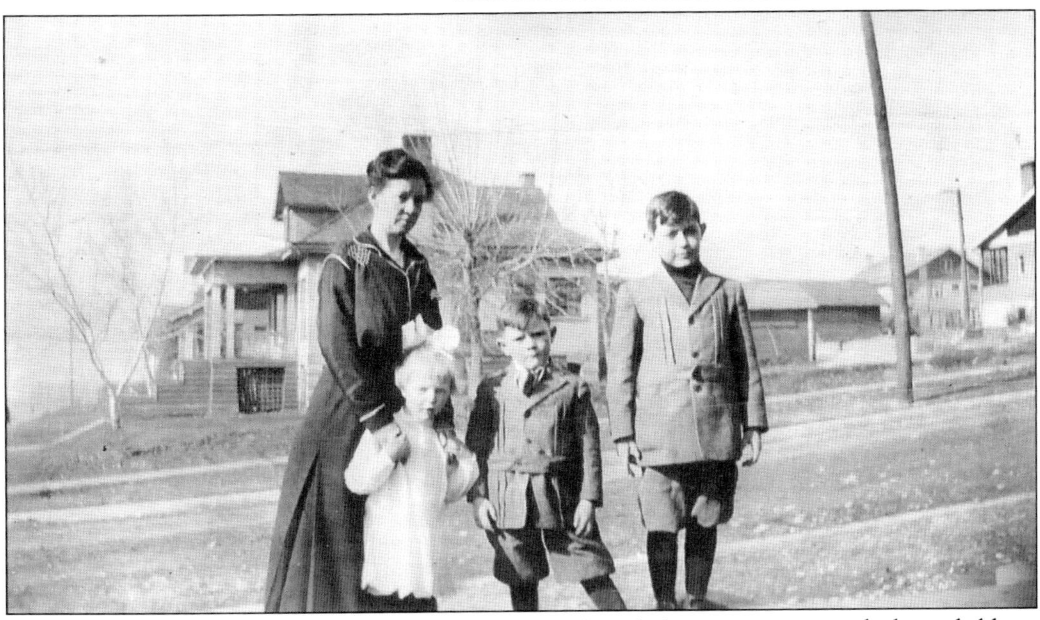

Although a candid shot, this photograph shows an unidentified woman posing with three children. The houses behind them are built relatively close together, signifying that this is not farmland. Throughout the county, families worked and played in neighborhoods like this.

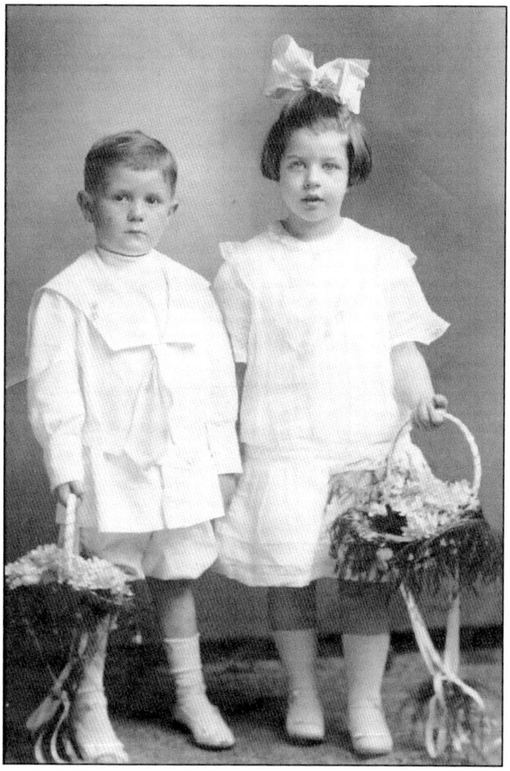

This image, labeled "Irish and Abell," shows two children who are presumably brother and sister. Of interest are the dress clothes and baskets of flowers. Unlike the candid snapshots that abound in local family albums, this photograph is clearly posed.

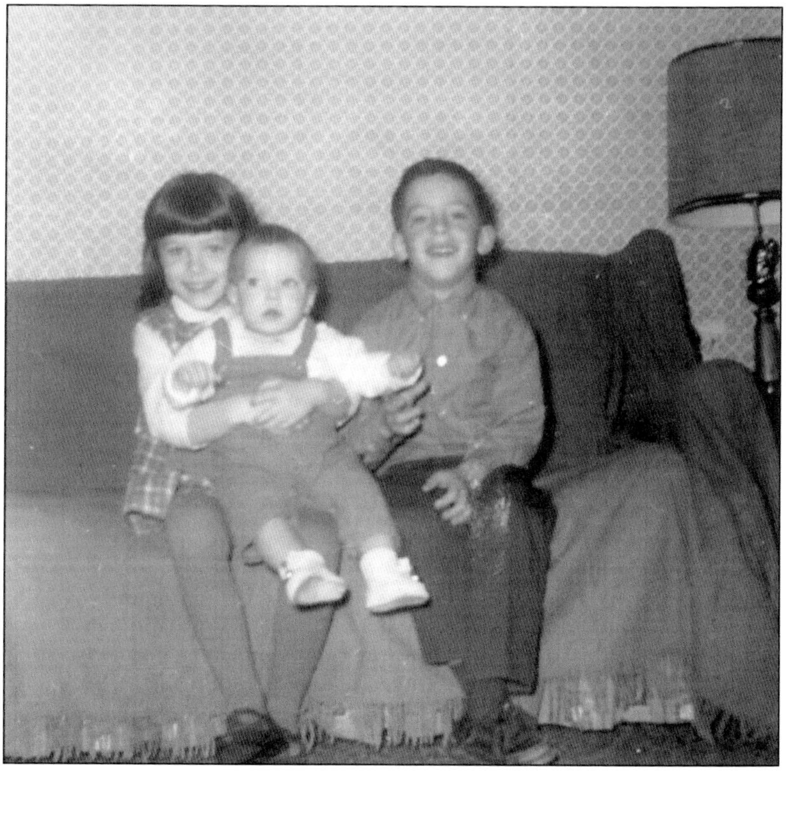

Diane (left), Teri Anne, and Ronnie Leonard are shown in Ellenburg on Christmas 1969. Notice the changed clothing and hairstyles, as well as the still posed (though less formal) image.

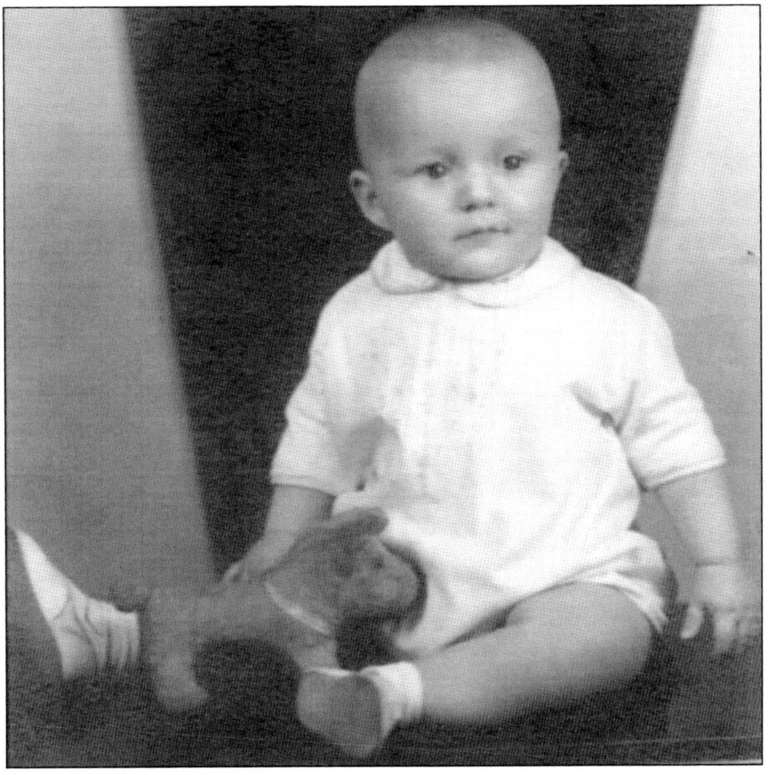

The baby in this portrait sits alongside his toy, a stuffed dog. For children throughout 18th-, 19th-, and early-20th-century Clinton County, playthings were created from handy objects. Although catalogs and general merchandise stores offered some mass-produced and marketed toys, most kids first played with handmade dolls and hand-carved objects. Leaves, cornhusks, sticks, trees, and other found objects were also used, becoming, among other things, toy guns, slingshots, forts, and brooms.

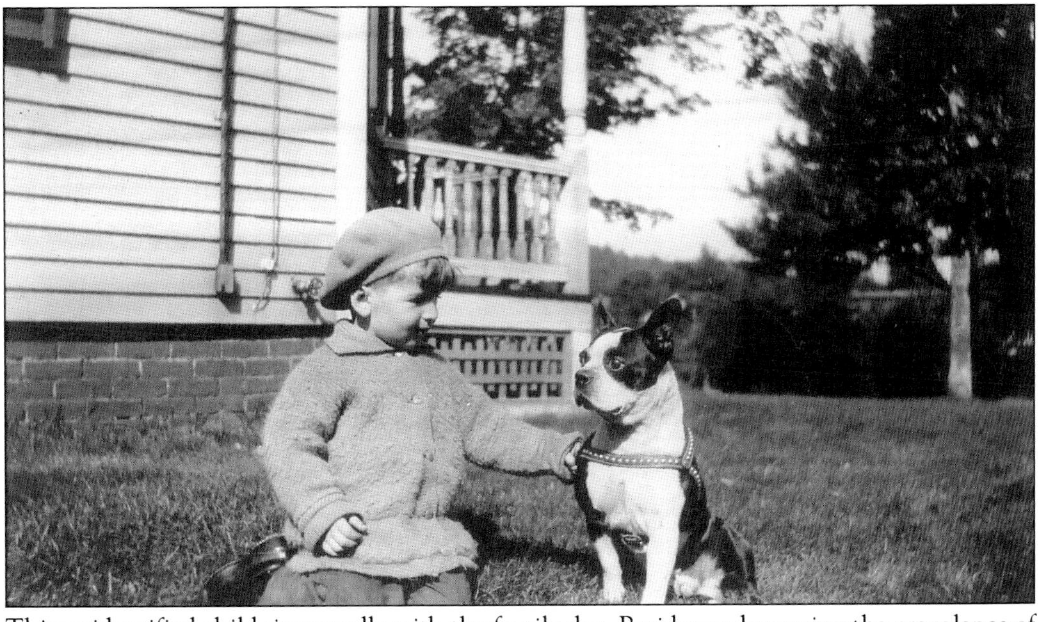

This unidentified child sits proudly with the family dog. Besides underscoring the prevalence of family pets in Clinton County, the image shows the relative comfort of this family. Notice the electrical wires running up the side of the house, the porch and manicured lawn, and the elaborate collar and harness worn by the dog.

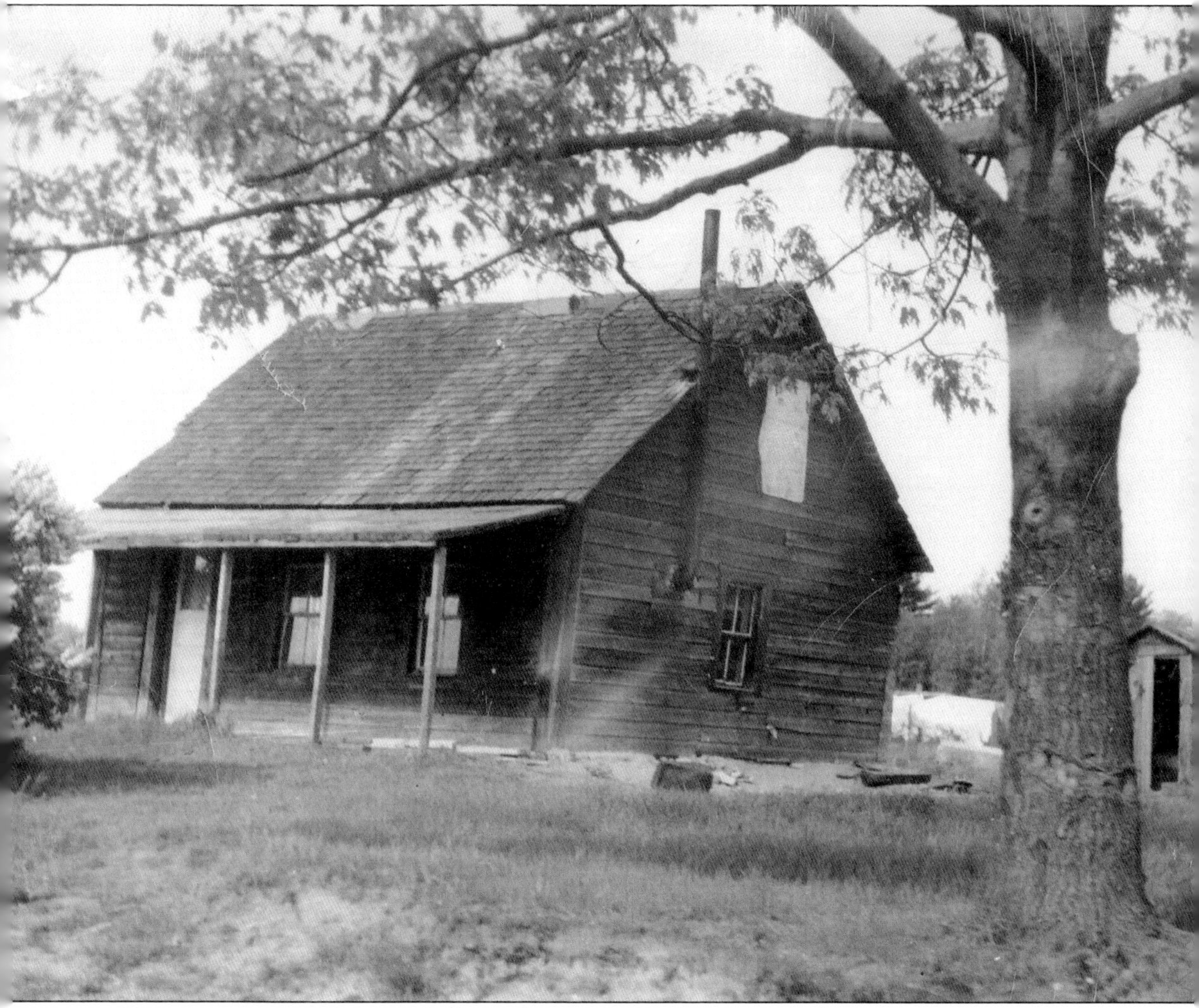

This May 20, 1949, photograph shows the standard architectural style of the county—gable ended, one-and-a-half to two-story clapboard structures. This one is located in Treadwell's Mills. Using the Saranac River as a power source, area mills generated a variety of products. In his journal, David S. Kellogg, a local doctor, wrote about his experience in a house like this: "The house was heated by a defective cooking stove in the kitchen . . . The wind blew the curtains. There were no double windows and the house itself, a thin-shelled frame house, not warm enough for a barn. But all were happy inside. The man worked at the pulp mill at Treadwell's Mills and had a fine job. He works every day, Sundays and all, but once in two weeks, while shifting from the day to the night tour, he got in an extra day by working 18 hours."

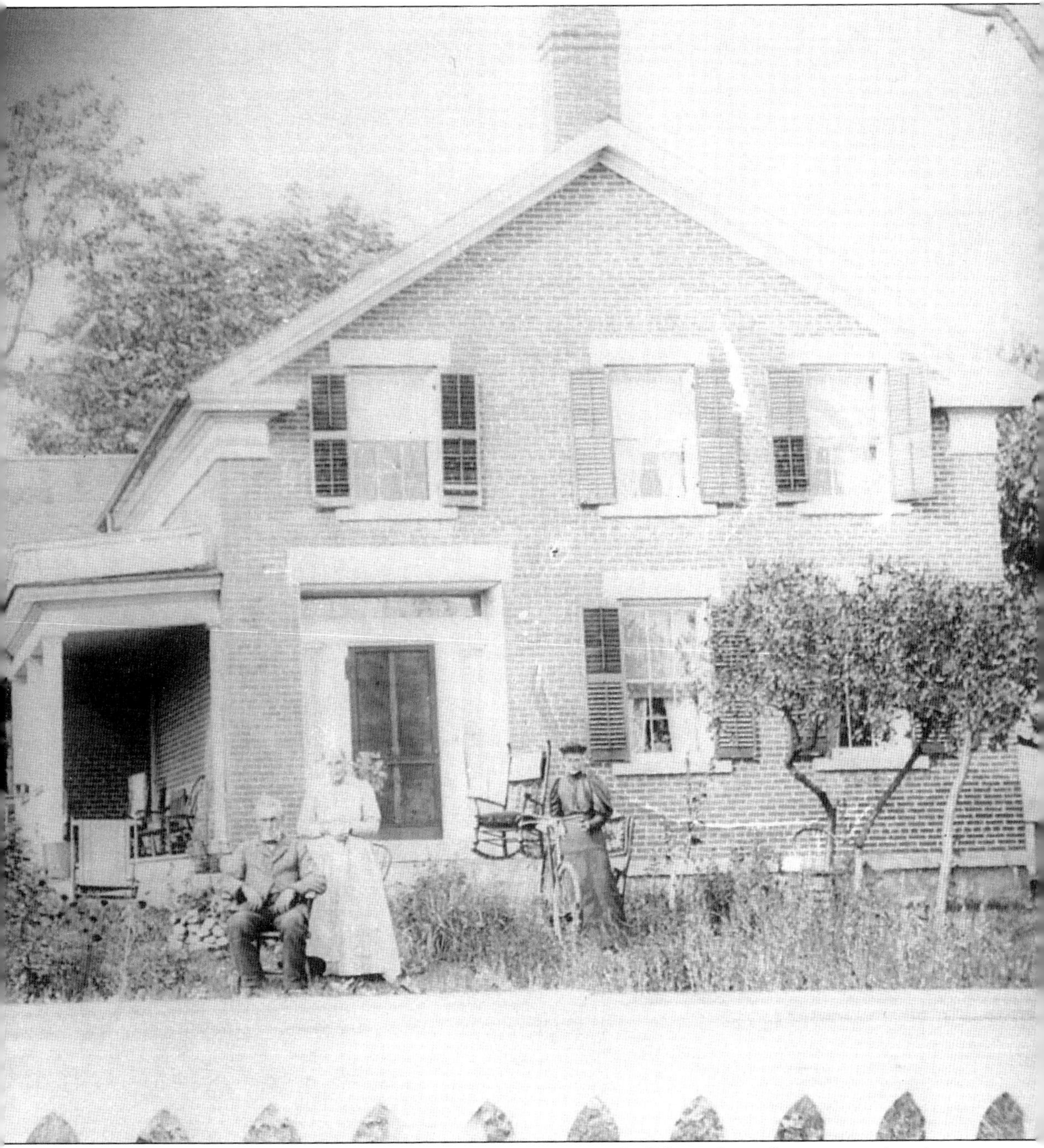

The Brand House was part of an active farm in Peru. Located off from the military turnpike, the farm grew apples in an adjacent orchard, raised dairy cows and chickens, and harvested a variety of crops in nearby fields. Photographed in the late 1800s, this house was one of some 849 brick dwellings in Clinton County, the total value of which was more than $2,115,000. Members of the Brand family showed off their skills at a variety of Clinton County's fairs. In 1893, Miss M. A. Brand received honors for the best set of lady's underclothes, the best crochet tidy, and her knit bedspread. Hiram Brand received a variety of awards for his thoroughbred cattle in successive years.

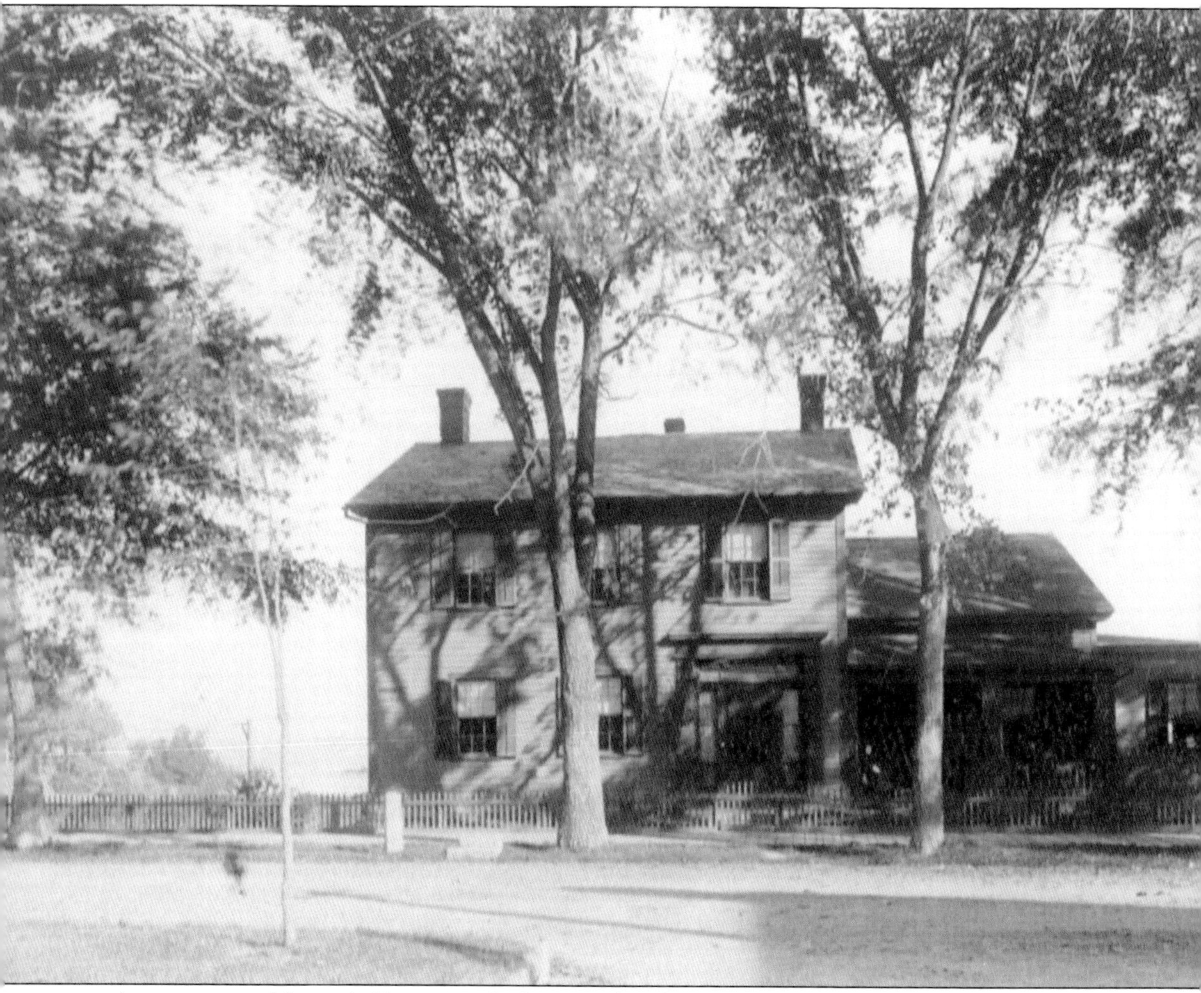

A two-story gable-roofed house with three ranks, three chimneys, and a one-story gable-roofed extension, this structure is one of 6,122 frame houses reported in Clinton County during the late 19th century. Frame houses were common because local timber resources could be milled locally to produce framing members and clapboard siding. Although wood and nails were produced locally, mass-produced alternatives were eventually brought to Clinton County from other locations. Those products, created in factories or at least on a larger scale, often lowered construction costs considerably and allowed more Clinton County residents to build houses like this one. That increase shows in local statistics from the end of the 19th century, when the county's frame houses were collectively valued at almost $4 million.

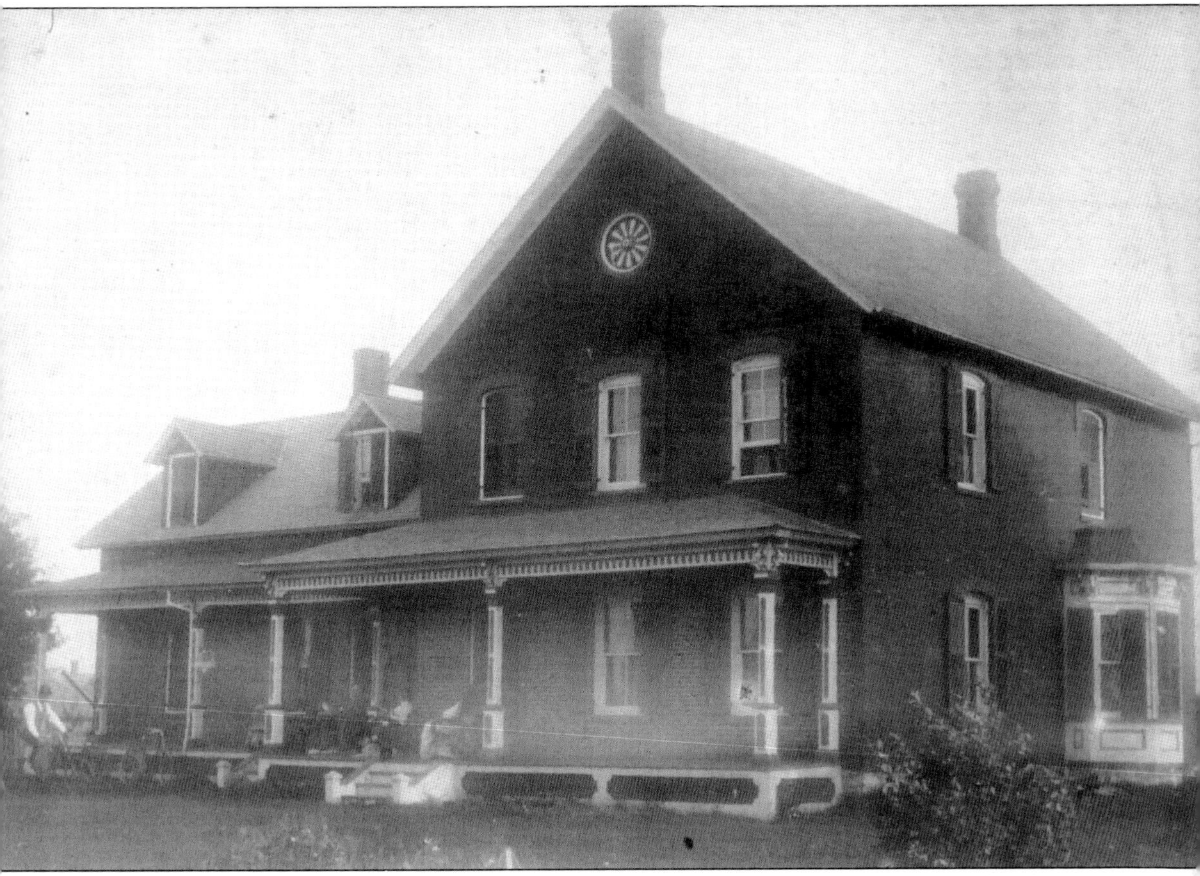

An ornamented brick, L-shaped and gable-roofed structure, the Humphrey Homestead is shown in this photograph. Shutters surround each window, corbelled caps finish off the house's three chimneys, a bay window extends from the side of the house, and gingerbread features characterize the porch's support poles and trim. That ornamentation, along with the bicycles in front of the house, emphasizes the relative wealth of the family that inhabited this structure in the Town of Clinton. The Humphreys were an active Churubusco family, with Thomas B. Humphrey serving as a notary public and as the Town of Clinton representative for the Resource Committee of the Home Defense League, H. H. Humphrey serving on the Home Defense Corps Committee of the Home Defense League, and George B. Humphrey attending the 1907 special session of the Clinton County Board of Supervisors. All three men, along with John M. Rufus Humphrey, brought the families to Chateaugay Lake for summer vacations.

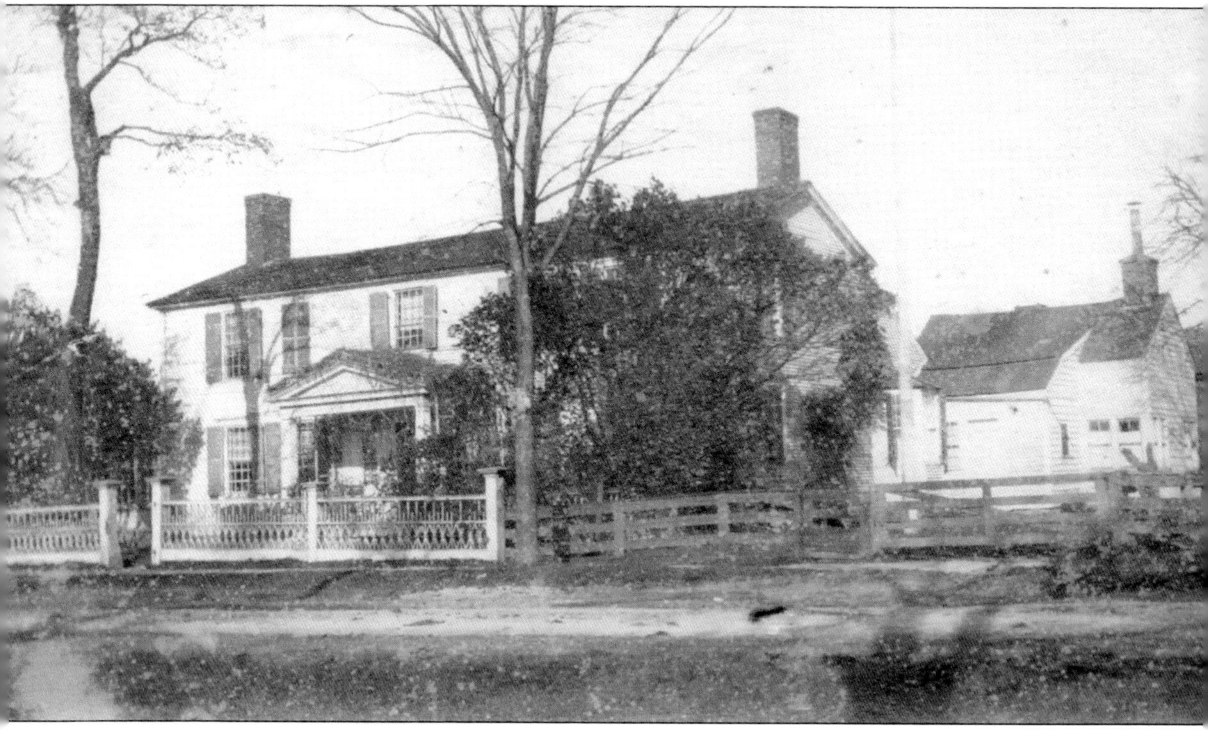

Built in 1797, the Kent-Delord House is one of Plattsburgh's oldest structures. Henry Delord and his wife, Betsy, bought and remodeled the house in 1810. Their family inhabited the dwelling until the 1913 death of Fanny Hall, the last direct descendent of the family. In addition to operating a farm, the family owned and operated the Red Store, which sold a variety of goods. During the War of 1812, Delord extended credit to soldiers; after the war, when Delord could not collect on those debts, he was financially ruined. However, the importance of the Delord family's political and social significance has long been recognized throughout the county. A push by the local Daughters of the American Revolution led to the purchase of the house in 1924 by local philanthropist William H. Miner. After receiving its absolute charter from the New York State Board of Regents to operate as a museum in 1938, the Kent-Delord House has maintained a collection of furniture, portraits, books, domestic objects, and personal possessions of the Delord family.

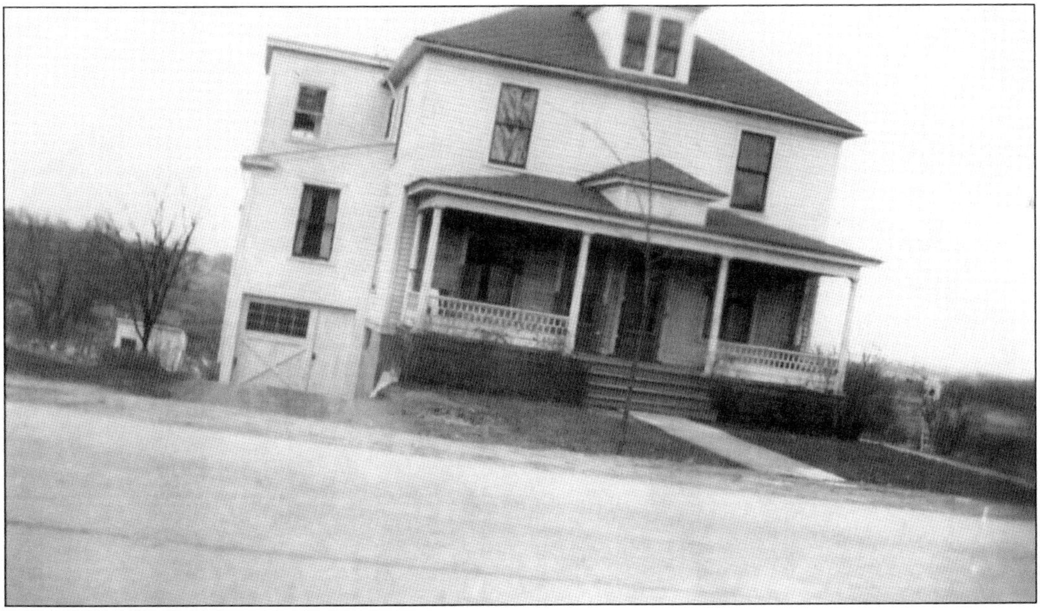

Located in Clinton, the Hazel and Fred Weil house was a two-story frame structure with a hipped roof. To the left of the house, a three-story addition rests on a fledgling garage. The dual doors visible on the front porch indicate that, at some point, the home was a duplex and housed two separate families.

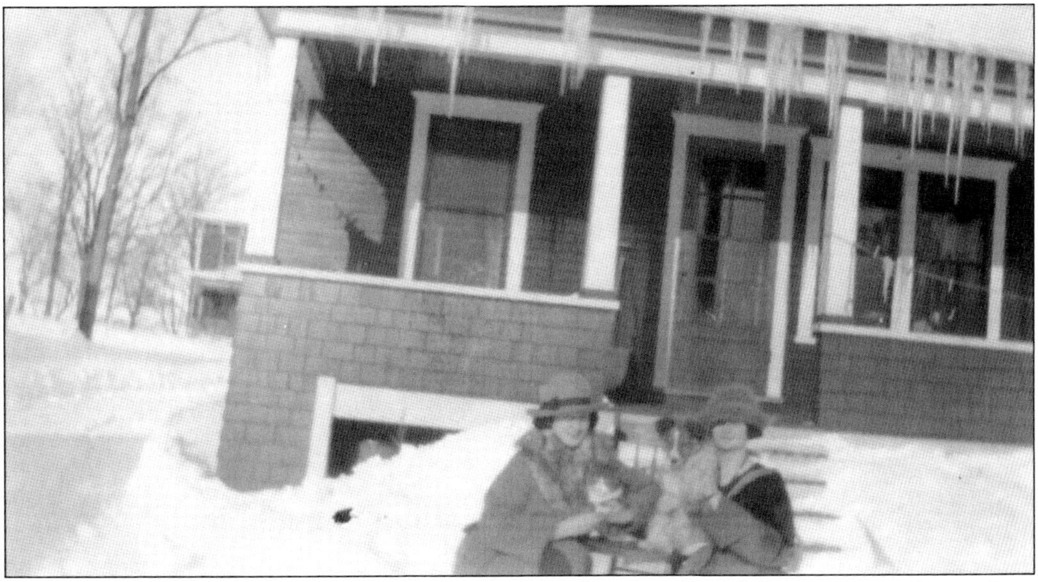

Kitty (left) and Mildred, shown here with their cat and "pup," offer a different vision of animals in Clinton County. While statistics for number and kind of farm animals exist in virtually every local census, the prevalence of domesticated animals in the county is virtually uncounted. However, family pets have been exceedingly common throughout Clinton County's history. Cats helped to keep barns and houses free of mice; dogs helped to track wild game and protect the home.

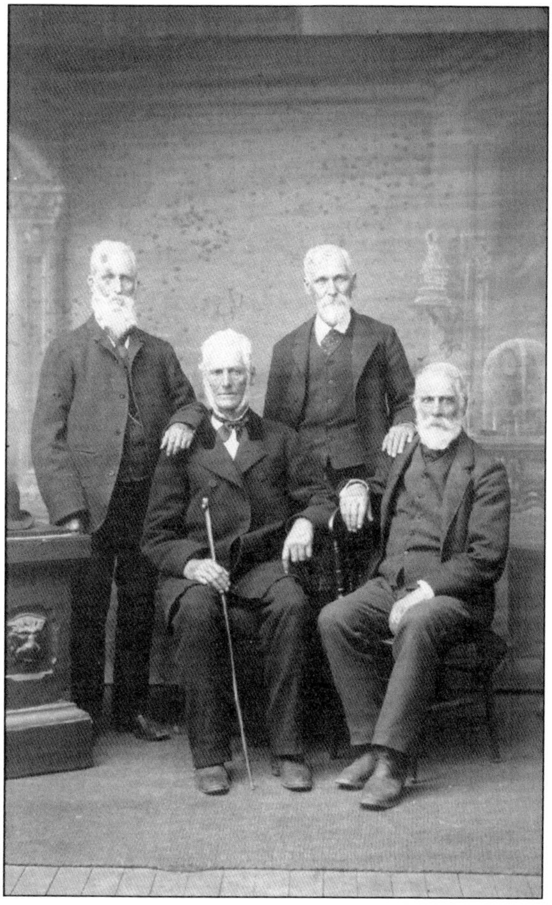

Pictured here are the sons of Henry Stratton. They are, from left to right, Cyrennus, Edward, Philander, and Jonas. John Stratton, their grandfather, was an organizing member of the Presbyterian church in Plattsburgh. He appears on the 1811 tax rolls for the town of Plattsburgh as the owner of 187 acres, with $900 in real estate and $190 in personal estate; Stratton's tax bill that year was $3.60.

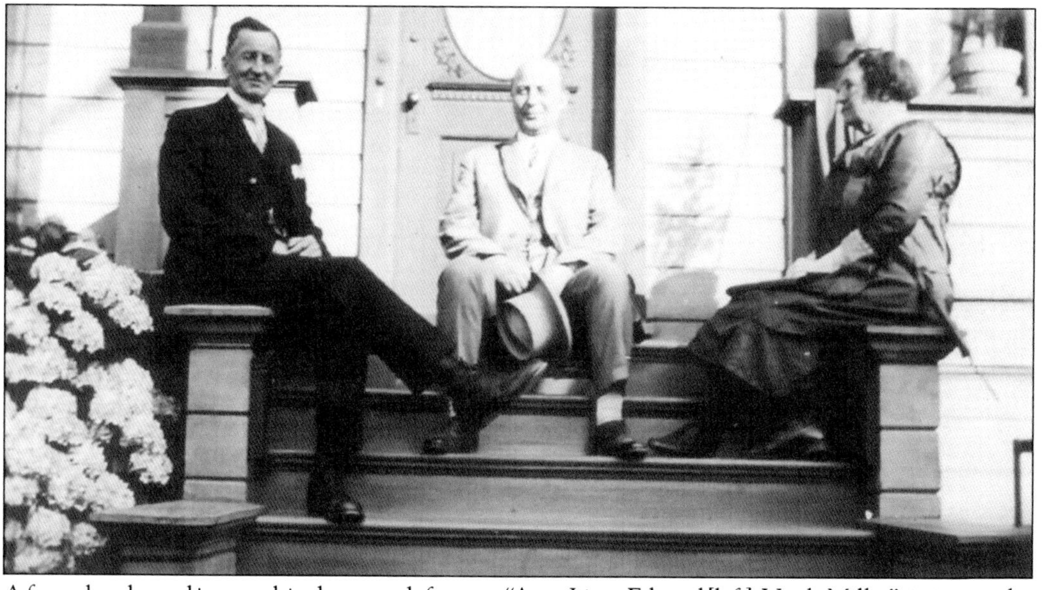

A formal and posed image, this photograph features "Aunt Lizze, Edward [left], Uncle Miller" sitting on the front steps of their home. The elaborate door indicates that the family was relatively well off.

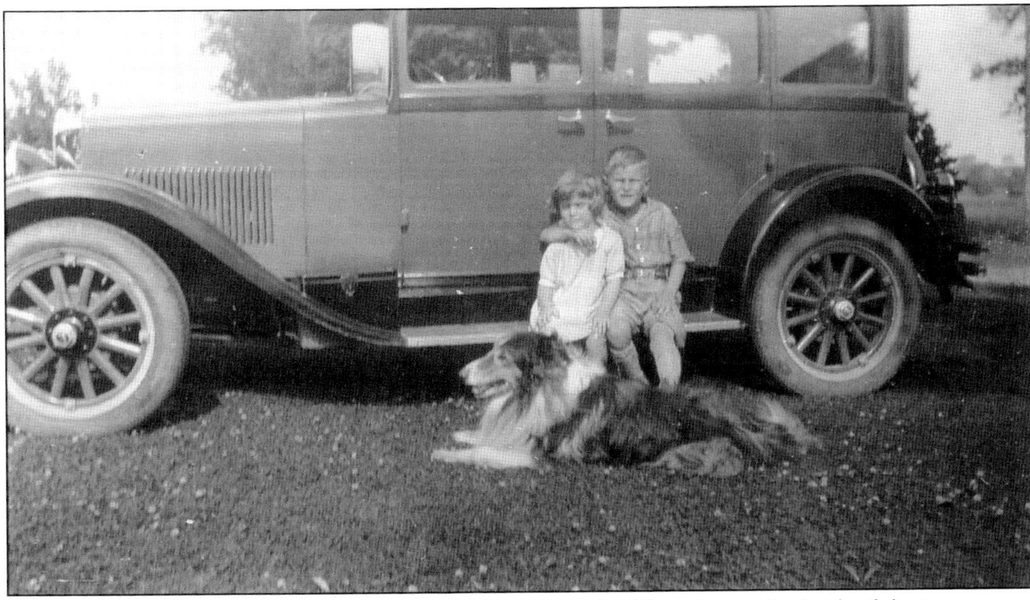

Photographs like this were sometimes used like postcards. The text on the back of the image says, "Taken last summer at Gilberts. My present car. Erskine." Sent to Maddie Cheeseman, this image features two children and a dog. Showing up frequently in the Cheeseman family photographs, often with Maddie's son Winford, these children are presumably relatives.

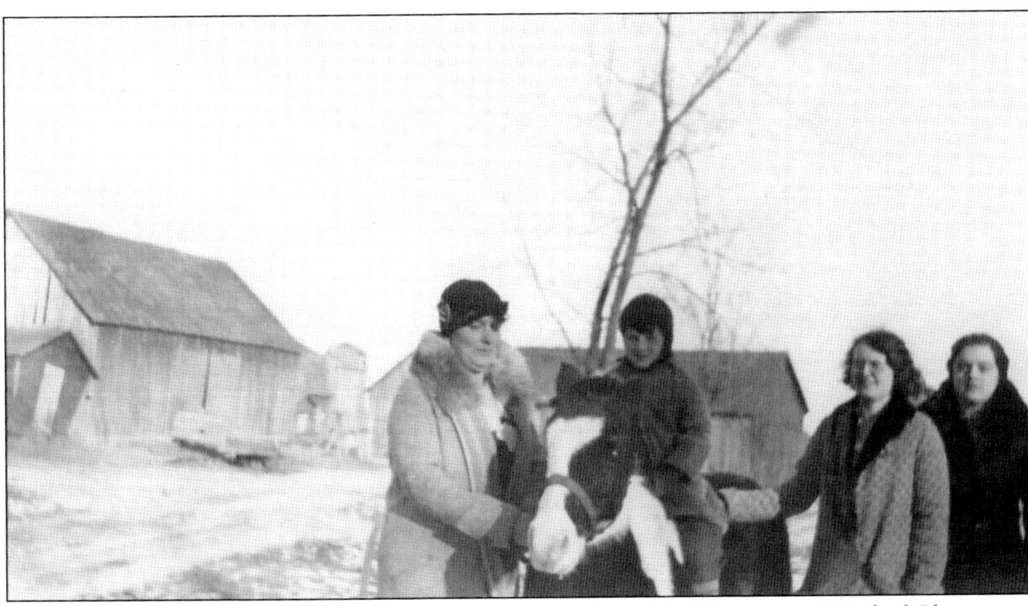

Visits from family members often gave rise to images such as this. Here we see Winford Cheeseman on his pony surrounded by his visiting aunts and his mother (second from right). Unlike more formal portraits, snapshots like this one emphasize the reality of a family's life. Thus, we see the barnyard of the Cheeseman family farm in the background.

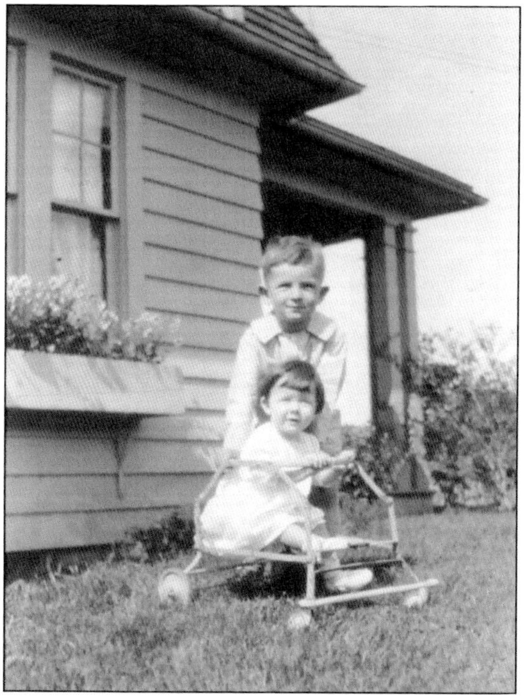

This picture shows a young Winford Cheeseman pushing a cousin in her baby walker, which sports an early metal frame. Also of interest is the clapboard house with a window flower box and manicured lawn. Taken together, these landscaping features point to the relative affluence of the family and the importance placed on external appearance.

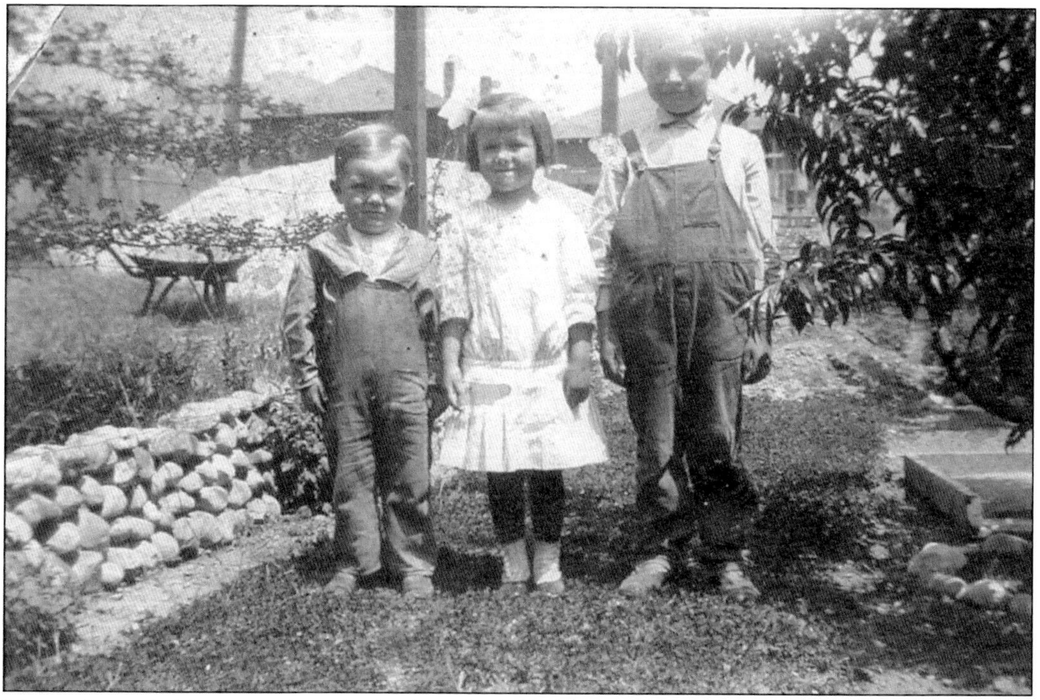

These three children stand in the backyard of their home. Notice the wheelbarrow to the left, the low stone wall, and the fledgling garden to the left. Whether in town or country, Clinton County residents planted gardens to increase their larders and to bring them the pleasure of fresh flowers. Given the rocky terrain of the county, stone walls are also common. Though the one pictured here is low, it is indicative of that trend.

Three children, each holding a large ear of corn, stand among the corn stalks of their family's farm in Ellenburg. Cornfields, in addition to being an important part of the farm's economic survival, offered myriad hiding spots. On special occasions or for festivals, farmers would dedicate a portion of their cornfield to the creation of a maze.

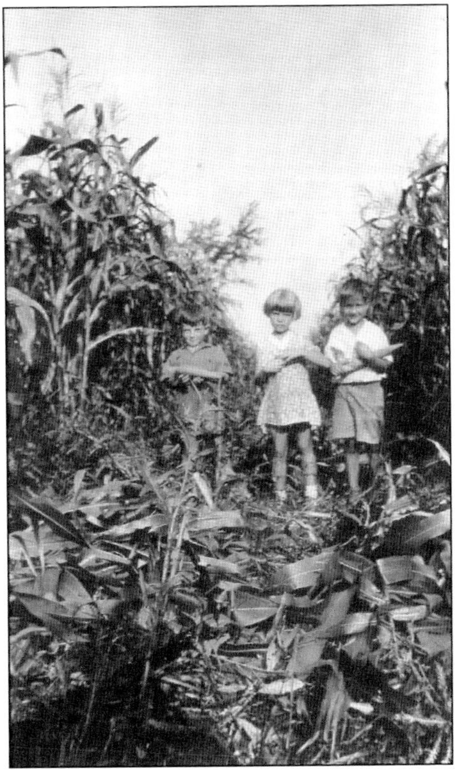

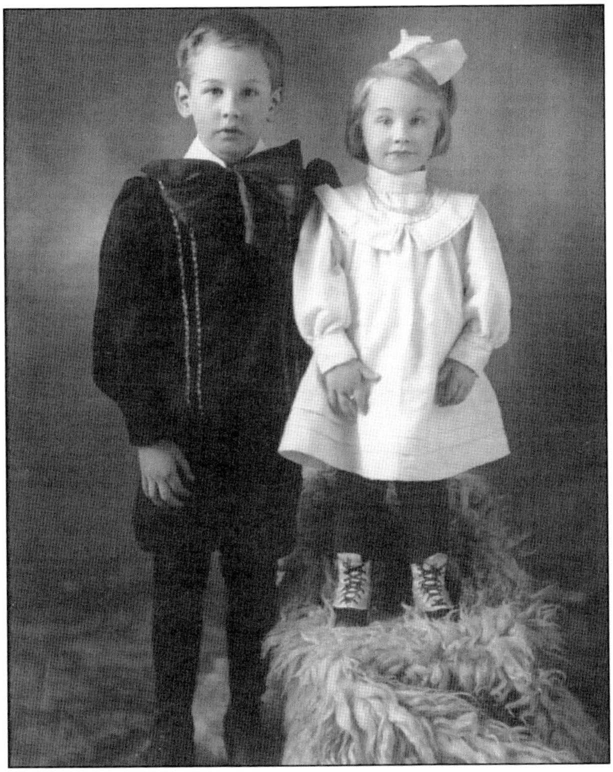

Harrison and Eva Hull pose in this photograph. Their father was an agent in Mooers. Notice the elaborate clothes and setting, which stand in stark contrast to those of the children pictured above.

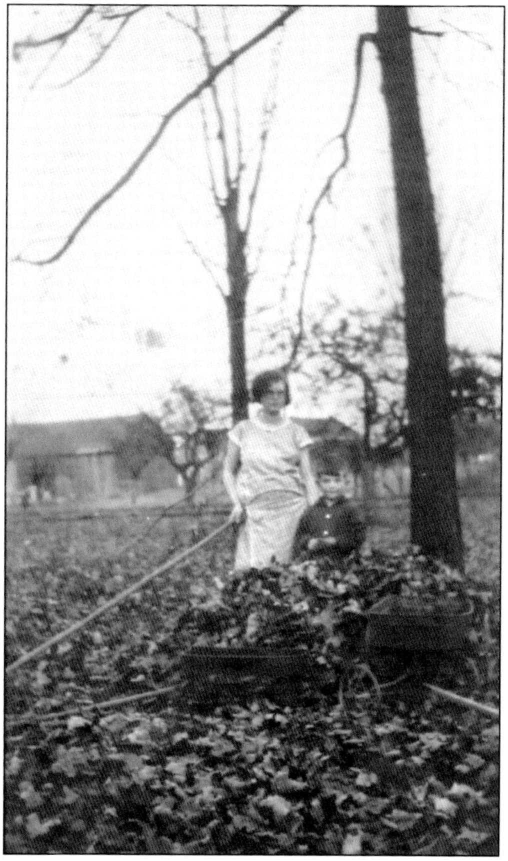

Though few families consider raking leaves a pastime, life in Clinton County necessitates the activity at least twice a year. Every fall, as the deciduous trees lose their leaves, families and landscaping companies head out to rake; every spring, as the snow melts and the wind-scattered winter debris appears, they begin again. Once the work of raking is complete, the leaves can be used for practical purposes (compost or bedding for animals) and for fun. Countless children find those piles of leaves perfect places to jump.

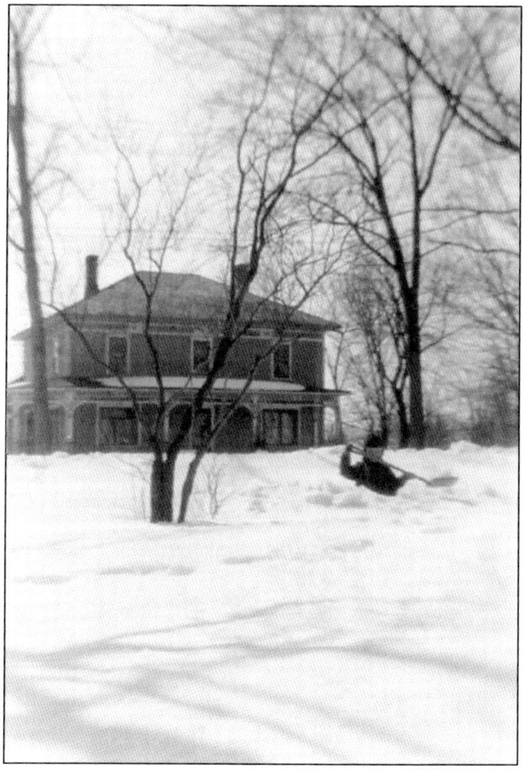

As with raking leaves, shoveling snow is a regular North Country activity. Necessary in order to clear paths, driveways, and roads, shoveling also allows for the creation of snow forts, snow sculptures, and snowmen.

Two

Religion

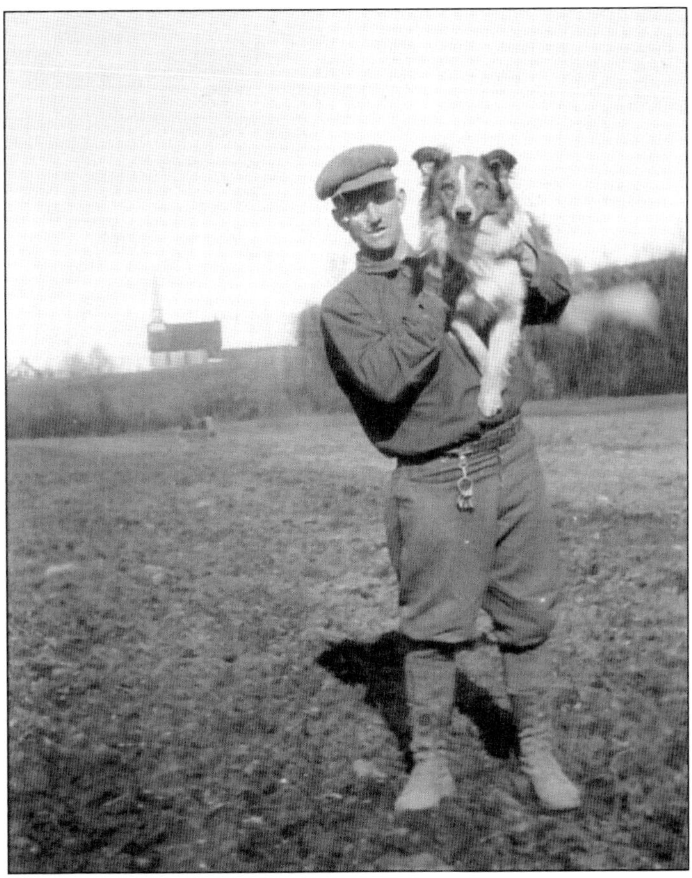

A typical Clinton County scene shows a church steeple in the distance. Church membership in the county has always been predominately Christian. In the late 1870s, more than 99 percent of local residents listing an affiliation said they were Christian, while less than 1 percent listed themselves as Jewish. Recent census reports have shown a similarly skewed breakdown of the county's religions, though Islam and Eastern faiths are now present as well.

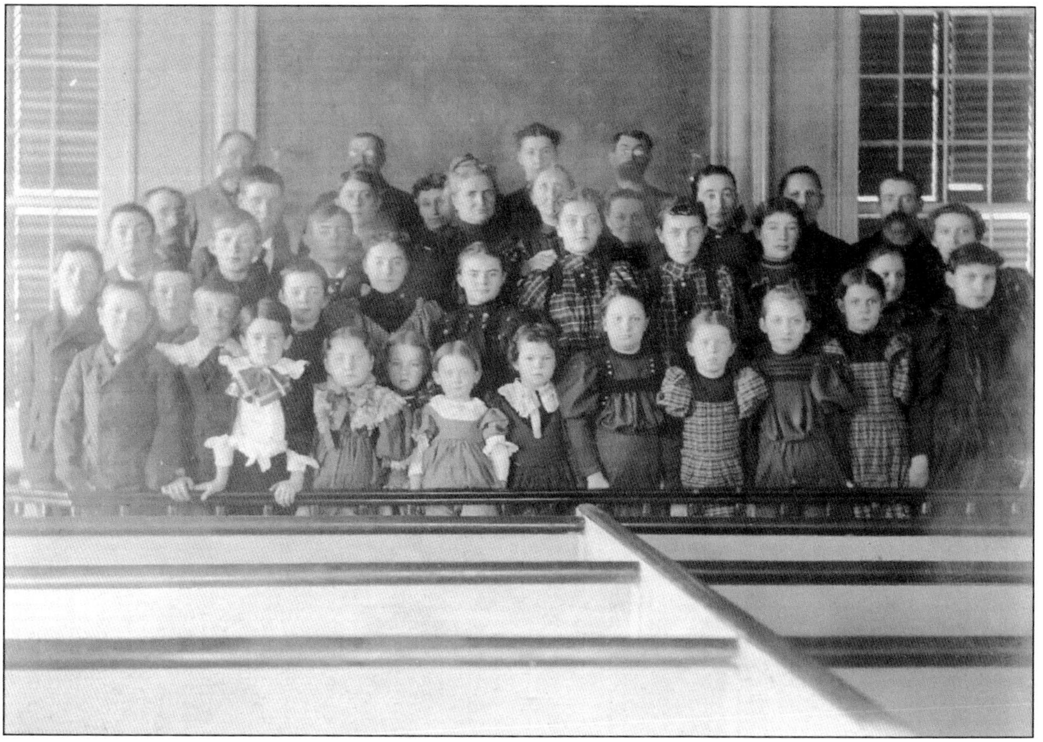

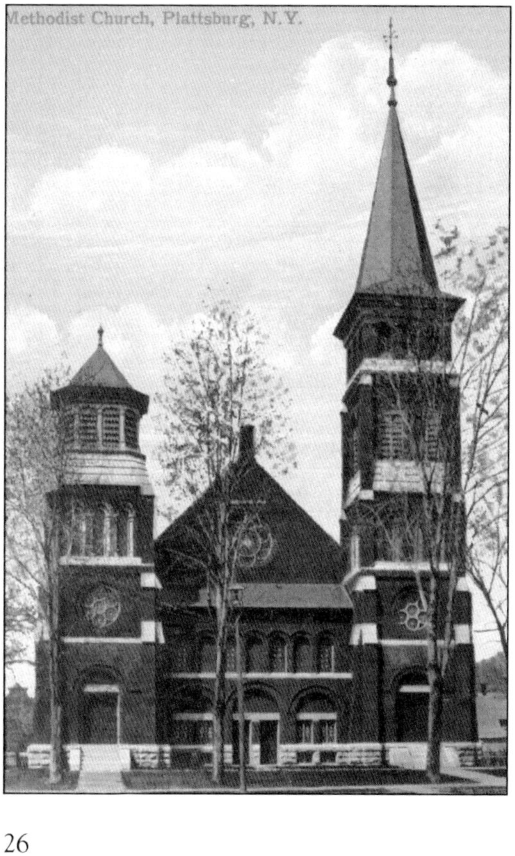

This unidentified group stands at the back of a Clinton County church. The wooden pews were built in a style common throughout the county. Churches like this were used for lectures, concerts, and community meetings in addition to worship services.

Before it burned down in 1956, this structure on the corner of Oak and Clinton Streets was the Methodist church. Built in 1885, this structure replaced an earlier Court Street structure. The congregation purchased a 22-acre lot at the corner of Beekman Street and Bailey Avenue to build its new church, which still stands today.

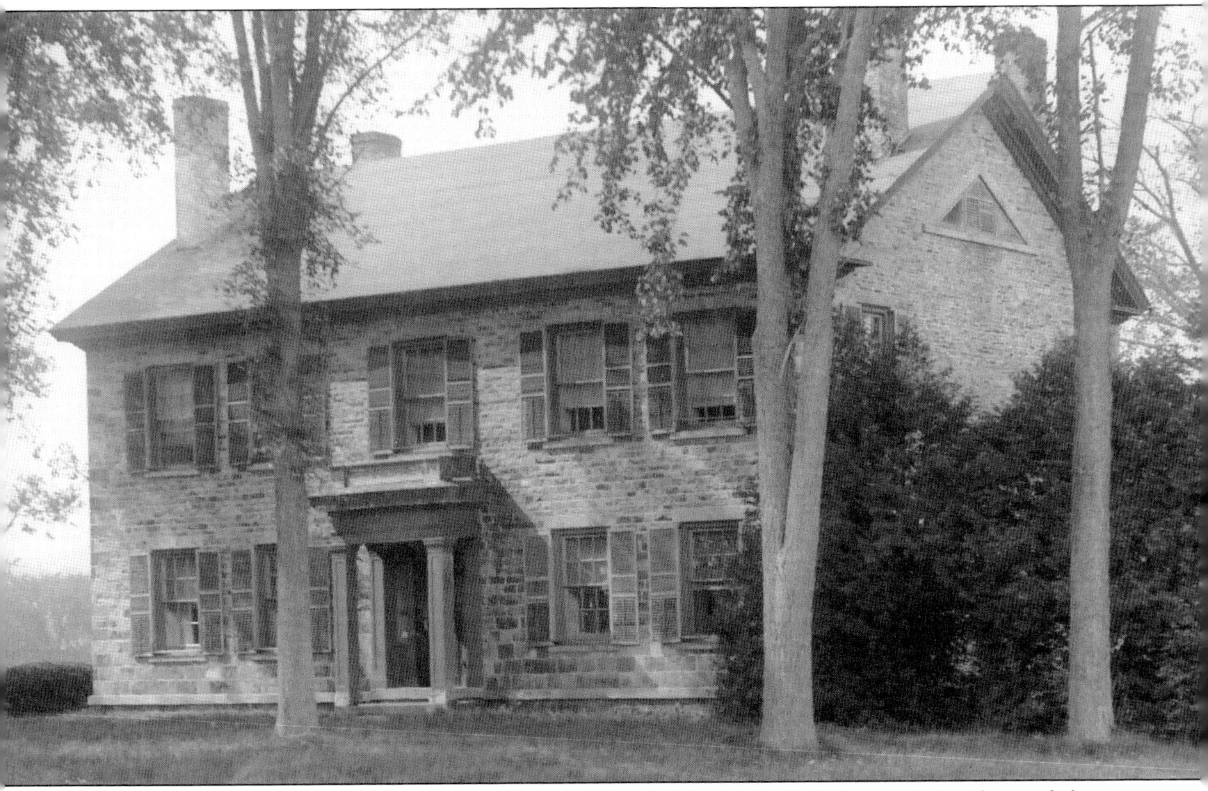

The Keese family, one branch of which owned this house in Peru, was active members of the Quaker Union. True to the tenets of their religion, the Quakers led the abolitionist movement in Clinton County and were active in the Underground Railroad, working to transport slaves to freedom long before the Civil War started. Houses like this one used barns with false walls and floors, houses with secret hiding spaces, and wagons with false bottoms to hide runaway slaves en route to freedom in Canada. Among the most famous members of the Keese family were Catherine R. Keese, who was president of the Female Anti-Slavery Society, and her husband, Samuel Keese, who was considered the head of the Underground Railroad in Peru.

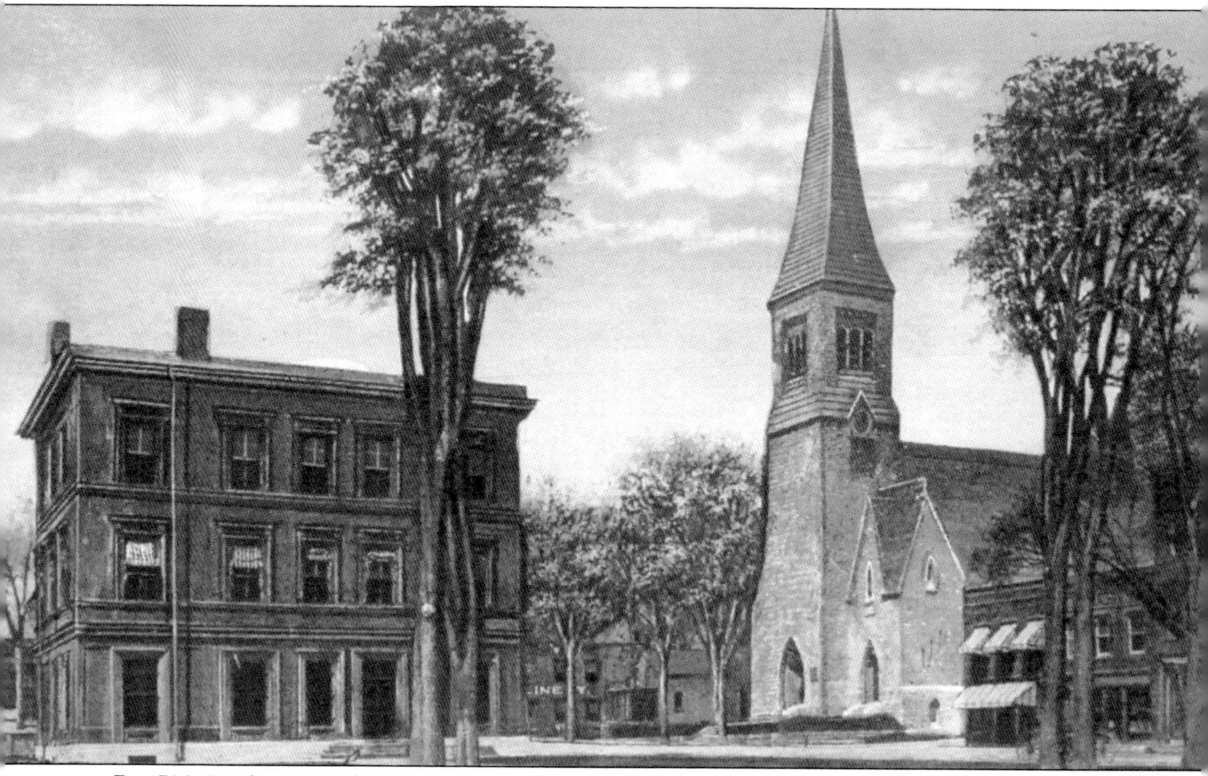

By 1792, Presbyterians had already organized in Plattsburgh, and by 1816, a parcel of land donated by Abraham Brinkerhoff Jr. was ready for the construction of a church. The resulting structure was destroyed in an 1867 fire, but a new church was begun in June 1868 and completed in 1873. That church, shown here, was created out of blue and gray limestone and included a 200-foot tower. During World War I, the church served Saturday evening suppers to soldiers stationed at the Plattsburgh barracks. Later, in the 1980s, the church continued to provide comfort to those away from home by housing refugees awaiting clearance to enter Canada. This postcard also shows the post office.

Built in 1830, the Trinity Episcopal Church was enlarged in 1852 and renovated again in 1866 and in the 1930s. This postcard highlights the blue limestone structure, with its stained-glass windows. Later renovations saw the replacement of the wooden spire shown here with a stone tower, the creation of a rectory, and the construction of Trinity Memorial Hall. Finished in 1962, Trinity Memorial Hall contains rooms for classes and the church choir.

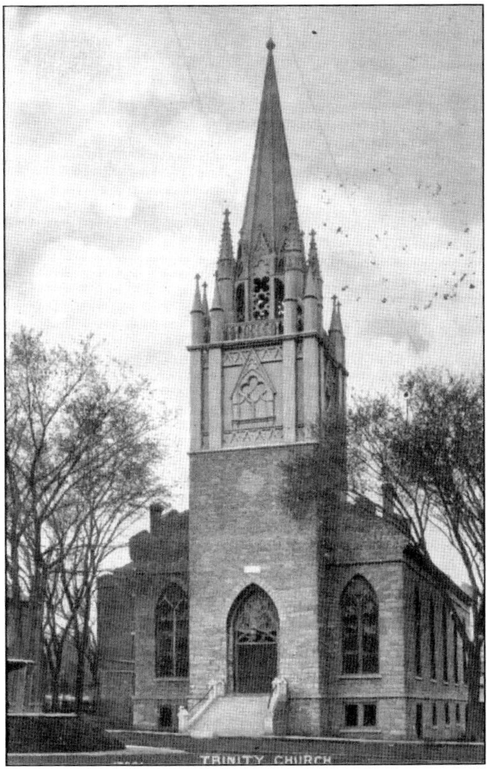

Located in South Plattsburgh, the Episcopal Mission Church shown here was affiliated with the Trinity Episcopal Church in the city of Plattsburgh.

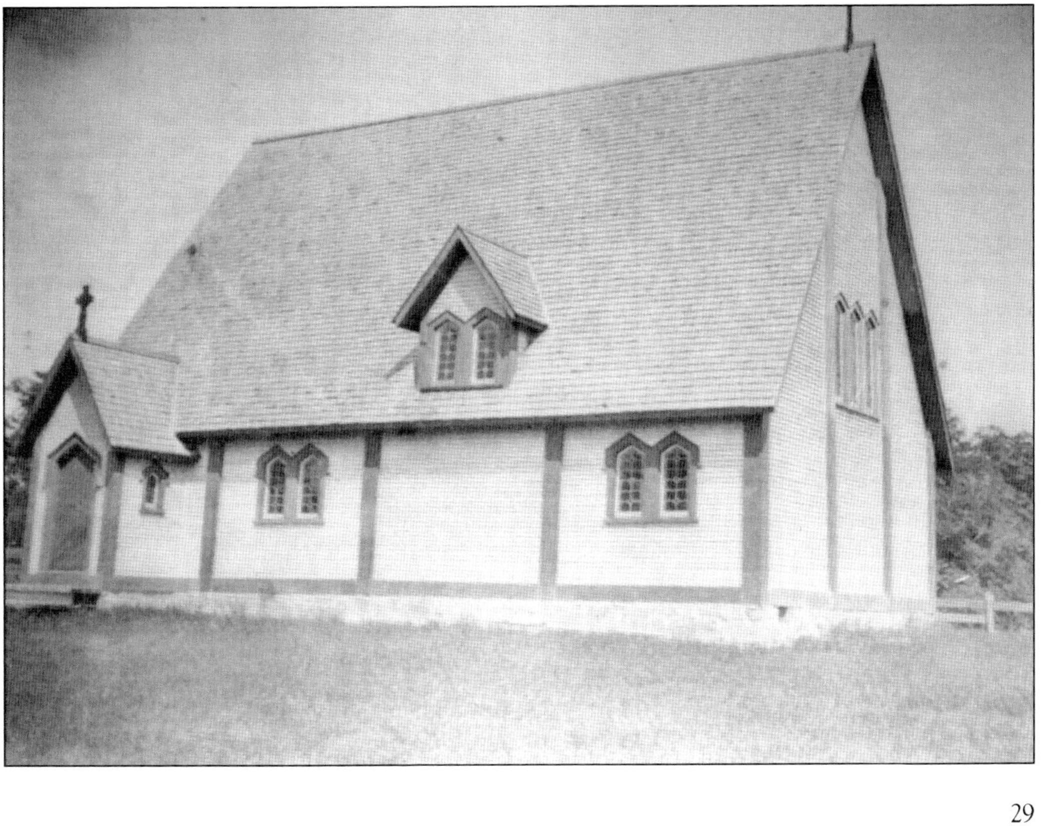

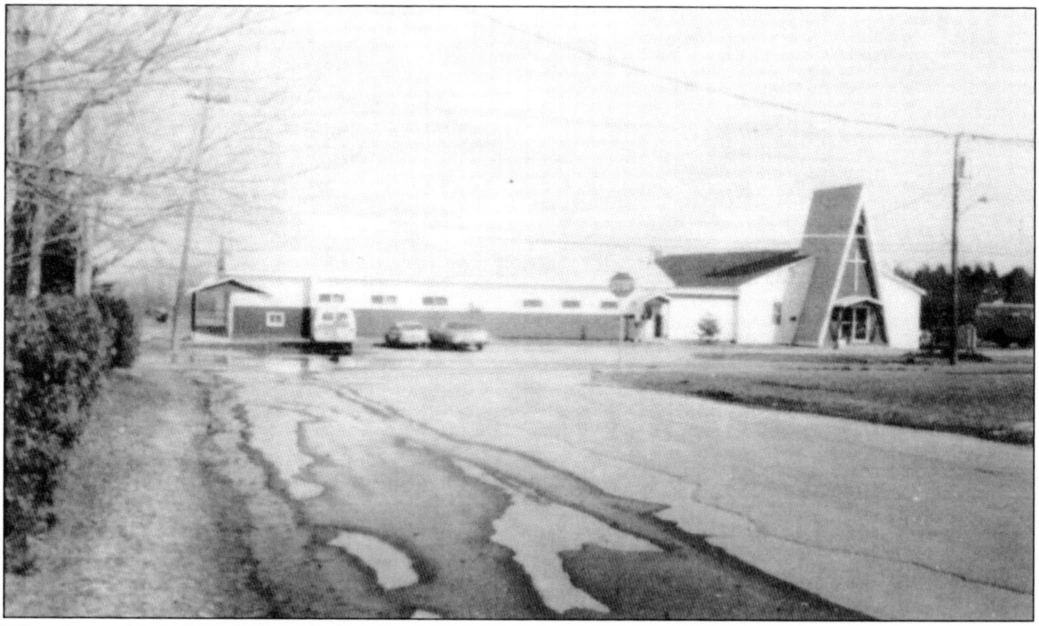

The Assembly of God church has been located on Prospect Avenue in the city of Plattsburgh since 1963. Established in 1954 by the New York District of Assemblies of God, the congregation moved to this location when the Daughters of the American Revolution Hall became too small. Later construction added the Christian Supply Center (1970s), the New Life Nursery (1980), the New Life Christian Academy (1981), and the parsonage (1987).

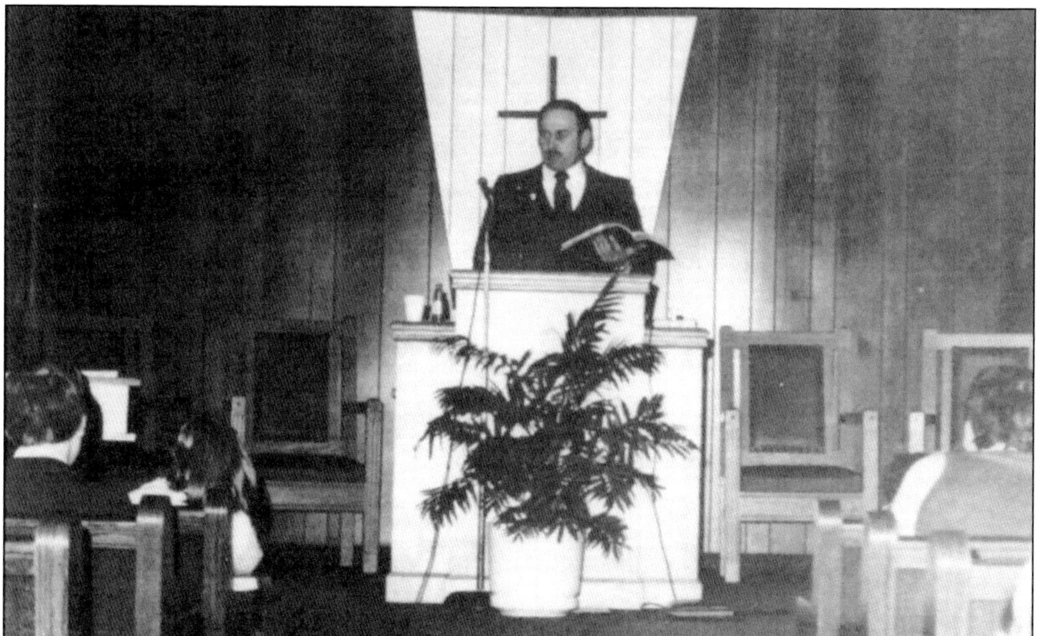

Pastor Mike San Soucie preaches at the Assembly of God church on Prospect Street. San Soucie and his wife, Elizabeth, began serving as the senior pastorate of the church in January 1970, taking over from Rev. and Mrs. Ronald Hale. Under the San Soucies' guidance, the church grew to include a school and Christian supply store.

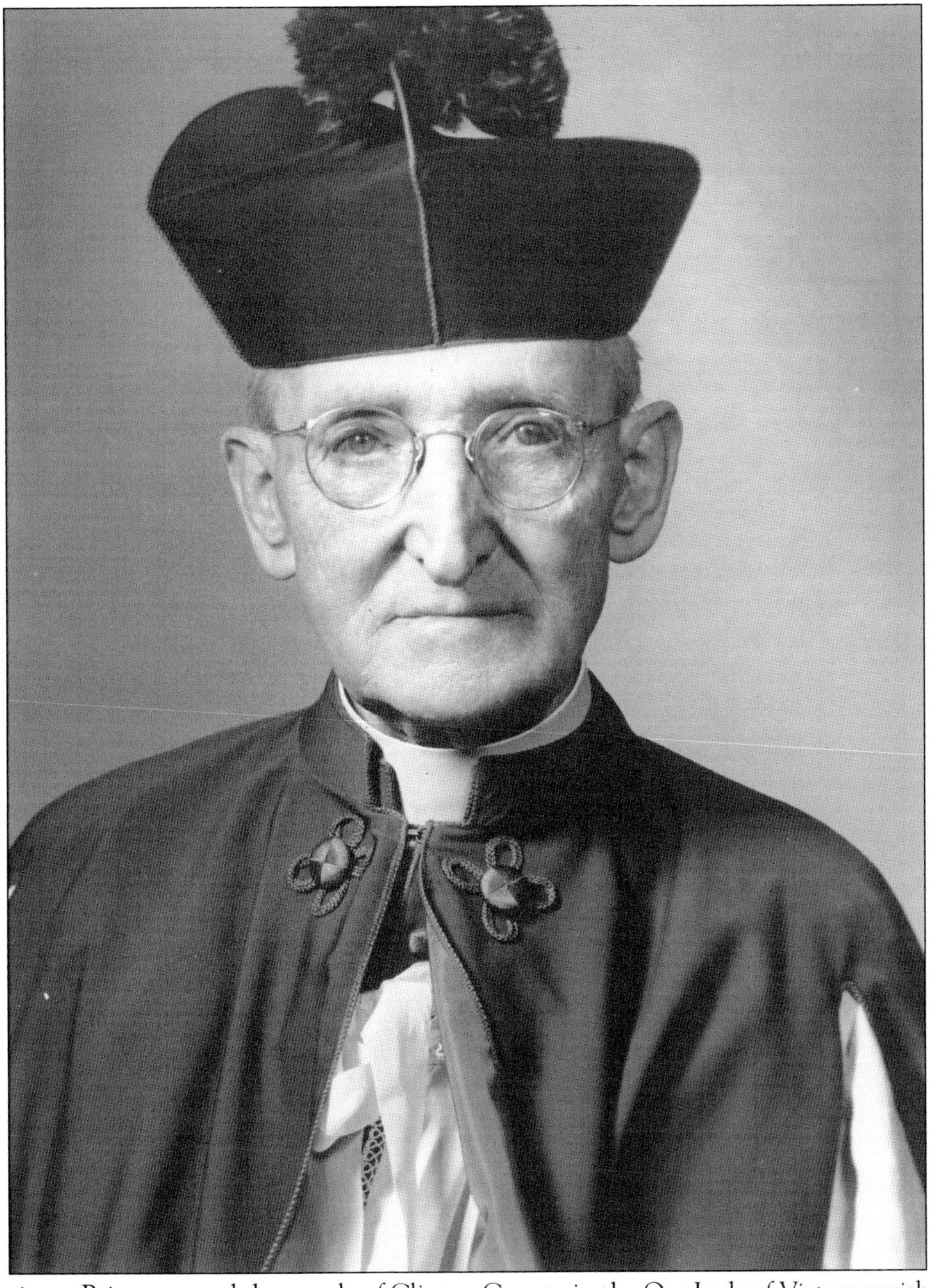

Monsignor Brisson served the people of Clinton County in the Our Lady of Victory parish, also known as the *Paroisse de Notre Dame de Victoires*, where he was pastor from 1950 until 1978. In addition to offering the normal array of Catholic services and rites, the church created Our Lady of Victory Academy to teach kindergarten through 12th-grade students and to provide a secretarial course for high school graduates. This photograph was used to celebrate Father Brisson's 50th anniversary as a Catholic priest. He was preceded as pastor by Fathers Desjardins (1907–1911) and Bachand (1911–1950) and succeeded as pastor by Fathers Rivette (1968–1973), Gagnier (1973–1978), Aubin (1978–1989), McGuinness (1989–1995), Edwards (1995–1996), Bleaux (1996–2006), and Hauser (2006–present).

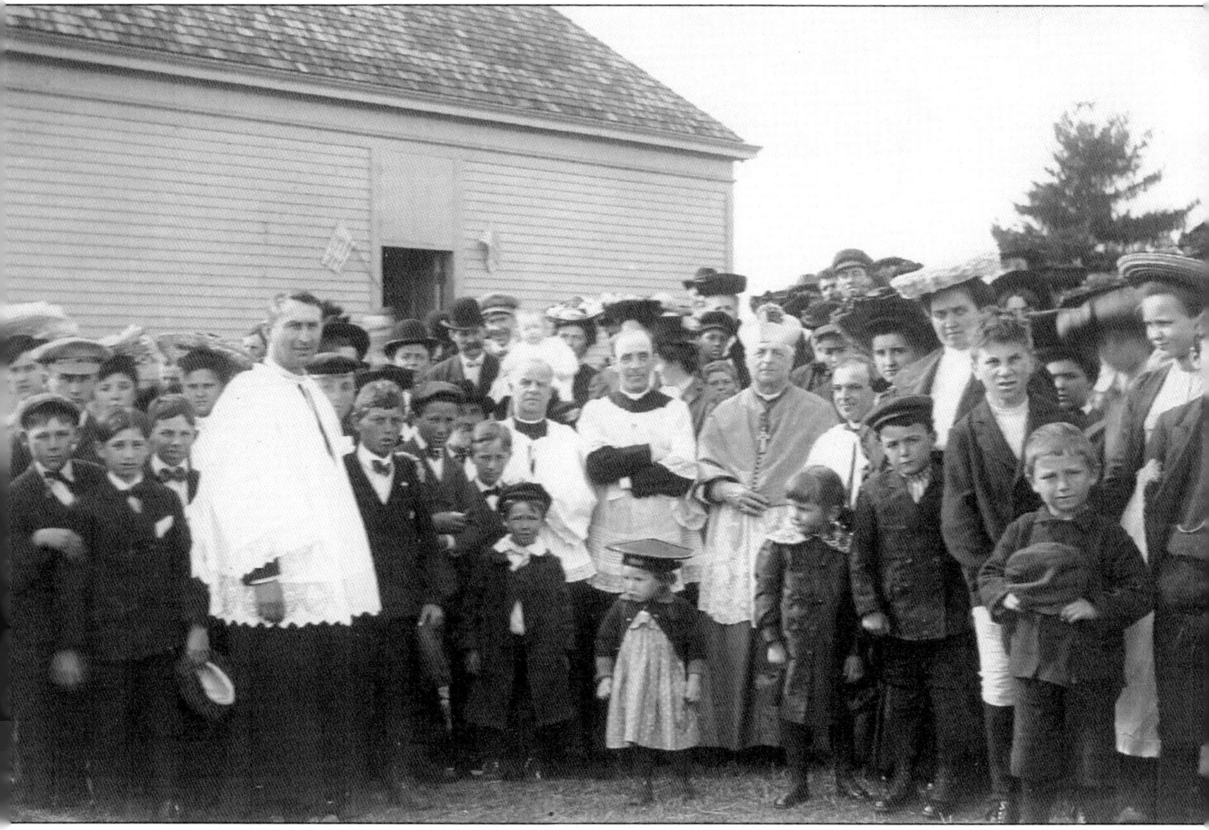

St. Peter's Church was created in 1853 to serve the French-speaking and French-descended families of Plattsburgh. Local citizens received word of the new parish from Fr. J. P. Bernard and Fr. F. M. Ruiz, who traveled through the city on their way to a retreat in Redford. Residents agreed to build a structure for the Reverend Oblate Fathers with all of the revenue from the pews and collections dedicated to the upkeep of the church and administered by that order. The church was built with funds raised by the area's working-class families. Eventually, the parish added two schools—the D'Youville Academy and St. Peter's Academy—and a convent. St. Peter's continues to be a vibrant and active parish, although the D'Youville Academy has long since closed.

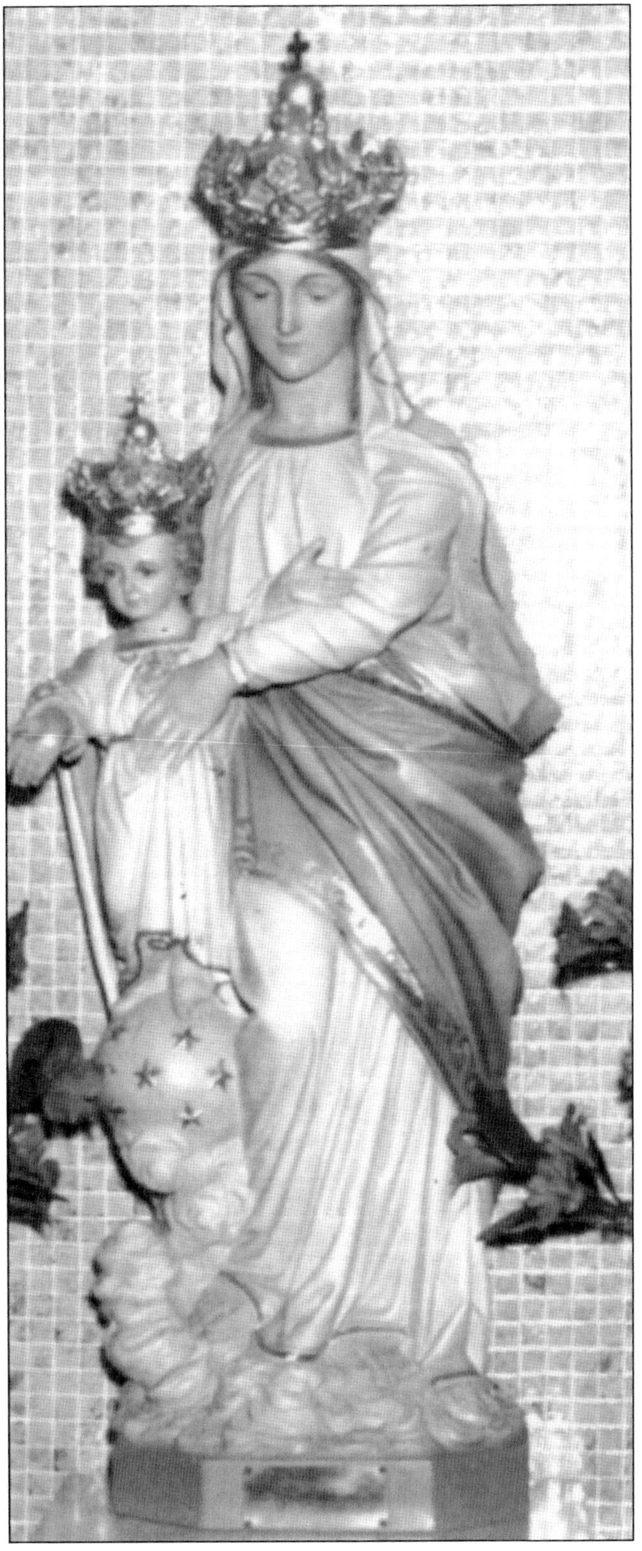

Our Lady of Victory Church, whose namesake is shown in this photograph, was established in 1911 after it became apparent that St. Peter's membership was too large to be easily accommodated within that church. The parish decided to build on South Catherine Street in order to better serve the French-Canadian families that lived between the Saranac and Salmon Rivers and between the city of Plattsburgh and Treadwell's Mills. Prior to the 1917 consecration of the church, members celebrated mass at the convent of the Sisters of Charity of Saint Louis. Eventually the parish added kindergarten–12th-grade and secretarial schools.

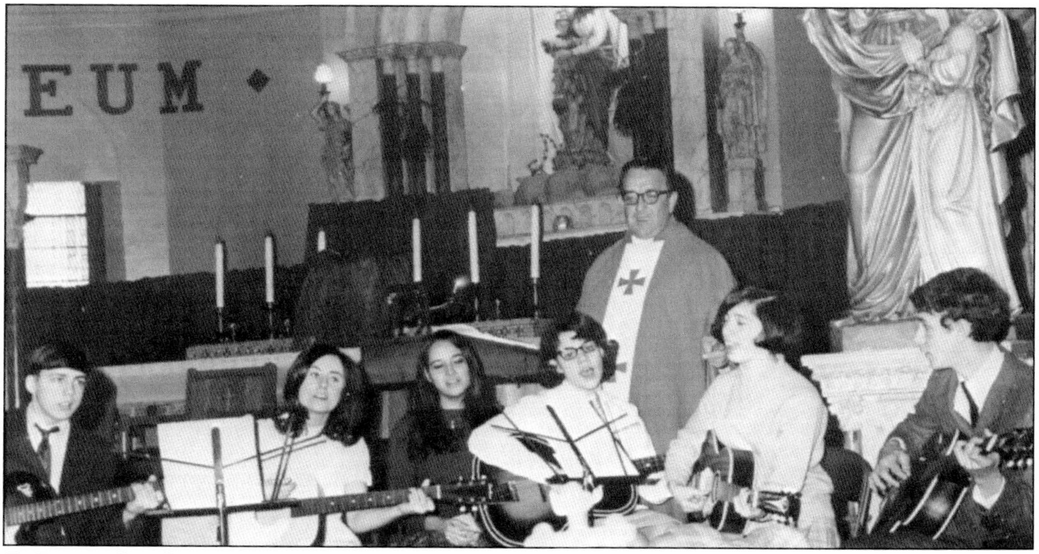

Fr. Bernard Kellogg watches as, from left to right, Douglas Dutilly, Debbie Payette, Linda Hall, Lory Clukey, Lita Kelly, and Joel Larocque perform as pat of the first Folk Mass at the 1968 OLVA retreat, an annual event for the school and church parish.

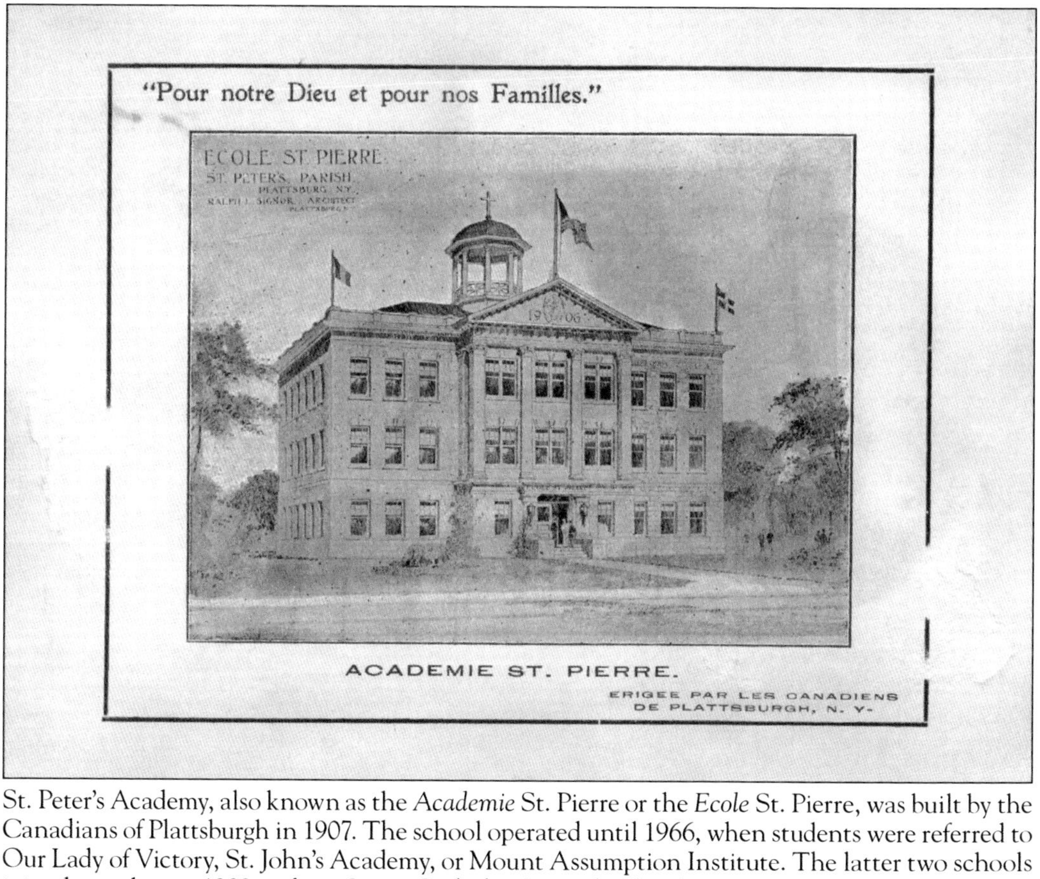

St. Peter's Academy, also known as the *Academie* St. Pierre or the *Ecole* St. Pierre, was built by the Canadians of Plattsburgh in 1907. The school operated until 1966, when students were referred to Our Lady of Victory, St. John's Academy, or Mount Assumption Institute. The latter two schools joined together in 1989 to form Seton Catholic Central School.

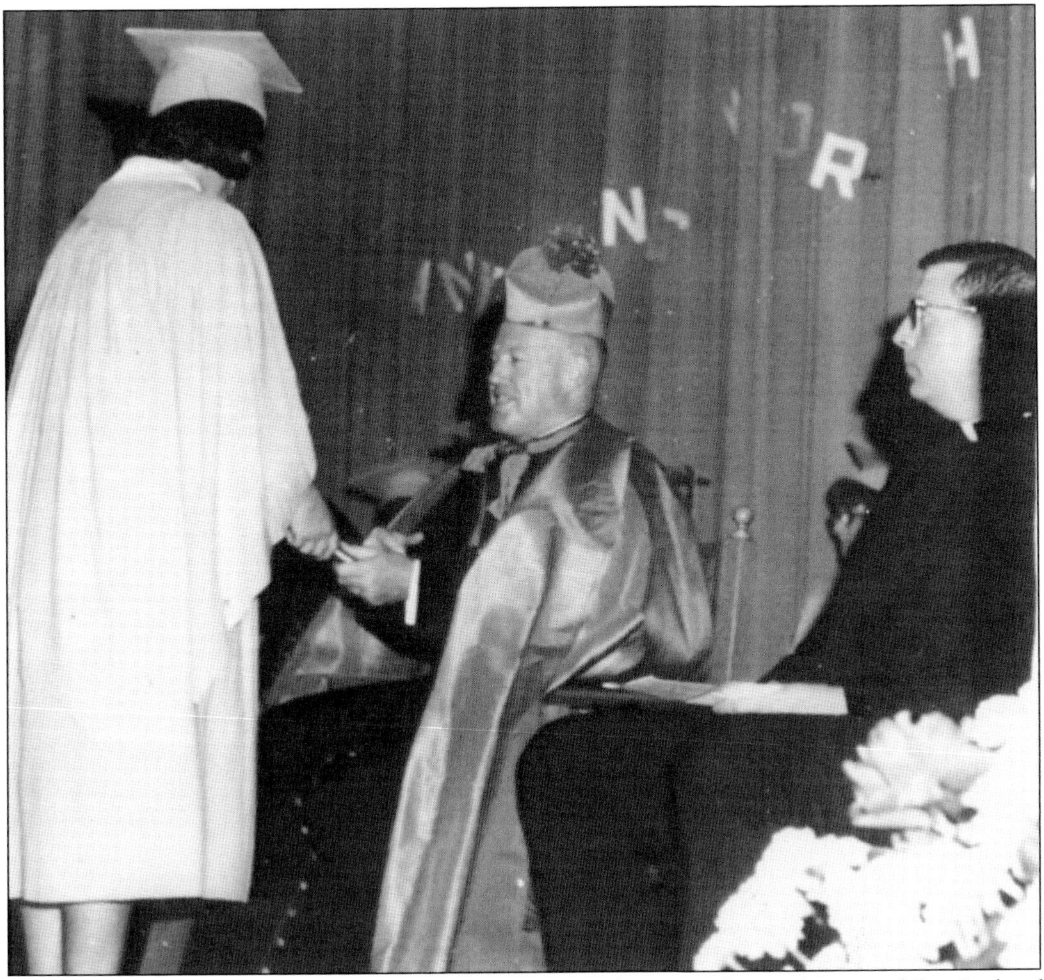

Bishop Thomas Andrew Donellan and Fr. John Senecal oversee the graduation of Our Lady of Victory Academy in 1968. The following year, OLVA ceased operating as a school, having reached a peak enrollment of 312 grade school and 97 high school students in 1950.

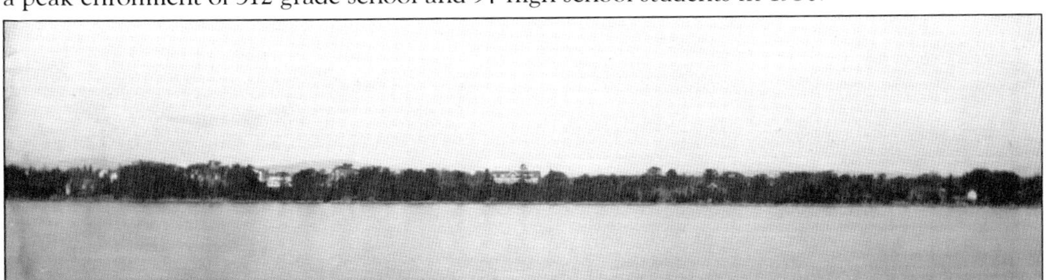

The Catholic Summer School at Cliff Haven, as seen from a steamboat on Lake Champlain, began operating in 1893, after receiving a charter from the Regents of the State of New York. In addition to several cottages, the school boasted an auditorium, a nine-hole golf course, a casino, tennis courts, a club house, boardinghouses, and, of course, a chapel. By the 1930s, the school fell into disuse and was purchased by developers who created a residential community still known as Cliff Haven.

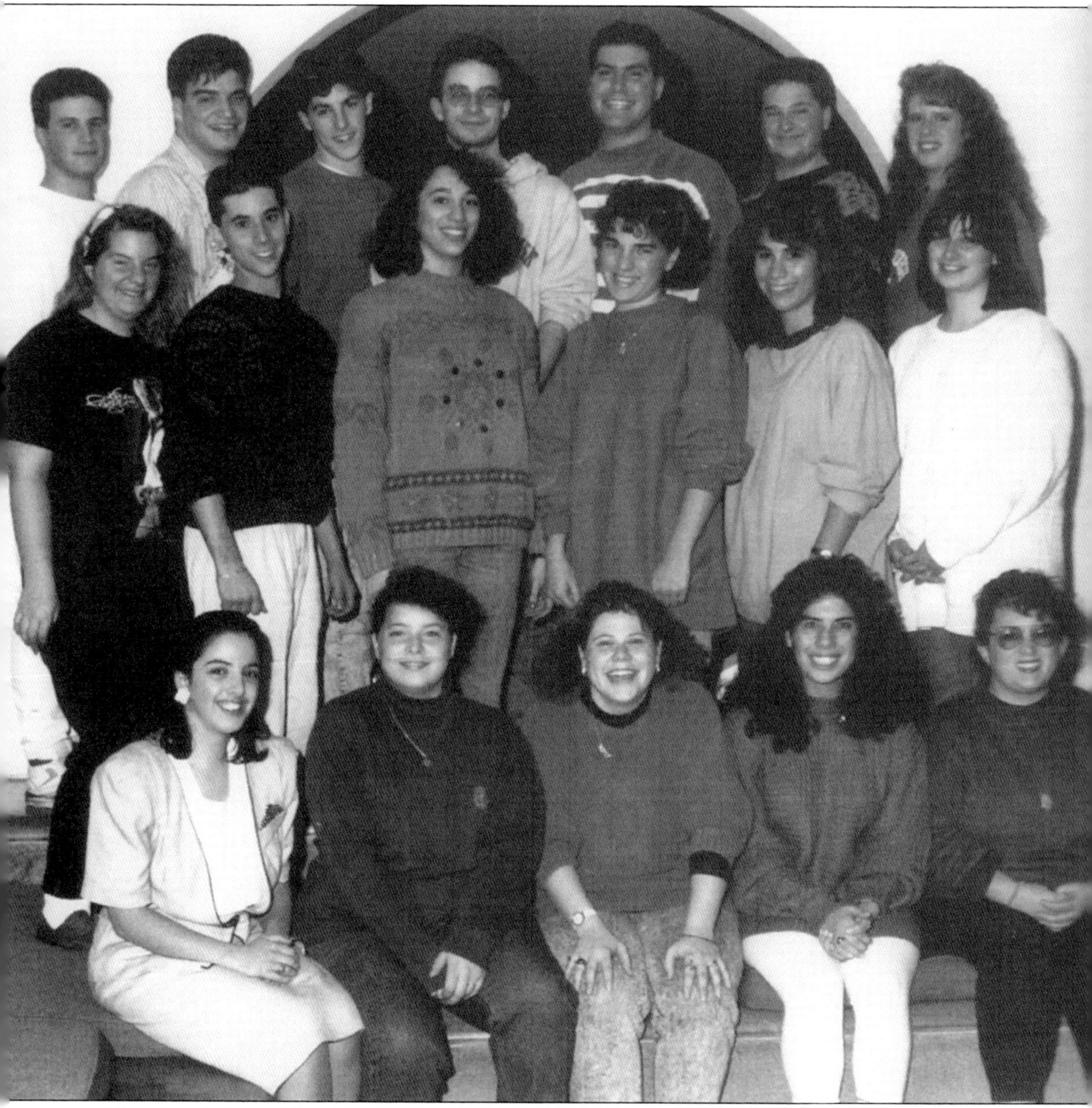

Plattsburgh State University, in its dedication to honoring the diversity of its students and of the community, includes Hillel among its student groups. Open to all students with an interest in Judaism or Judaic history, the group has ties to the local synagogue, Temple Beth Israel. Incorporated in 1861, the Jewish Congregation of Plattsburgh—which later became the Beth Israel Congregation—purchased the former Universalist church on Oak Street in 1866. They eventually moved to a new temple designed by Jeremiah Oosterbaan in 1970. Another, more traditional and orthodox temple was established in 1917. Known as the Congregation Ahavas Sholom, with a synagogue on Palmer Street, this group rejected the Reformed Judaism of the Beth Israel Congregation. Membership in the Congregation Ahavas Sholom dwindled until it formally closed in 1969.

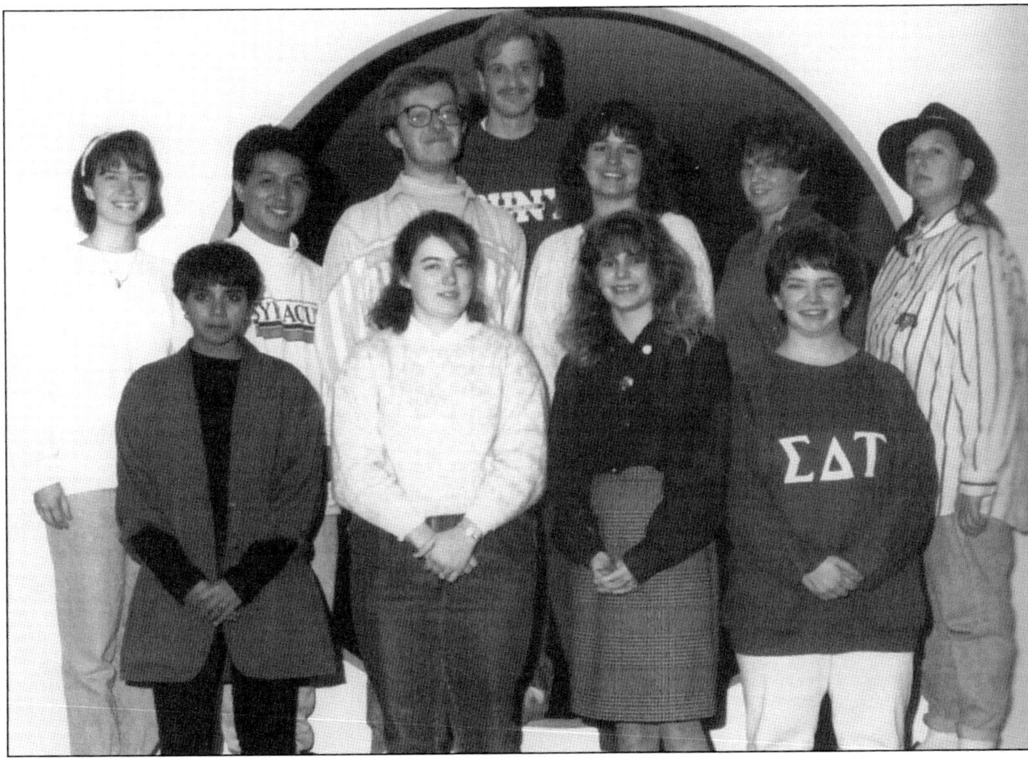

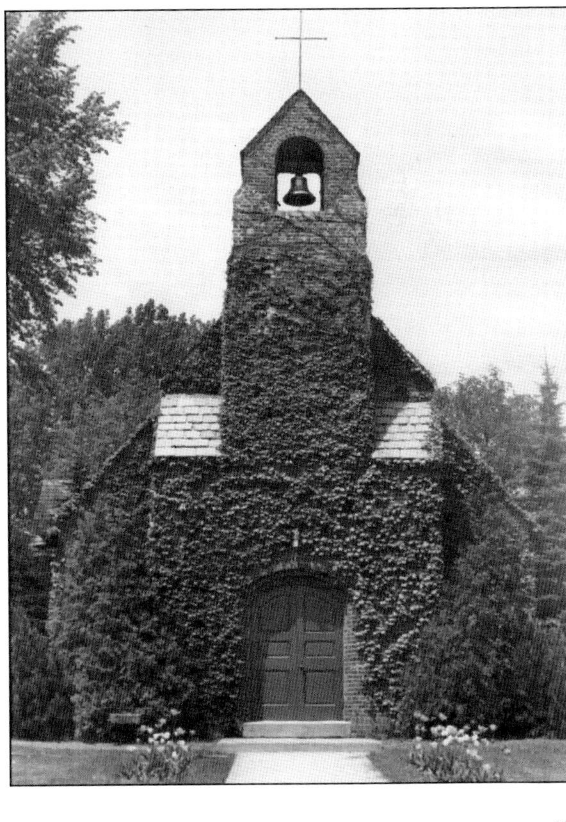

In addition to Hillel, Plattsburgh State University sponsors the Intravarsity Christian Fellowship, a nondenominational organization dedicated to serving the community. Clinton County's religious communities have long worked to improve life in the region. Food shelves, thrift stores, soup kitchen, coffee house, and relief shelter are all consistently maintained within the county. During times of increased economic hardship, natural disaster, and surging refugee populations, the Interfaith Network has supplemented their normal activities in response.

Dedicated in 1933, the Plattsburgh Memorial Chapel (commonly known as the Base Chapel) offered Protestant, Lutheran, Episcopal, and Catholic services for servicemen and women stationed at the base. Since the 1995 closure of Plattsburgh Air Force Base, the chapel has been used as a nondenominational facility open to the general public. Jewish services were not offered on the base.

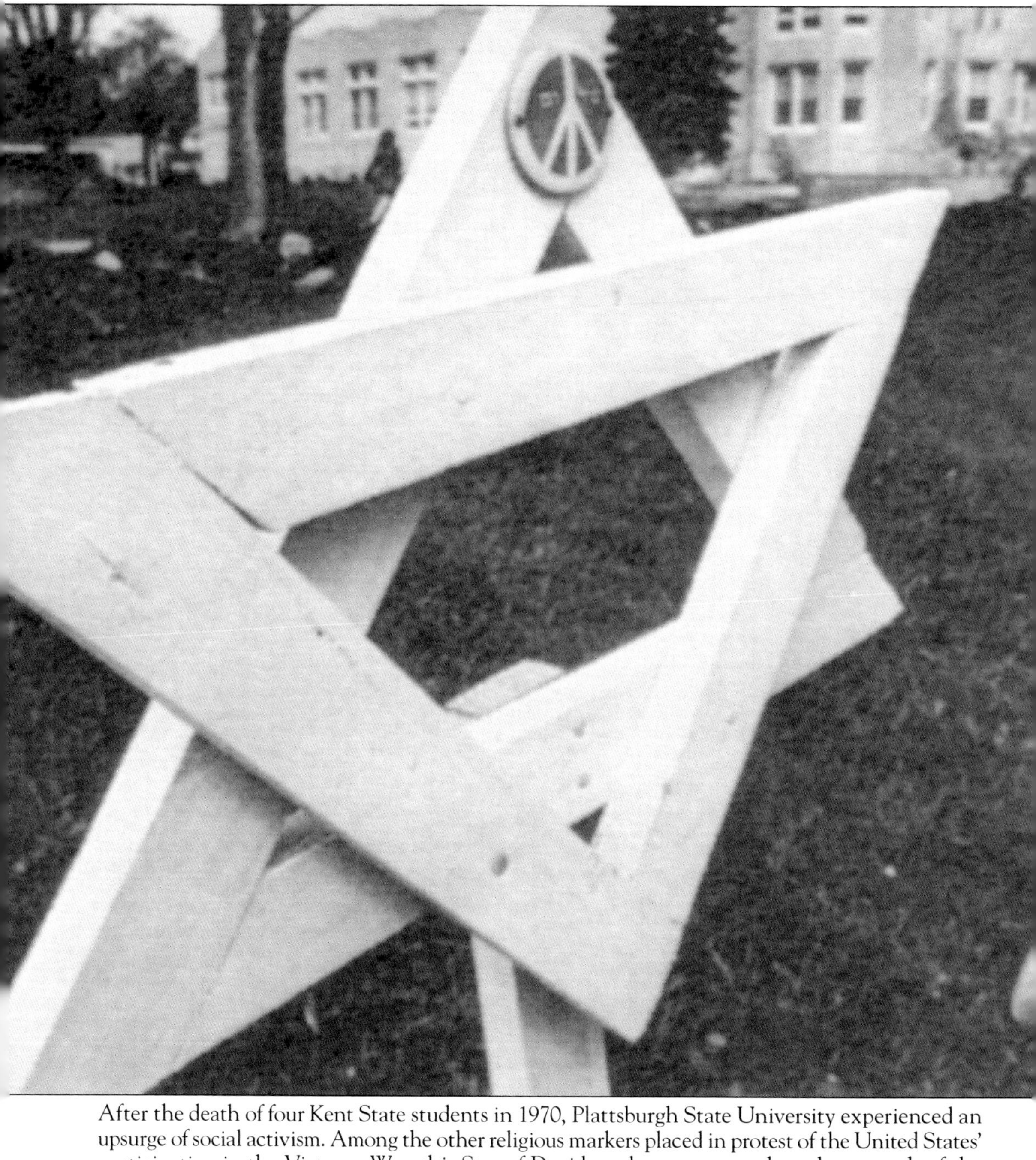

After the death of four Kent State students in 1970, Plattsburgh State University experienced an upsurge of social activism. Among the other religious markers placed in protest of the United States' participation in the Vietnam War, this Star of David marker was erected on the grounds of the college. Emblazoned with a peace symbol, the sign emphasizes the connections between religious belief, moral conscience, and political protest. The sign also underscores the social activism of the local Jewish community, which—among other things—organized itself to meet the needs of Jewish soldiers at the Plattsburgh training camp during World War I, to band together with local churches to provide food and shelter for those in need (including various refugees), and to honor civil responsibility (as with the B'nai Brith Lodge "Man of the Year" award).

Three

EDUCATION

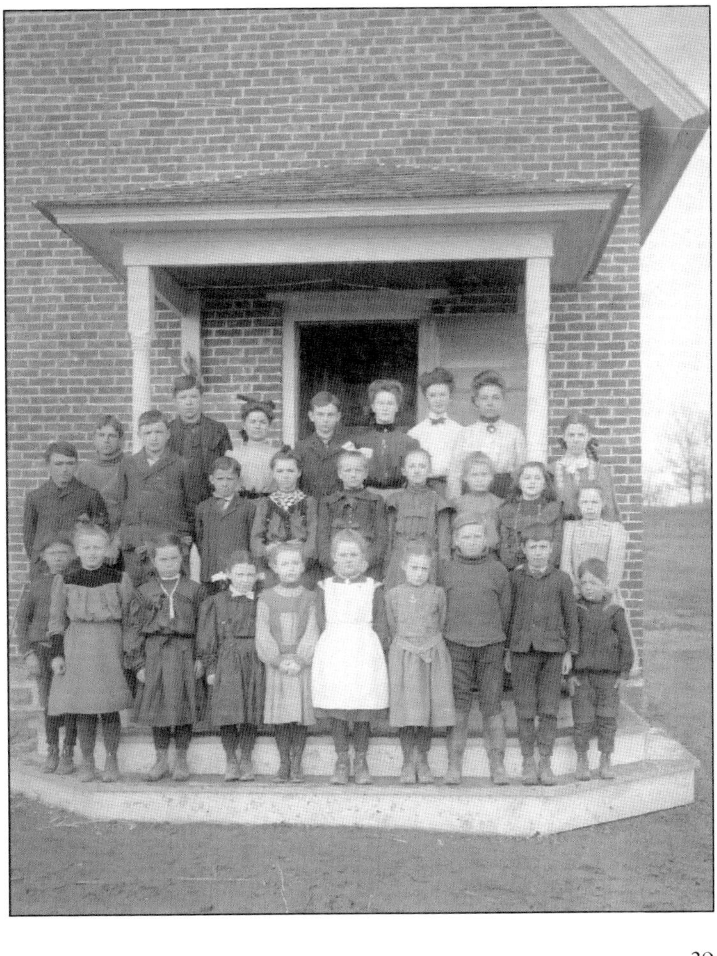

Standing outside of their brick schoolhouse, this unidentified group offers a sense of school life in Clinton County. The class was comprised of 17 girls and 10 boys; a majority of the boys pictured are young, possibly indicating that older boys were at work on their families' farms. Consolidation of local schools began as early as 1904, and eventually, eight distinct and centralized school districts were created.

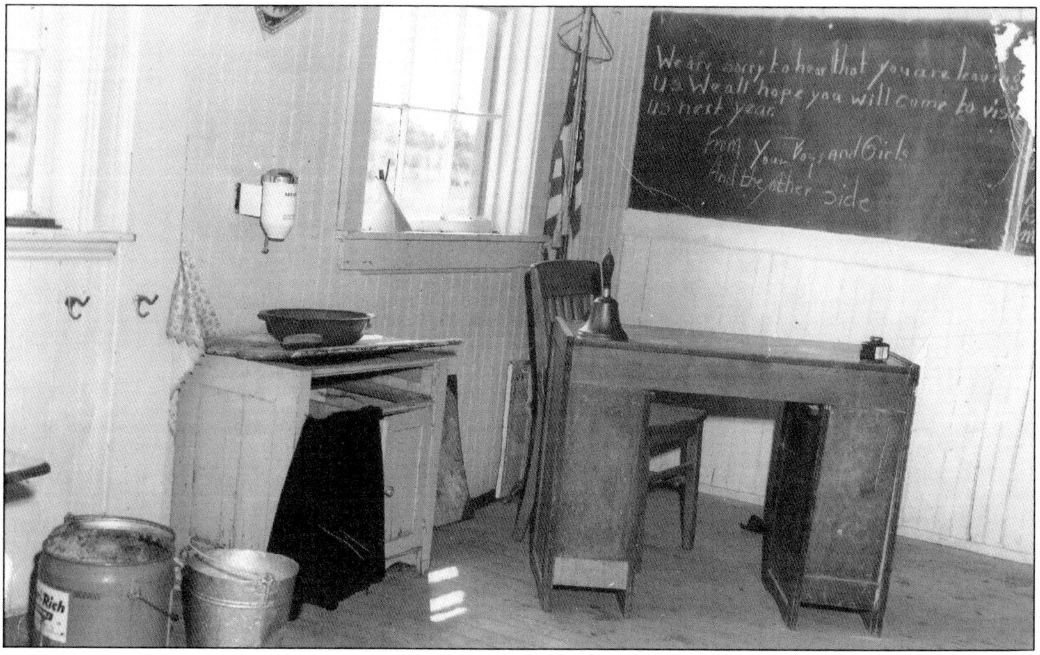

One- and two-room schoolhouses abounded in Clinton County. This Plattsburgh school, captured on film on July 20, 1949, used two rooms to educate students in the town of Plattsburgh. Notice the soap dispenser and wash basin, conveniently placed between the two windows. Indoor plumbing was not part of early school life.

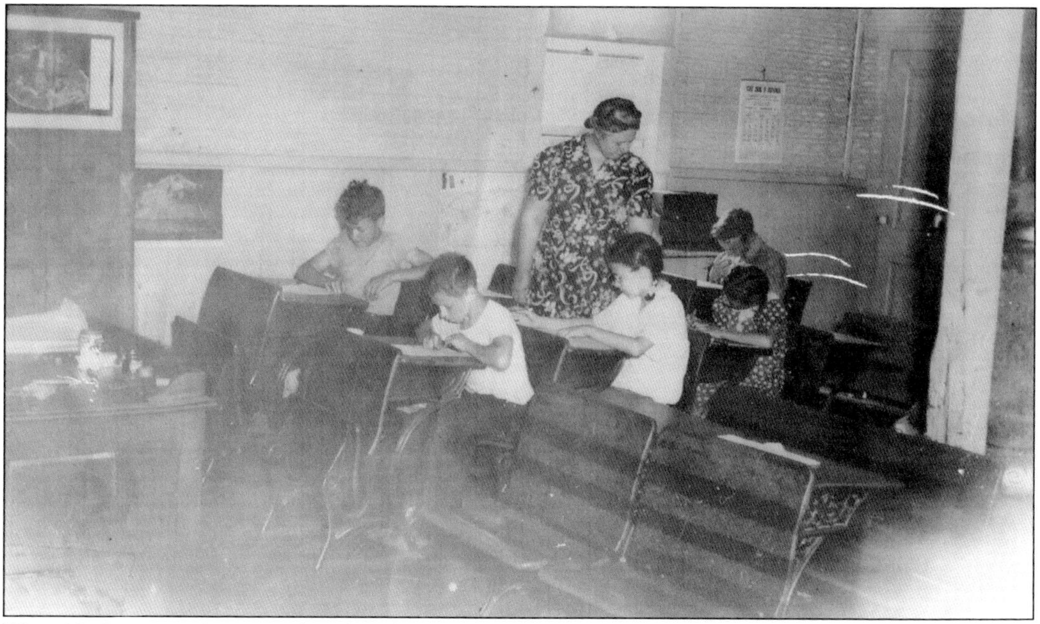

This 1949 image shows a Plattsburgh teacher assisting students in her two-room schoolhouse. After finishing at this school, children had the option of attending high school in Plattsburgh. Centralization of school districts, a process that first limited the number of one- and two-room schoolhouses, eventually created more high schools. Students in the town of Plattsburgh were then sent to Beekmantown, Peru, or Saranac depending on their location.

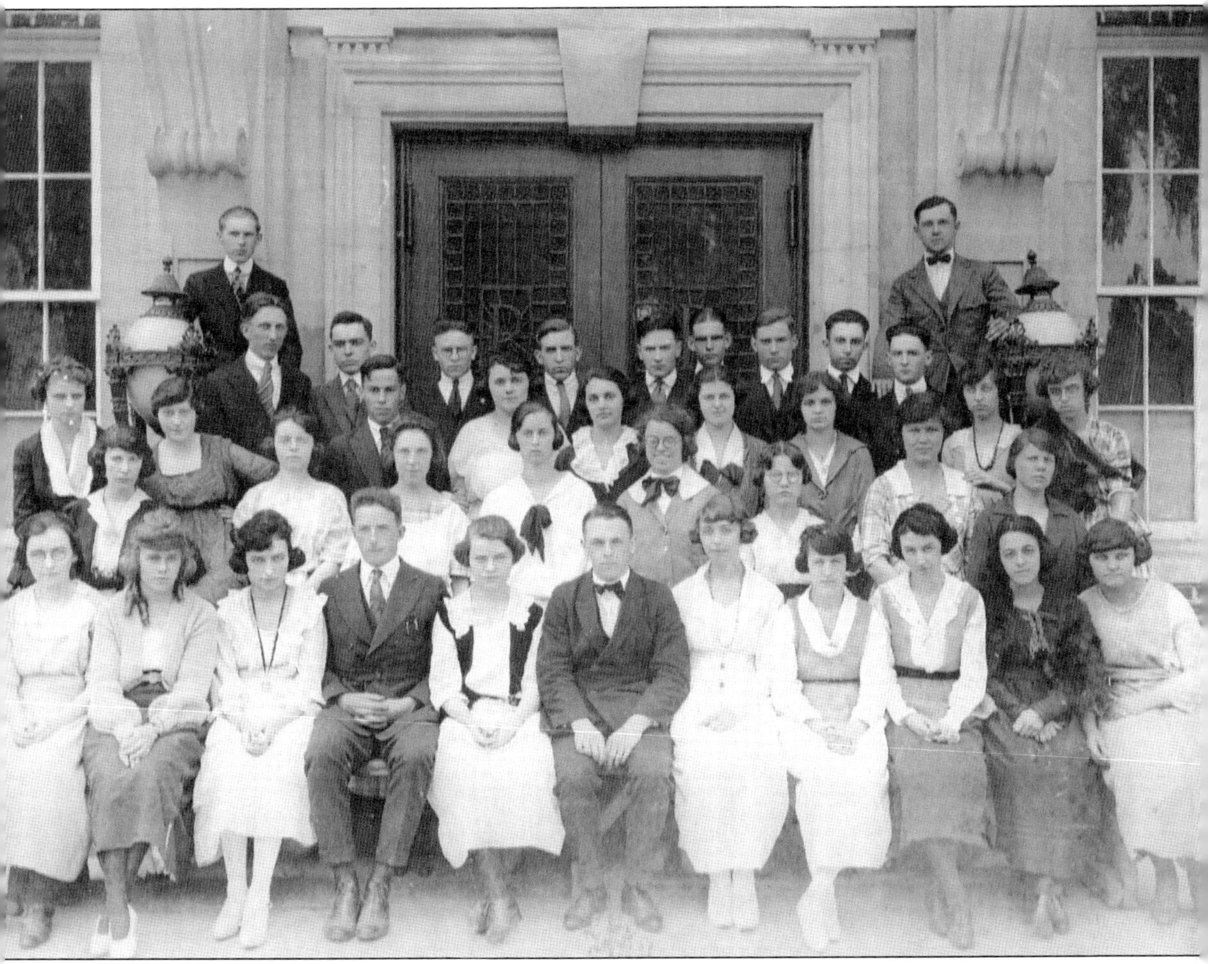

The Plattsburgh High School class of 1920 is shown here. Members of the class included, in no particular order, Leslie Wooton, Francis LaBombard, Arthur Bickford, Robert Conly, Francis Brennan, Donald Cameron, John Ryan, Carleton Bosworth, Malcolm Graham, Harold Stratton, Arthur Cogan, Edward Coville, Helen Delaney, Dorothy Hunt, Helen Hadley, Hilda Wright, Helen Carroll, Dorothea Freeman, Isabel Everest, Louise Honsinger, Nora McMartin, Leah Chapman, Katherine Phair, Cathirine Dwane, Helen Lewis, Hazel Stiles, Neila Atwood, Kathleen Graves, Marian Rooney, Gladys Herwirth, Gertrude Frazier, Joseph La Fleur, Martha Signor, Francis Gallagher, Grace Everest, Catherine Lucy, Flora Conway, Hazel Garrett, Mabel Westcott, and Delia Thurlow (not pictured).

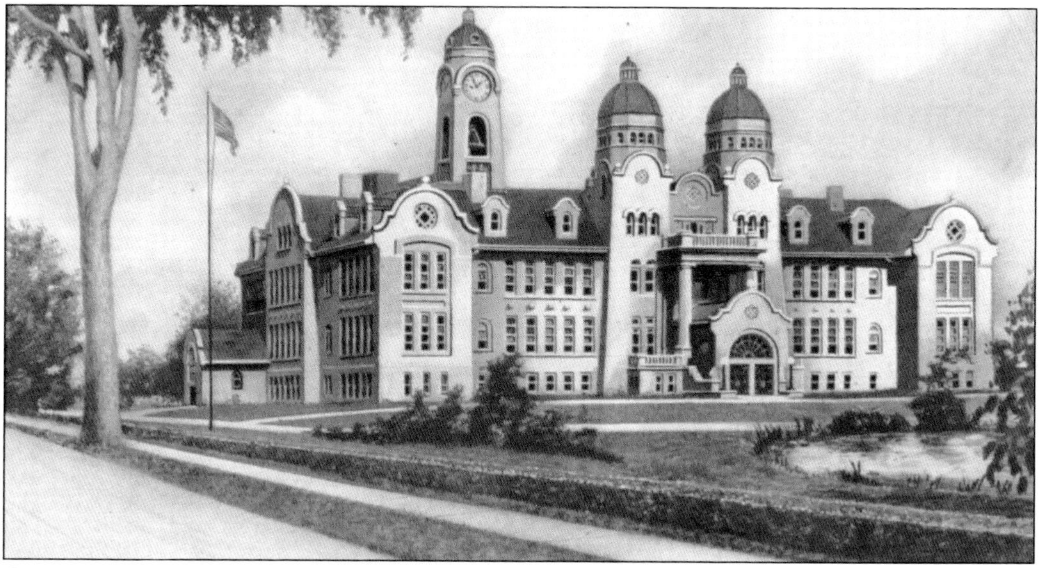

Operational by 1916, the Chazy Central Rural School was built by local businessman and philanthropist William H. Miner. The first consolidated school in New York State, CCRS included modern toilet facilities, swimming pools, a large auditorium, laboratories, workshops, and regular classrooms. Although a new building has replaced this structure, Miner's contributions are honored through the incorporation of statues, portraits, and artifacts from the original school.

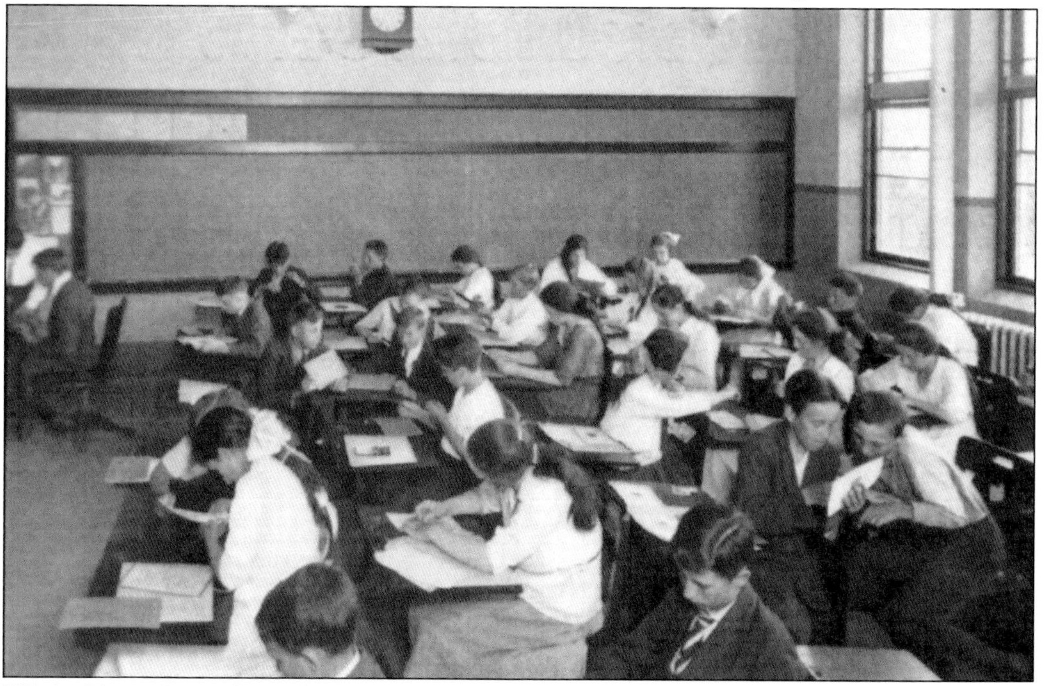

While Chazy Central Rural School highly valued traditional course work, the school district also emphasized the importance of the arts. Although other schools in the county also showed their commitment to the arts by offering classes, few had facilities like CCRS. This 1921 image shows a drawing class at the school. Notice the high ceilings and large windows, both features of highly effective studio space.

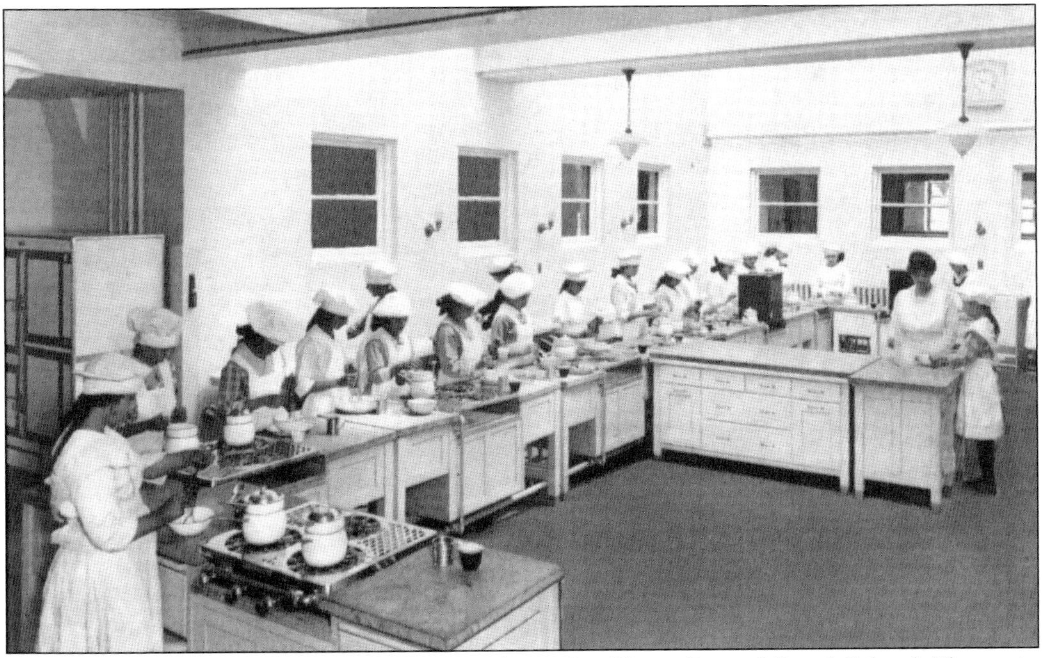

Household arts were among the courses taught at the Chazy Central Rural School. Shown in 1921, this classroom includes 20 female students and their teacher. The gender division was intentional: girls learned about the domestic arts of cooking, sewing, and cleaning; boys were given the option of learning other skills.

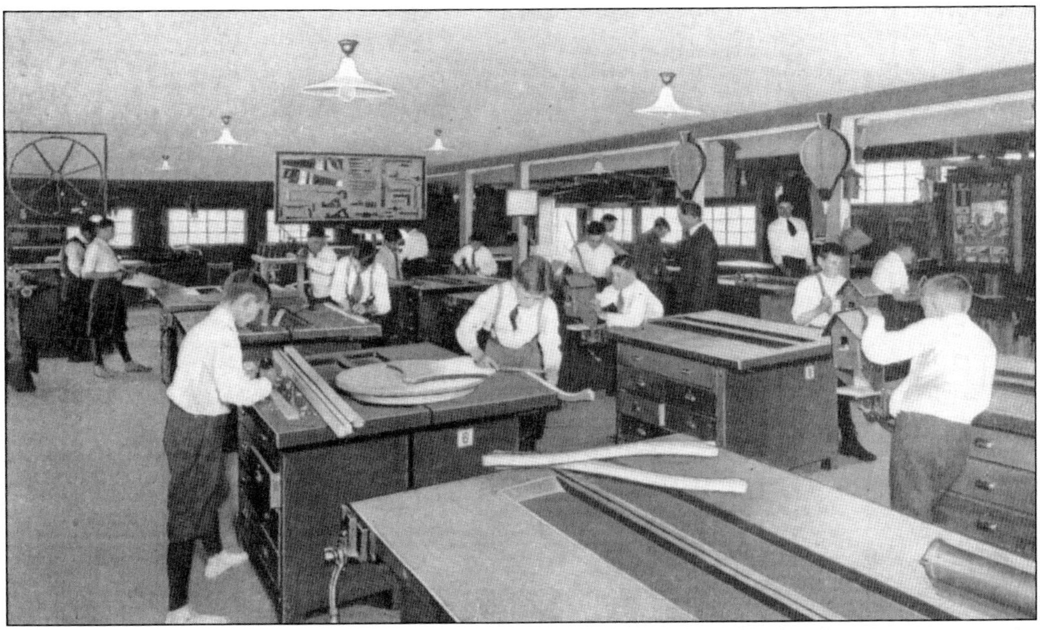

One of the choices available to boys at the Chazy Central Rural School was carpentry. As evidenced in this 1921 image, boys learned to identify and use tools to create objects of use in the school and around the community. Other options available to boys included the machine shop and drafting.

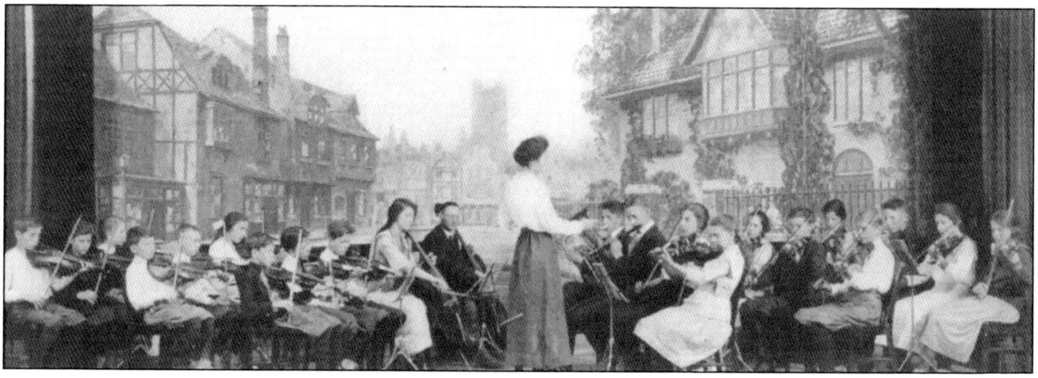

Music classes were another added feature of the Chazy Central Rural School. Though students in one- and two-room schoolhouses sang and presented concerts (mostly recitations), CCRS really offered the first formal musical training classes. This 1921 photograph indicates the depth of that music program: in addition to singing classes and a chorus, the school sponsored a string orchestra.

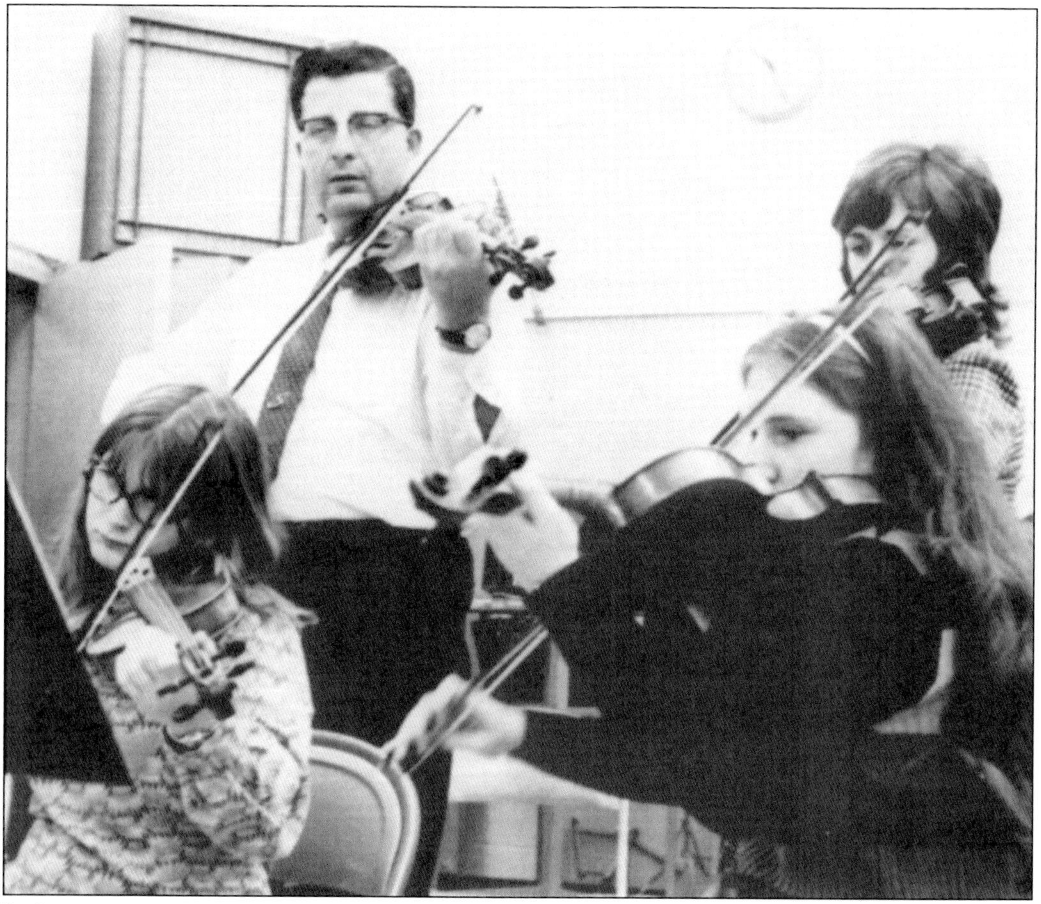

In later years, string instrument programs were adopted by the Peru Central and Plattsburgh City Schools, while band programs were developed by all of the county's schools. This 1974 image shows longtime Peru Central School orchestra director George Slosson with students in his string program.

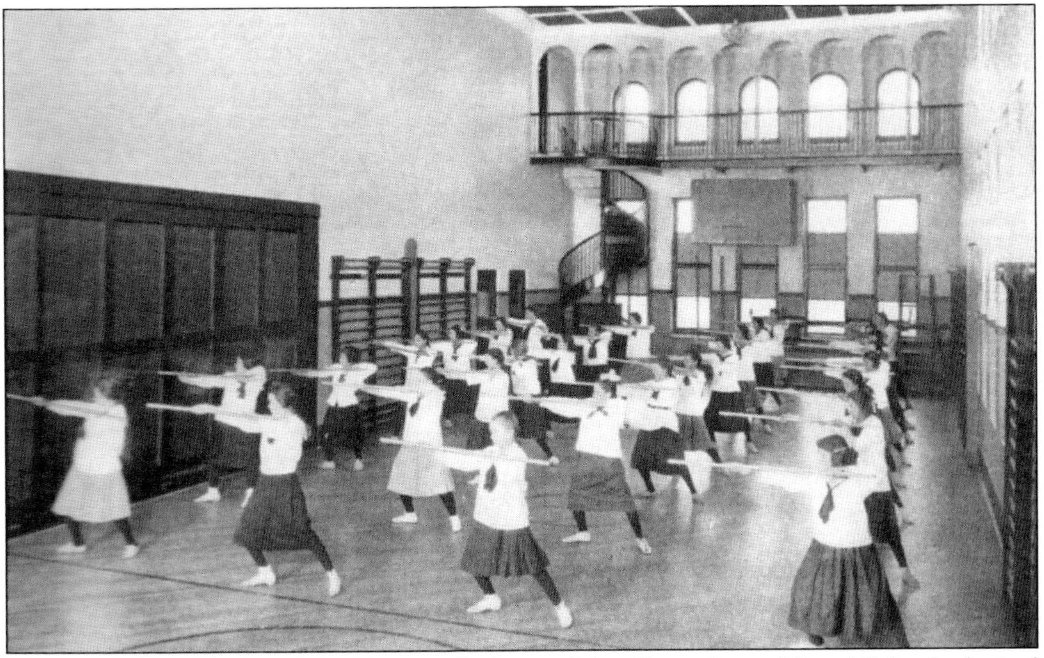

Although few schools had the extensive facilities of the Chazy Central Rural School, physical education classes were divided by gender throughout the county. Here, a group of girls exercises in the girls' gymnasium. In addition to this gym, the school had a boys' gymnasium and separate pools for both boys and girls.

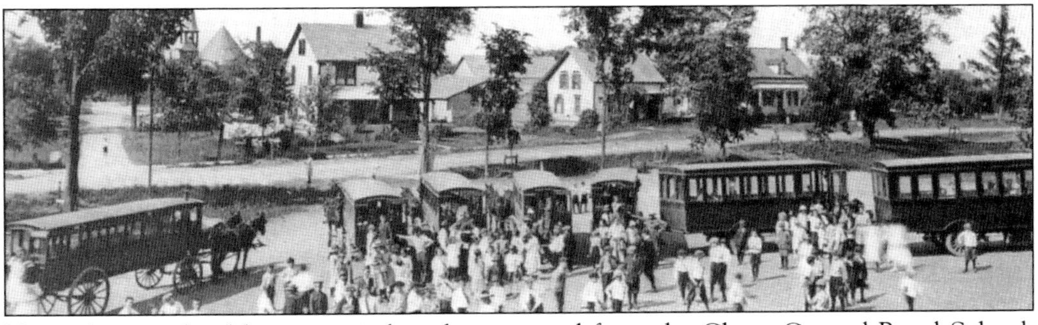

Horse-drawn school buses carried students to and from the Chazy Central Rural School. Centralization and consolidation required transportation of students from more remote locations; thus, all of the school districts (except the Plattsburgh City School District) needed to maintain a fleet of school buses.

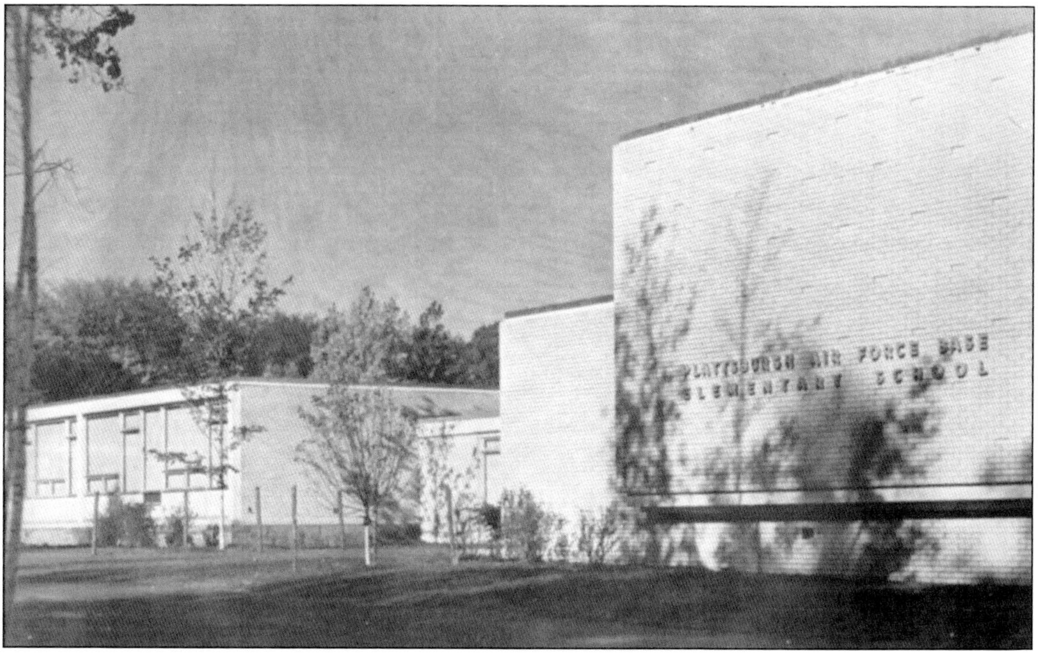

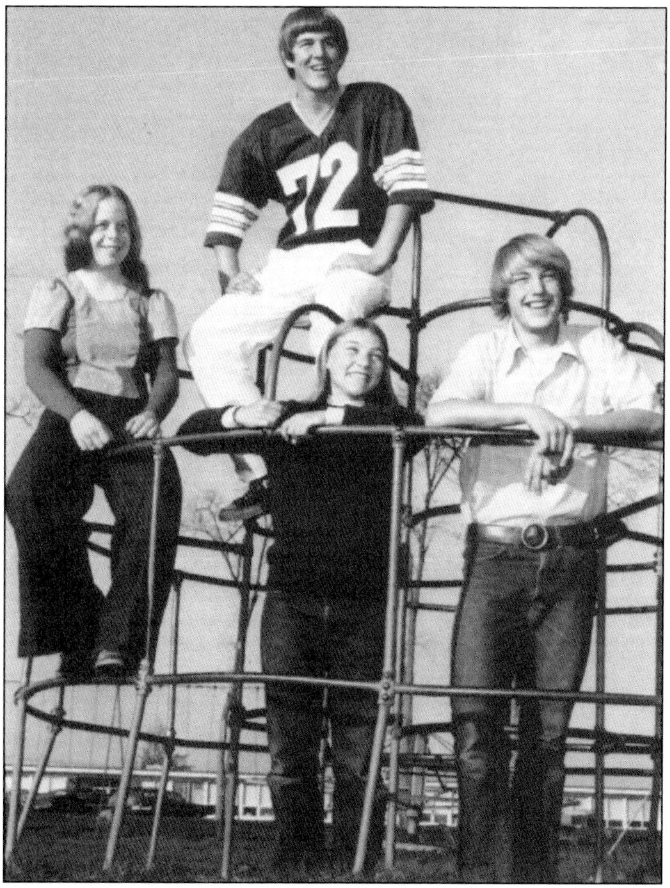

Plattsburgh Air Force Base included two schools. While most of the students at Northside Elementary School lived on the Air Force Base and moved from that school to the Plattsburgh City School District, Southside Elementary School students were mixed. Run by the Peru Central School District, Southside (shown here) included students from the Air Force Base and students from throughout the school district; similarly, Peru's home elementary school included both base and non-base students.

Peru Central School's 1974 freshman class officers pose on the elementary school playground. The primary school building, a one-story brick structure with a cafetorium and gym, stands in the background.

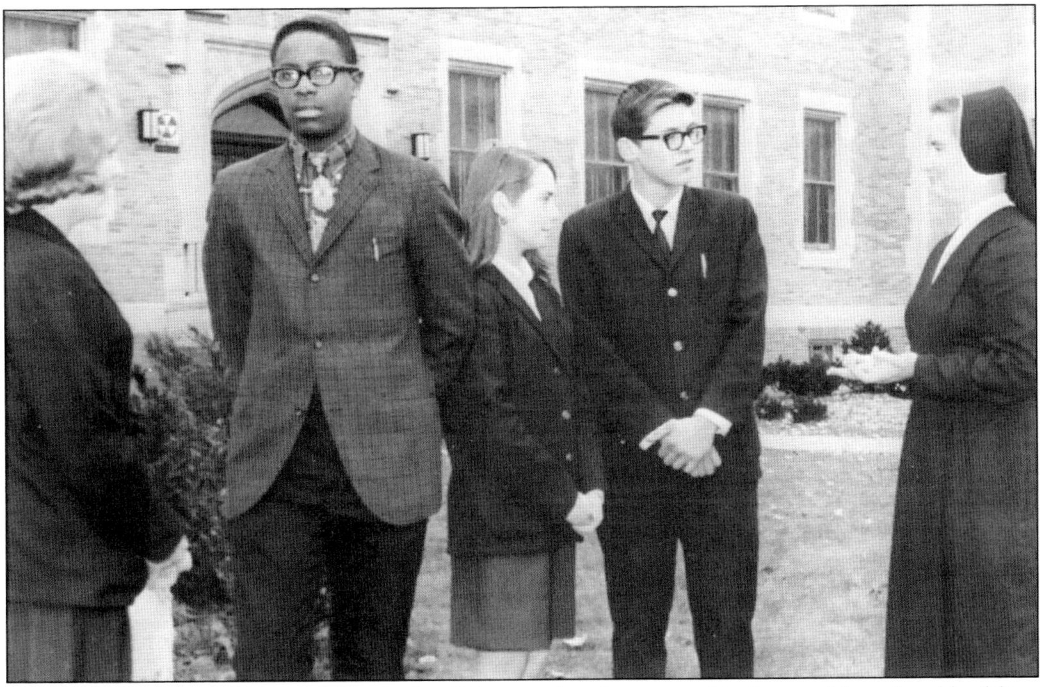

The freshman class officers of Our Lady of Victory Academy stand in front of the school building with Sister Mary Vincent. Serving for the Class of 1968 were Pamela Armstrong, president (third from left); Stephen McDonald, vice president (fourth from left); Lawrence Carlswell, treasurer; and Barbara Perry, secretary. Student governments are used throughout the county to teach civic responsibility and to give students a sense of empowerment.

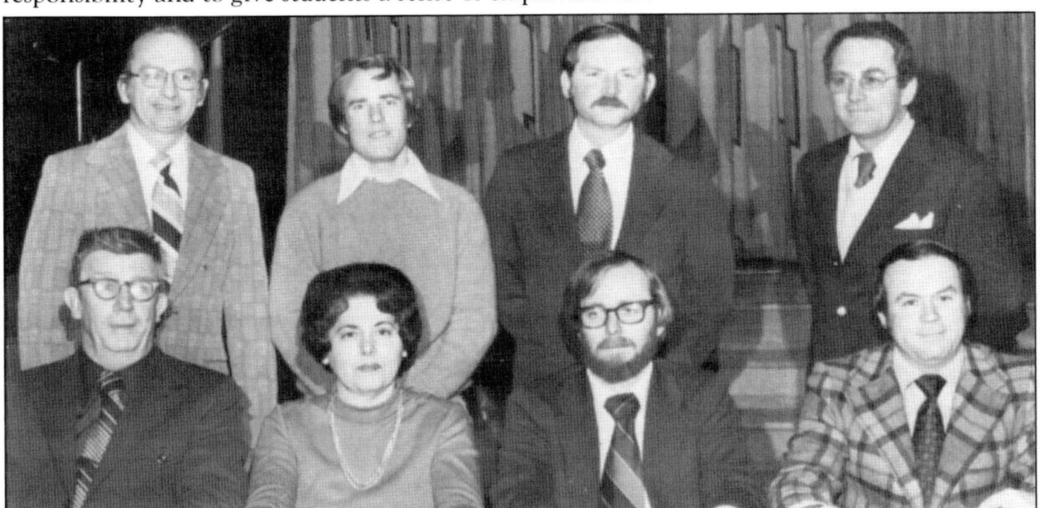

The 1976 Plattsburgh City School District Board of Education is shown here. Throughout the county, boards of education are elected to represent taxpayers and make budgetary decisions about schools. Seen here are, from left to right, (first row) James Lombard, June Heming, Ira Barbell, and Ed Fitzgerald; (second row) Charles Farrington, Dr. Robert Heins, William Cogan, and Michael McMartin. One school board member, Edward Bleeker, was not present when this photograph was taken.

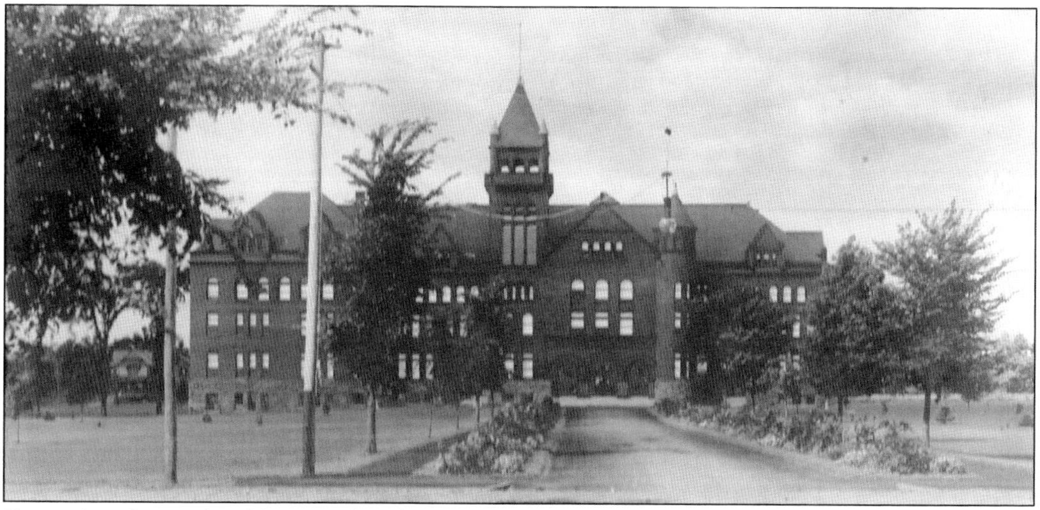

Opened on September 30, 1890, the Plattsburgh Normal School was the last of 11 Normal Schools to be built in New York State. Fox Holden, A.M., LL.B., became the first principal of the school, officially known as the New York State Normal and Training School at Plattsburgh. Under his guidance, the first commencement exercises were held on June 23, 1891, at the First Methodist Episcopal Church.

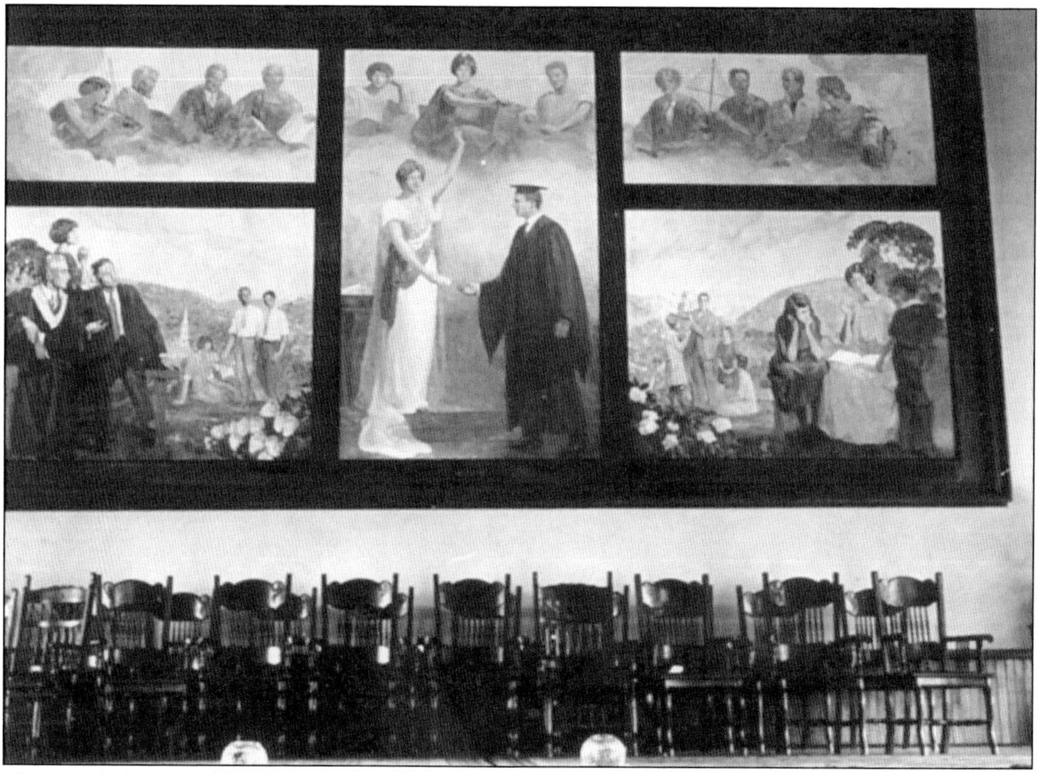

This symbolic mural by George L. Nelson was given to the Normal School by the classes of 1923, 1924, 1925, and 1926. The painting, lost in the fire of 1929, offered a vision of a Normal School student receiving his diploma from the State of New York. Surrounding him are representations of every field taught at the school.

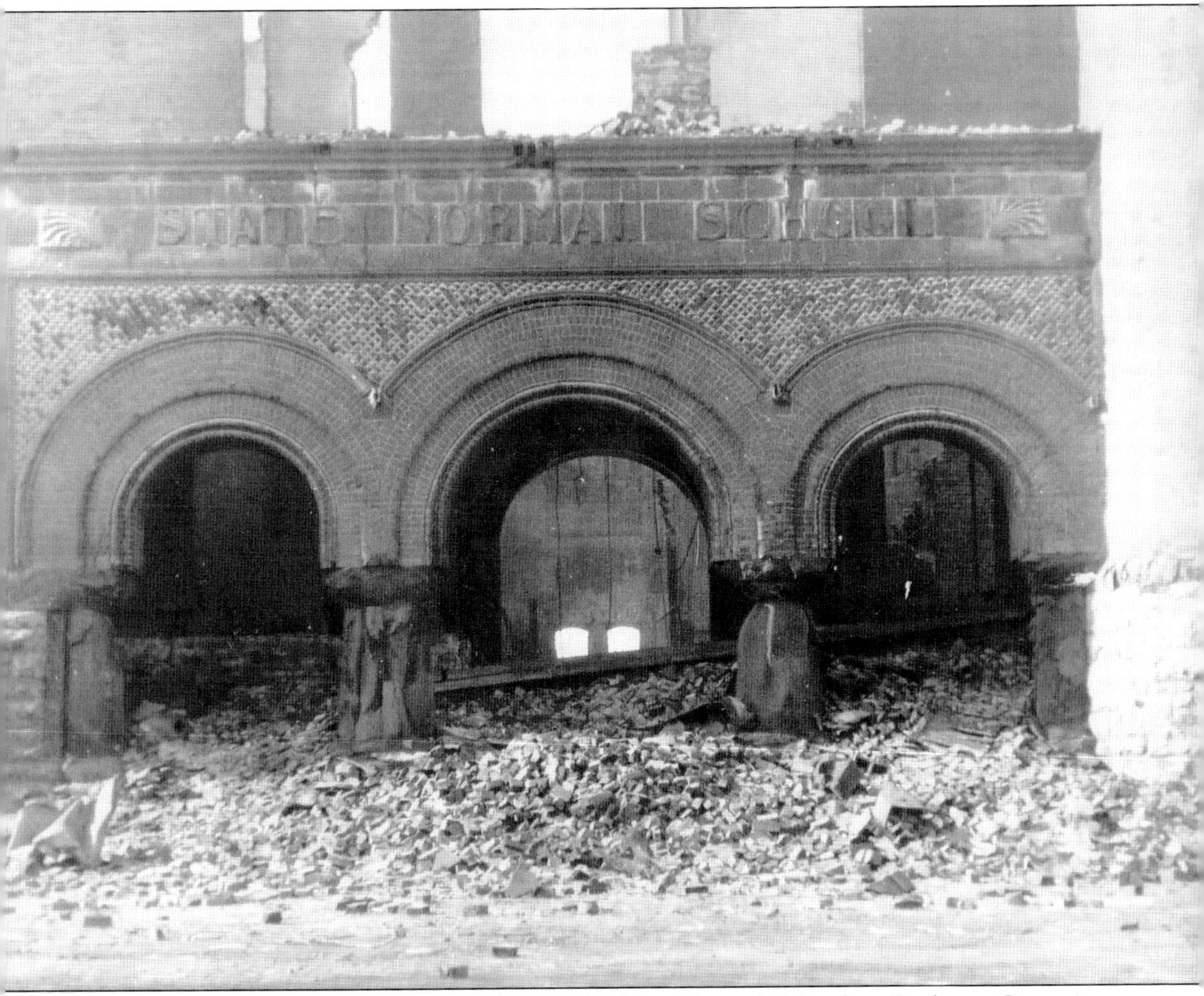

In 1929, fire destroyed the original building of the State Normal School on Beekman Street in Plattsburgh. Established in 1889 by the New York State Legislature to train teachers, the Normal School housed classrooms for students in the Model School, classrooms for Normal School students, lecture halls, and an auditorium. Once it was completed in 1932, the building grew to include classrooms, a few small lecture halls, a full-size auditorium, offices, and, after a 1990s renovation, a smaller recital hall. After the 1929 fire, the building was renamed Hawkins Hall in honor of George K. Hawkins, who was principal of the Normal School from 1898 until 1933.

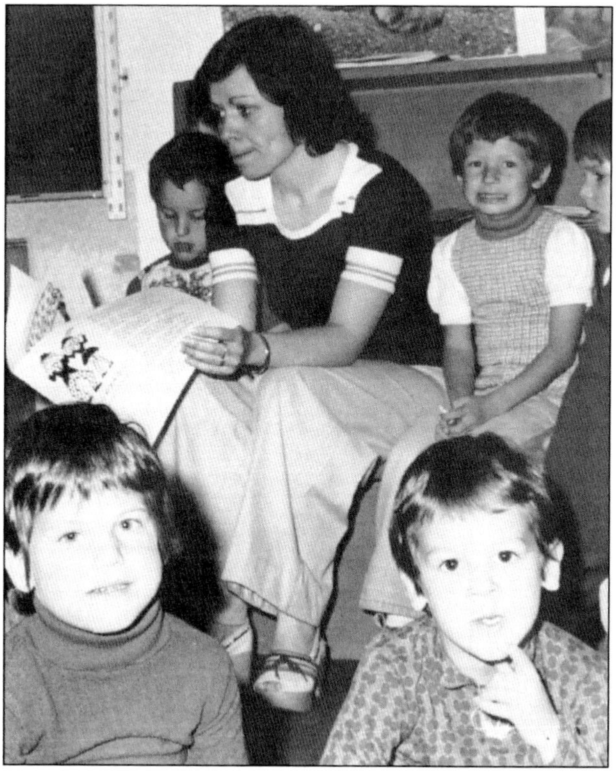

Even after the Normal School became the Plattsburgh State Teachers' College (1942), the State University Teachers' College at Plattsburgh (1948), the State University College of Education, (1959), the State University College of Arts and Science at Plattsburgh (1961), and Plattsburgh State University of New York, education has remained a hallmark of the institution. Education majors like the one shown here have observed and taught in local schools throughout the region since 1889.

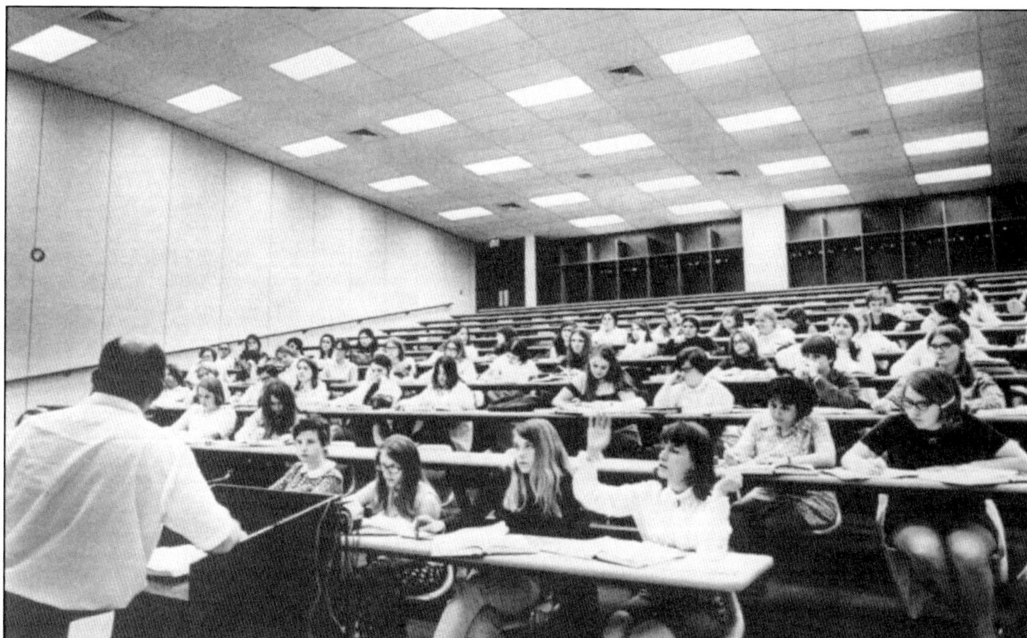

Under construction in 1969 and finished in 1970, the George E. Yokum Communications Lecture Hall houses the Communications Department and several lecture halls like the one shown here. Used by the largest classes at Plattsburgh State, these lecture halls hold between 100 and 500 occupants.

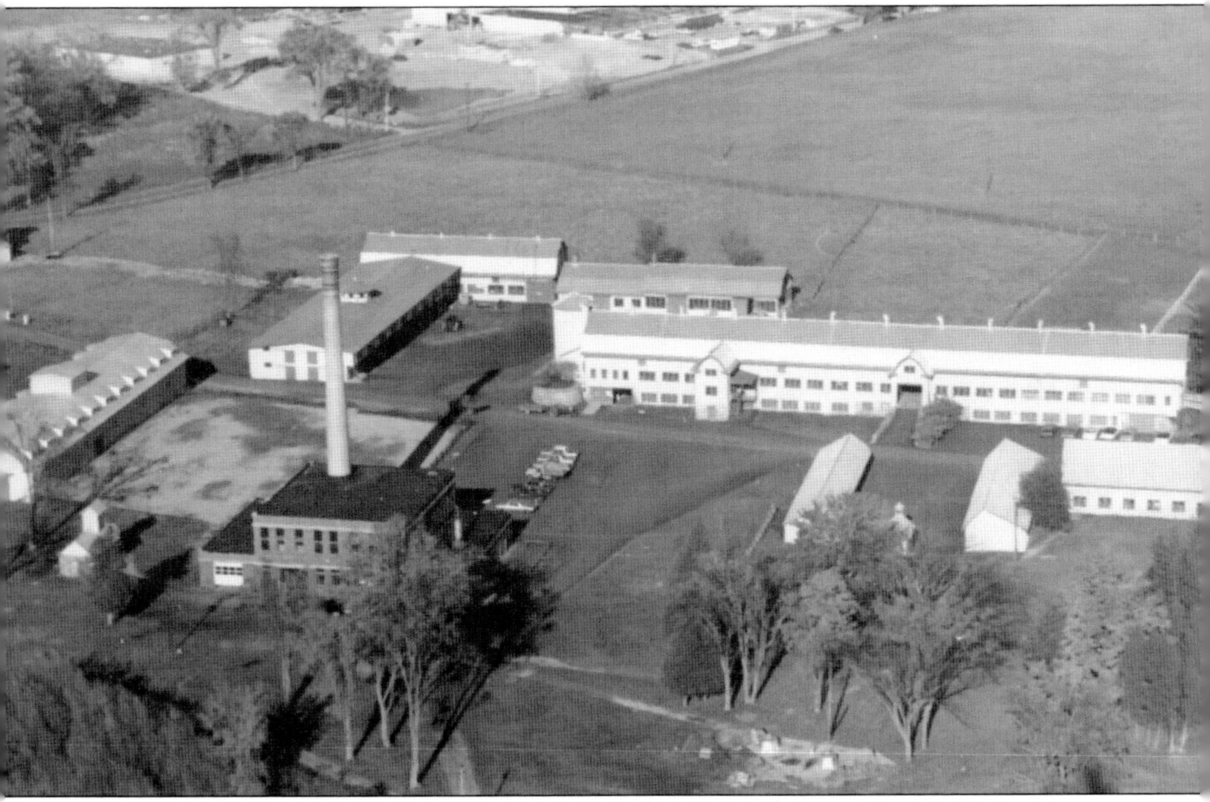

The William T. Miner Agricultural Institute, shown here from above, was originally known as Heart's Delight Farm. The original 144-acre family farm, to which 16,000 acres were eventually added, became the heart of the Miner Institute. Now affiliated with Plattsburgh State University, the Institute offers a residential program, established in 1972, that allows students to focus on Applied Environmental Science (AESP). Other Institute activities include an Agriculture and Environment program offered through the AESP since 2004 and an Advanced Dairy Management Program offered through the Vermont Technical College/University of Vermont 2+2 program. In addition to these educational programs, the Miner Institute also sponsors a series of research programs, including some related to horses, cows, dairy farming, and crops. A demonstration farm is also maintained by the Institute.

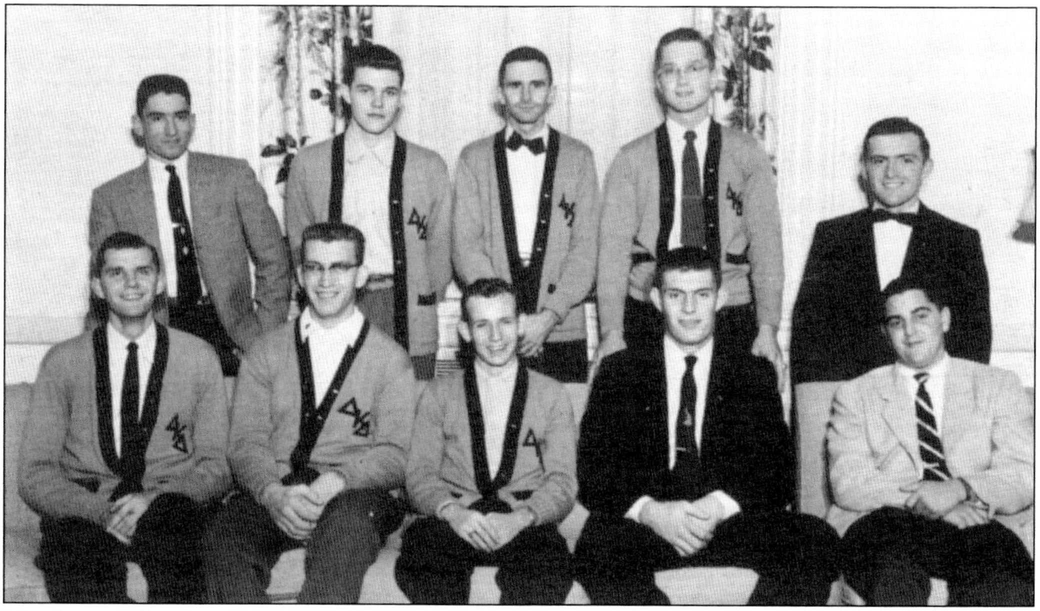

Members of Plattsburgh State University's Delta Kappa Delta fraternity pose in this 1956 photograph. From left to right are (first row) J. Duell, C. Winch, G. Kibler, H. Davey, and D. Riani; (second row) D. Proulx, M. Nye, B. Walker, H. Sheldon, and D. Henry. Newly developed when this photograph was taken, the fraternity fostered fellowship, brotherhood, and school spirit throughout the college and alumni communities.

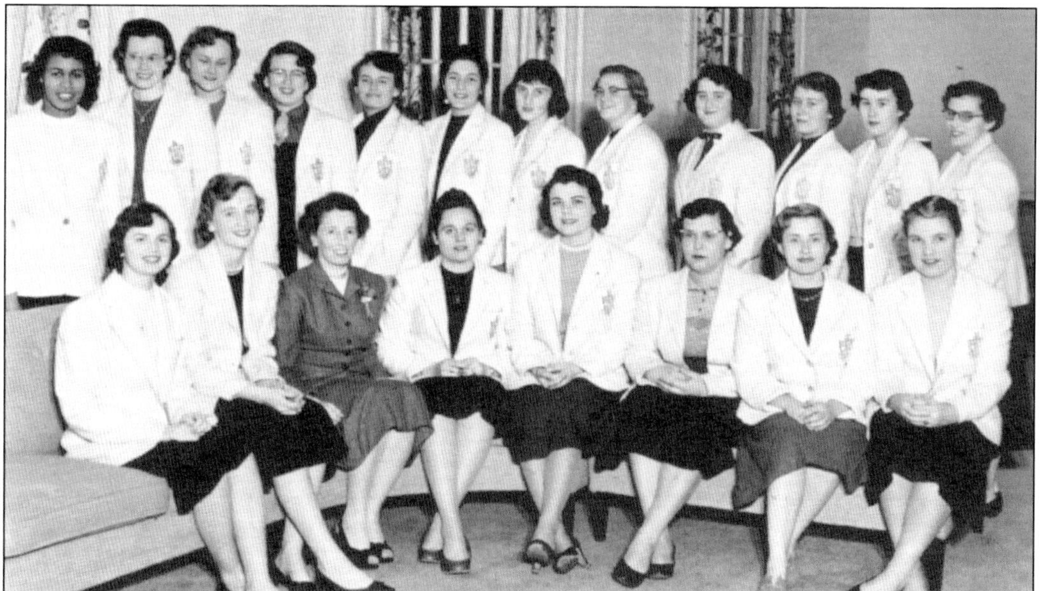

This 1956 image shows some of the members of Plattsburgh State University's Alpha Delta sorority, organized in 1925 to promote intellectual, social, and character development among its members. From left to right are (first row) R. Smith, E. O'Connor, Dr. Alice Backus (advisor), C. Garrant, J. Ward, B. Trudeau, C. Sullivan, and M. McIntyre; (second row) B. Sterling, M. DeYoungh, R. Harzmann, H. Poggenburg, H. Rote-Rosen, H. Foote, M. Allen, E. Fitzgerald, K. Main, K. Jackson, N. Ladue, and L. Knapp.

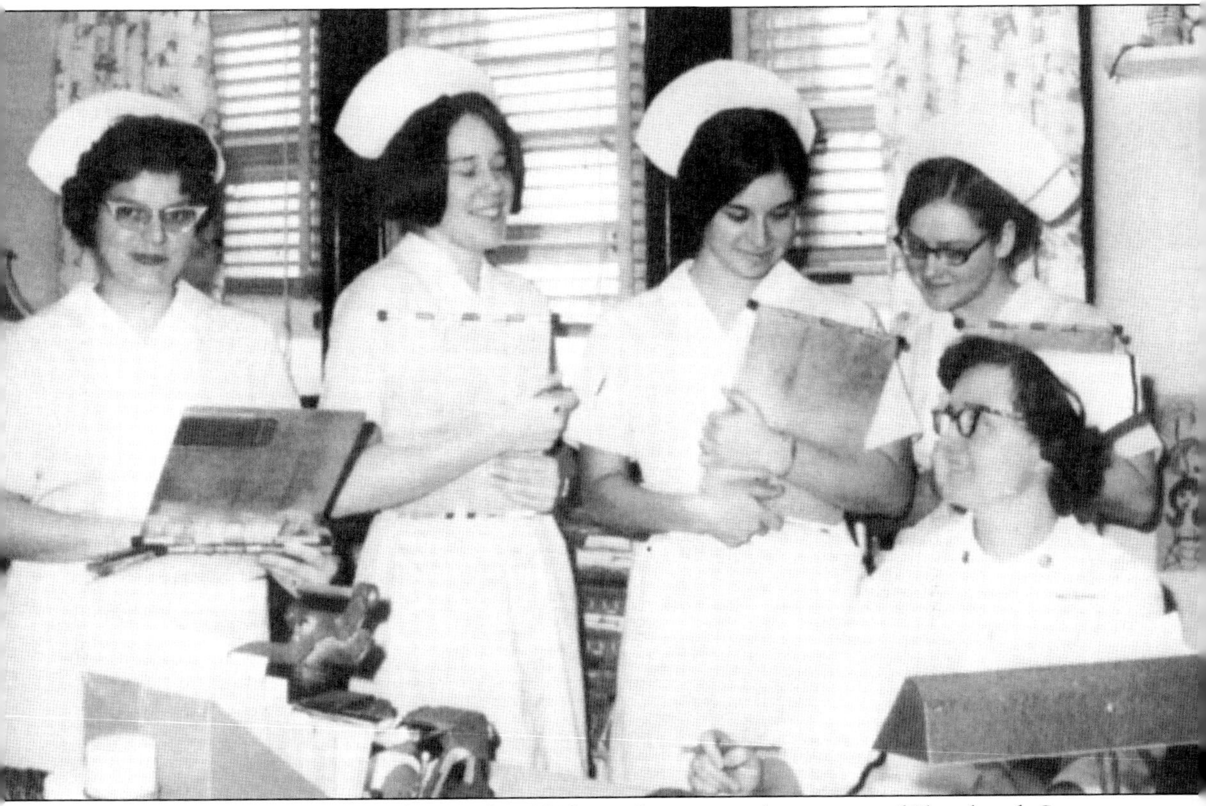

The Champlain Valley Hospital opened in 1910 on what is now the campus of Plattsburgh State University. The Order of the Grey Nuns of the Cross, who had arrived at the D'Youville Academy in Plattsburgh in 1860, petitioned local businessmen to create the hospital in 1903. Once the hospital was founded, the Grey Nuns trained nurses and ministered to the sick. To accompany an elaborate three-story stone hospital, a nursing dormitory was erected in 1926. Students completed their classroom and laboratory work, as well as their clinical observations, within this hospital and dormitory. Nonsectarian, the hospital welcomed patients of all incomes and abilities to pay.

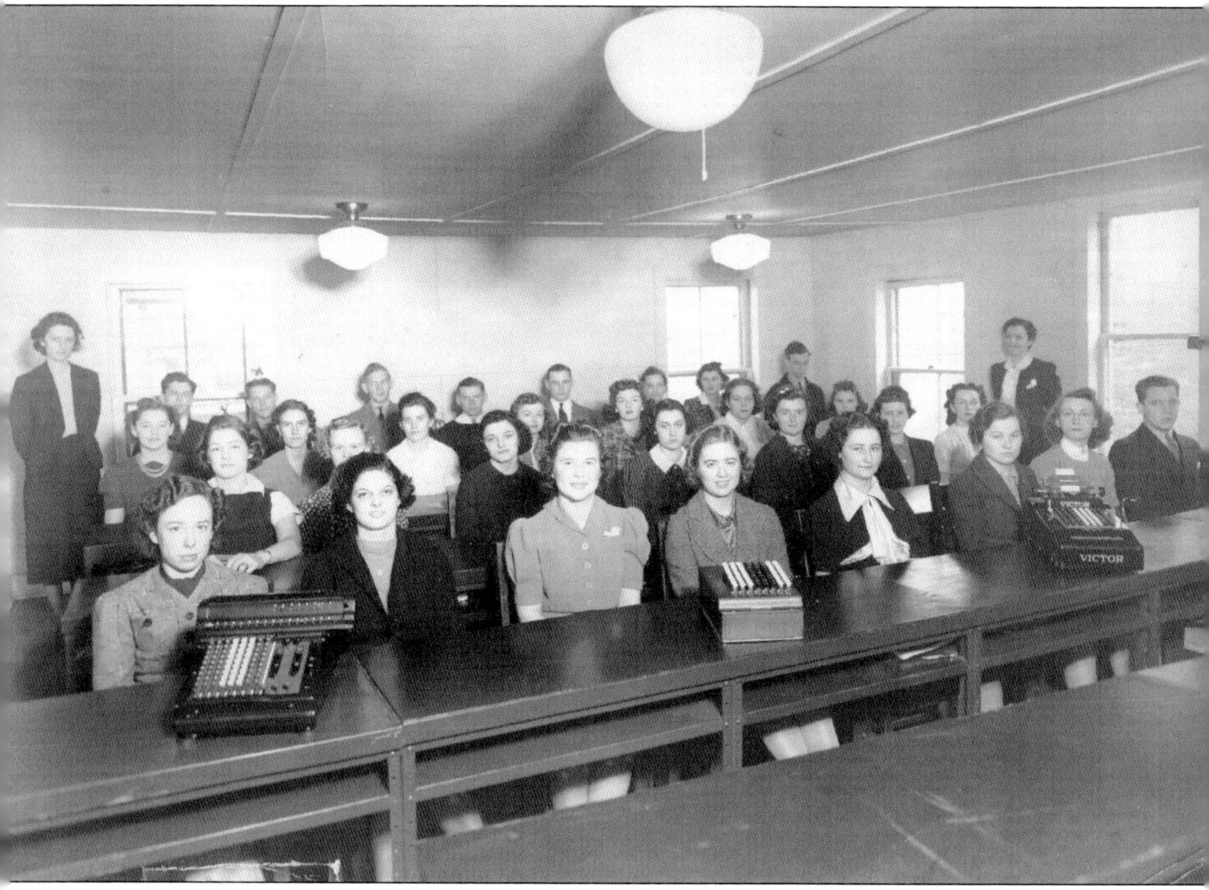

Shown here is the 1939 graduating class of the Plattsburgh Business Institute, along with their teachers, Mrs. Genevieve Lyons (left) and Mrs. Margaret Sullivan. Leona Newell and Wallace P. Gadway, each of whom has been marked with an "x," later married; their daughter donated this photograph to the Clinton County Historian's Office in their memory. The Plattsburgh Business Institute taught commercial, stenographic, and secretarial courses. Situated in second-floor rooms on Oak Street, the school was created in 1930 by Samuel Todd. Leo Nash's bus company offered service to Oak Street, making transportation easier for students. Prior to 1929, the Plattsburgh Traction Company offered trolley service on roughly the same route, which covered Broad, Beekman, Cornelia, Montcalm, Bailey, Oak, Riley, Margaret, Bridge, Macdonough, Hamilton, and Peru Streets.

Four

AGRICULTURE

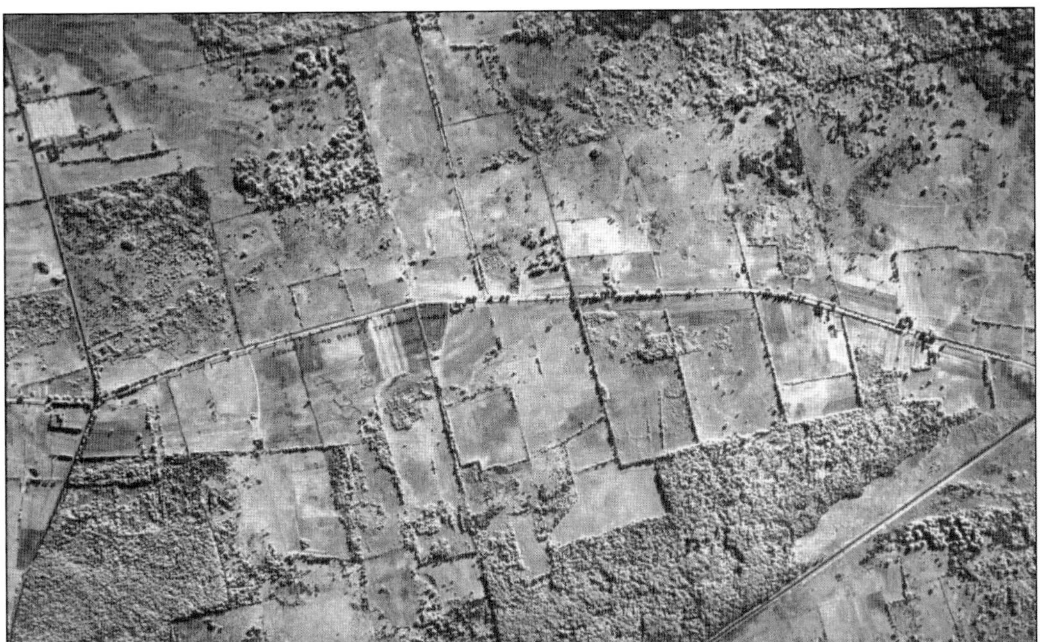

This aerial view of Spellman Road, in the town of Beekmantown, shows carefully delineated plots of land. Of particular interest are the wooded areas and the fields, most of which have been used to plant crops for local farms. Major local crops include corn, potatoes, and apples, while dairy cows and chickens are among the most common county livestock.

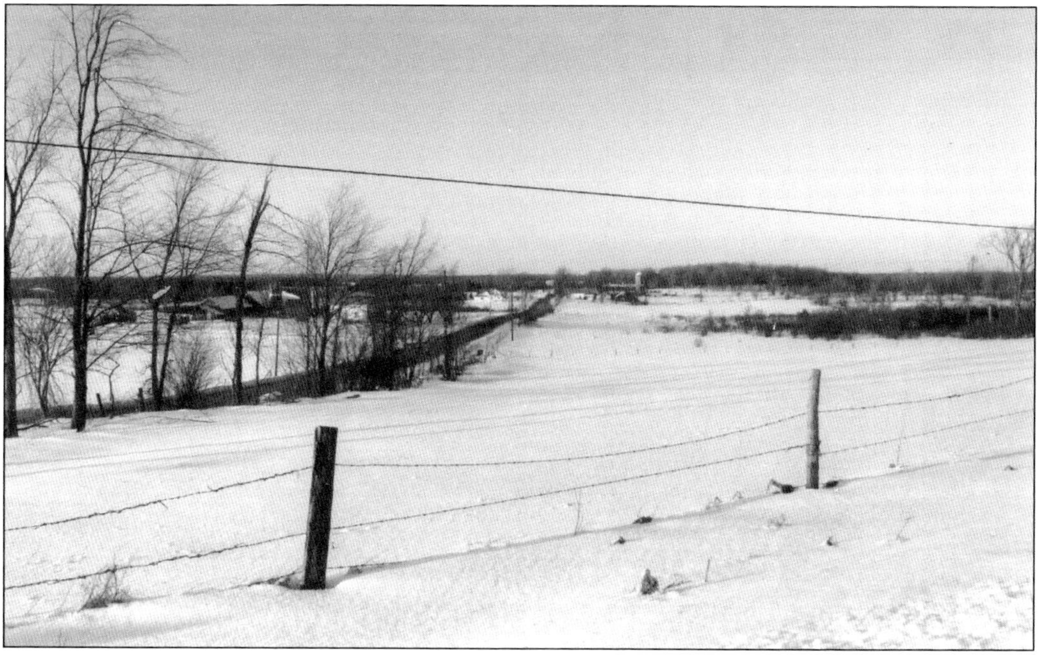

A typical image of Clinton County's rural areas, this 1984 photograph of Old Route 190 in Ellenburg shows fields bounded by barbed wire fences and two fully functional farms in the distance. New York State continues to boast about 7.55 million acres of farmland, which produced more than $3.6 billion in 2005.

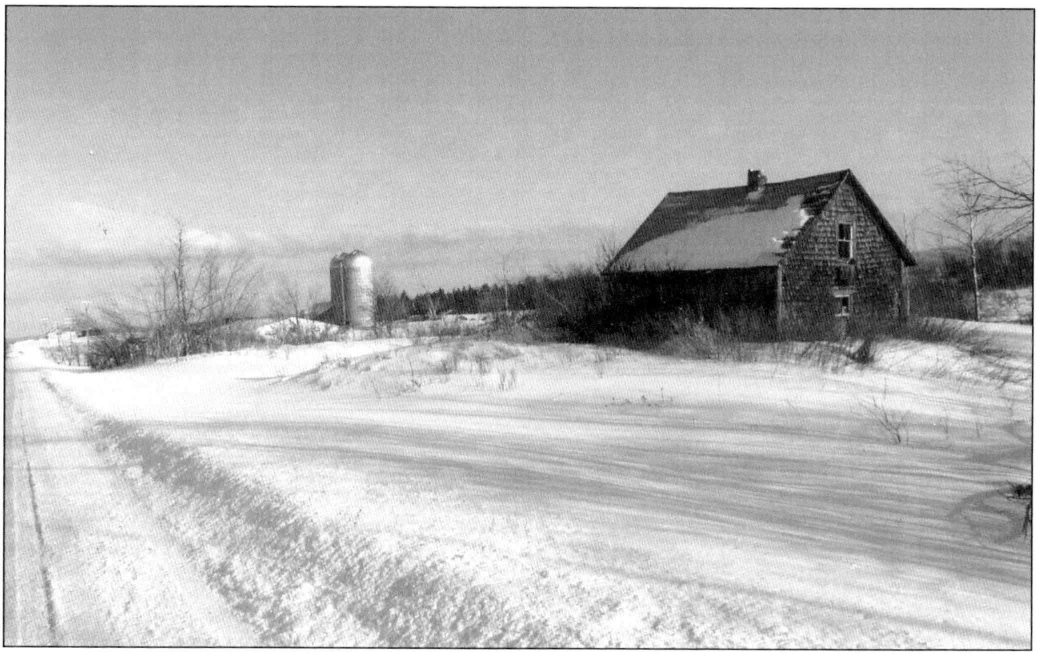

This 1984 image of the Frances Boyea Moore homestead on West Hill, Ellenburg Center, also shows Route 190, looking east, and the Floyd Peets' farm. Farms such as these generally raise dairy cows, thus contributing to the sale of New York's largest agricultural product, milk. Other popular county crops include potatoes, corn, and apples.

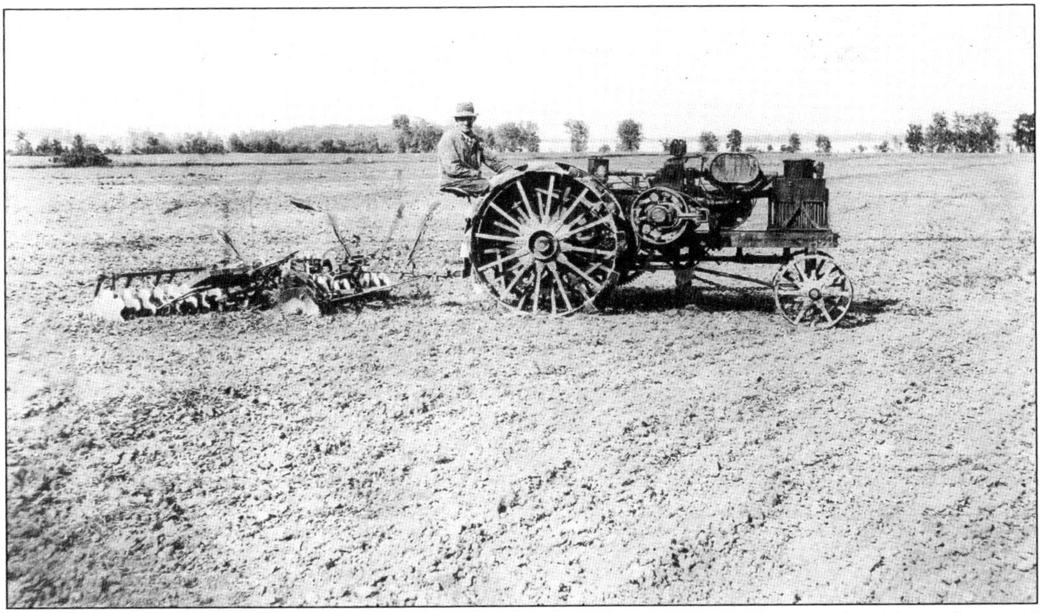

George LaPlante works the land of Jackie Reynolds' farm around 1860. Notice Lake Champlain and the Green Mountains in the distance. Many of Clinton County's farms are situated in such picturesque spots, benefitting from the relative proximity to water and the general freedom from flooding.

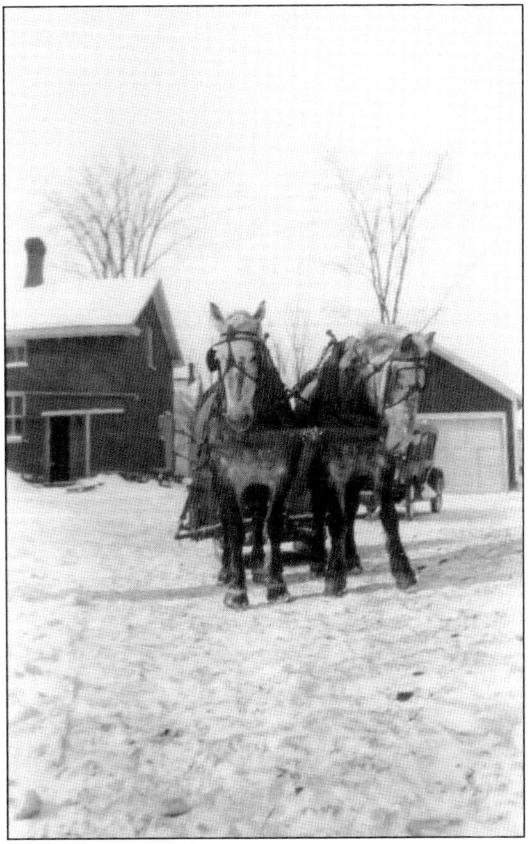

Long after automobiles and tractors were widely available, horse and oxen teams continued to be used for farming. This photograph offers an interesting view of the changing technologies of the farm, with a team of horses leading the way and an automobile following.

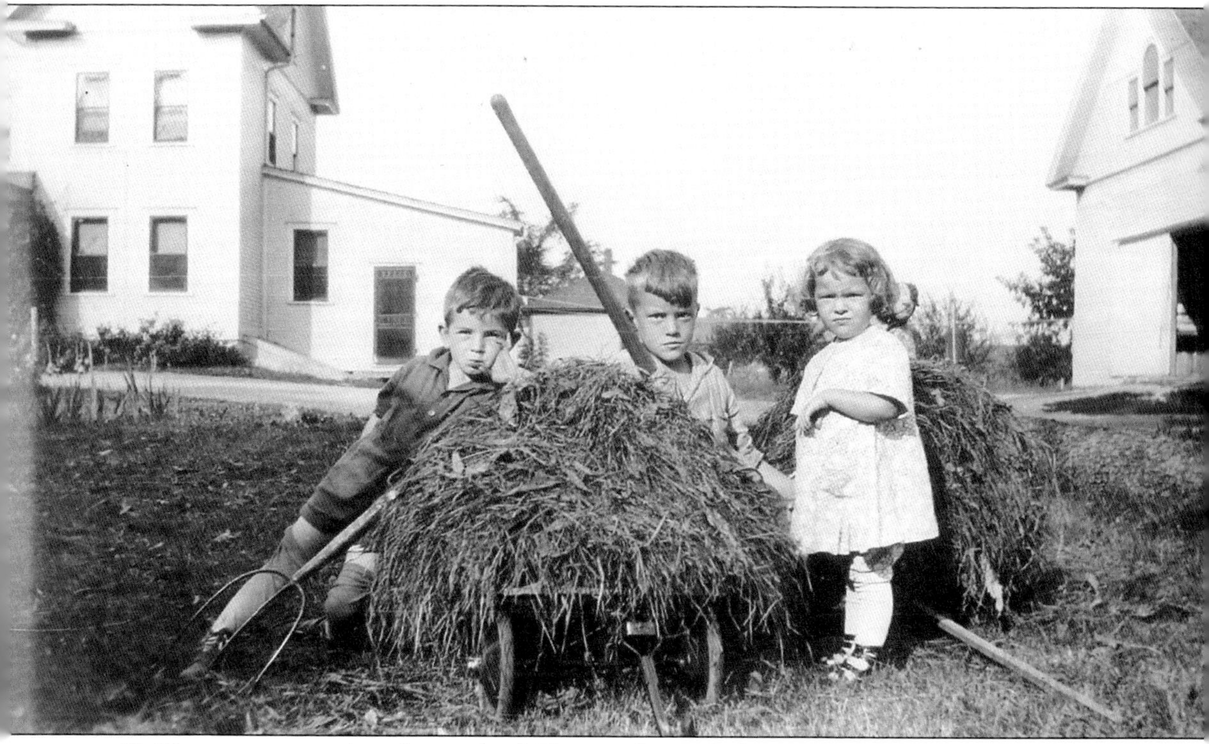

Children participated in the work of Clinton County's farms. Here three children (Winford Cheeseman is on the left) play at raking hay. They have used their pitchforks to load a wagon full of hay to be used as bedding and food for the animals. As these children grew older, they would have been assigned jobs on the family's farms—for the boys, those jobs would have included baling hay. In 2005, New York State's farms produced $282 million worth of hay. Though earlier generations did not earn such a substantial sum, they relied on locally grown hay heavily, both as an important farm supply and a source of cash income.

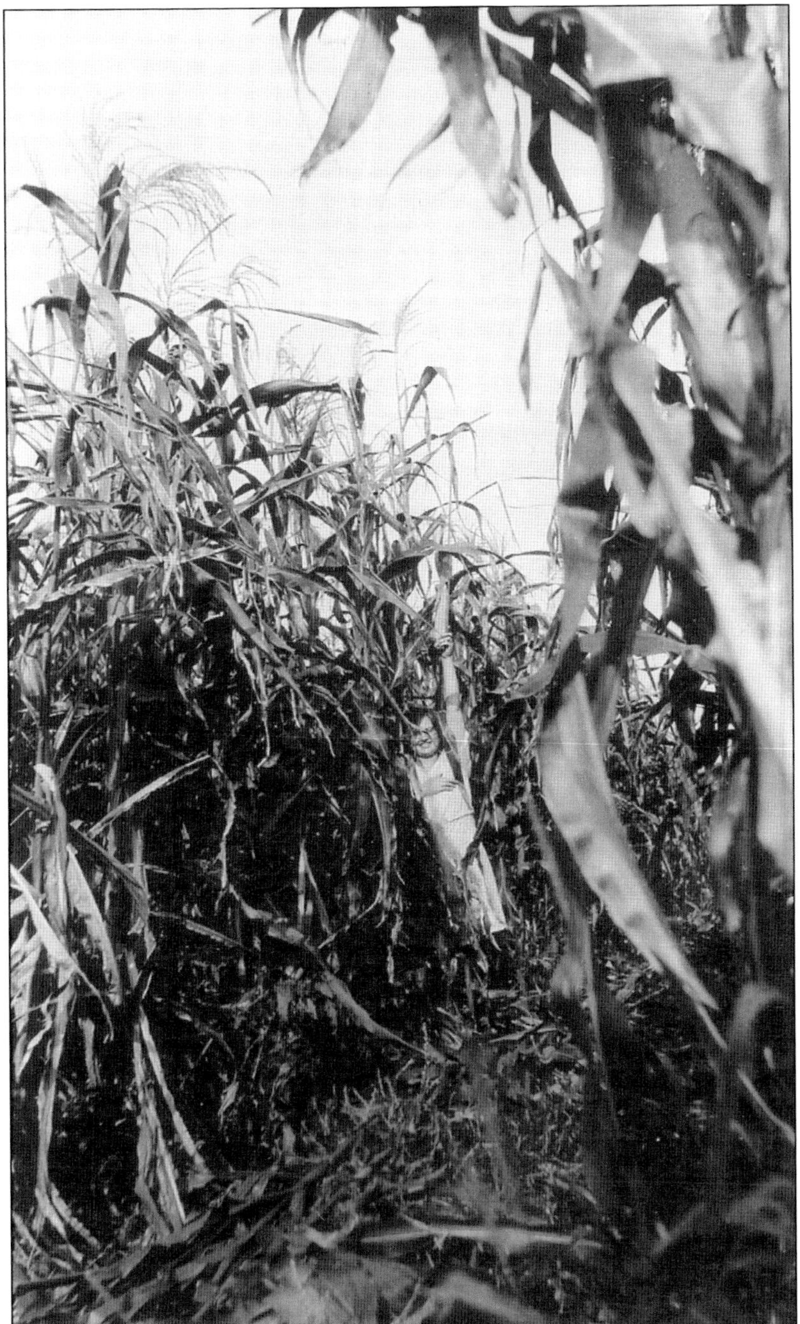

Corn has long been one of Clinton County's principal crops. Grown for human and animal consumption, residents count on corn to be "knee-high by the fourth of July." The Ellenburg crop shown here is truly exceptional, rising at least 2 feet higher than Maddie Cheeseman. Throughout the second part of the 1800s, more than 250 acres of corn and more than 4,000 acres of Indian corn were sown throughout the county. According to the New York Agricultural Statistics Service, corn continues to be a valuable state crop: in 2005, New York raised $227 million of corn silage and $117 million of grain corn.

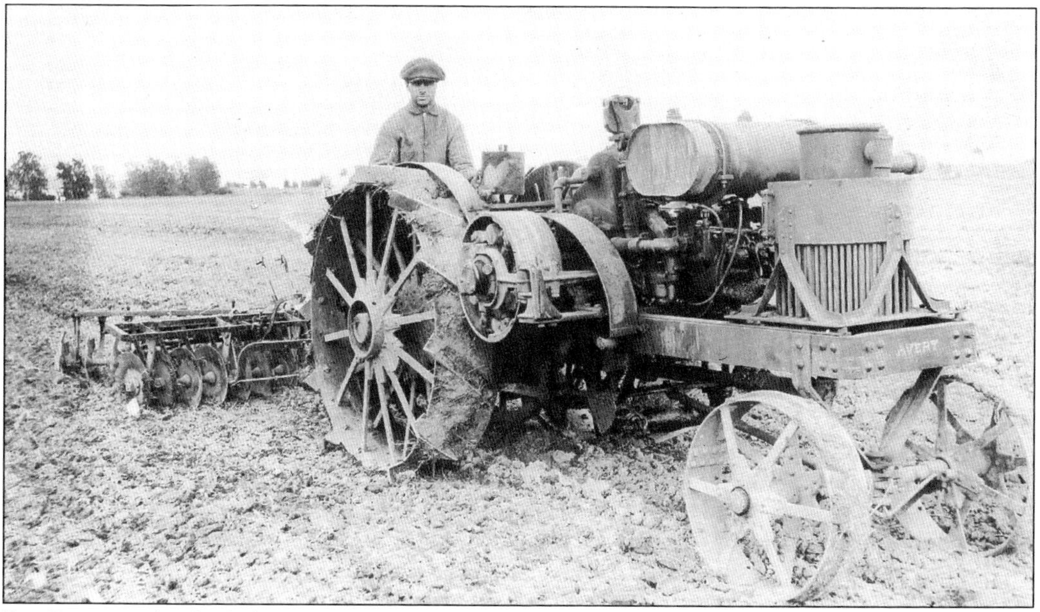

Ben Bruce works the fields with an Avery tractor. Fieldwork included plowing the land, harrowing, planting seeds, harvesting the crop (with subsequent steps of tedding and baling), and plowing again. Tractors helped to speed many of these processes, though horse-and-oxen teams remained useful throughout the first half of the 20th century.

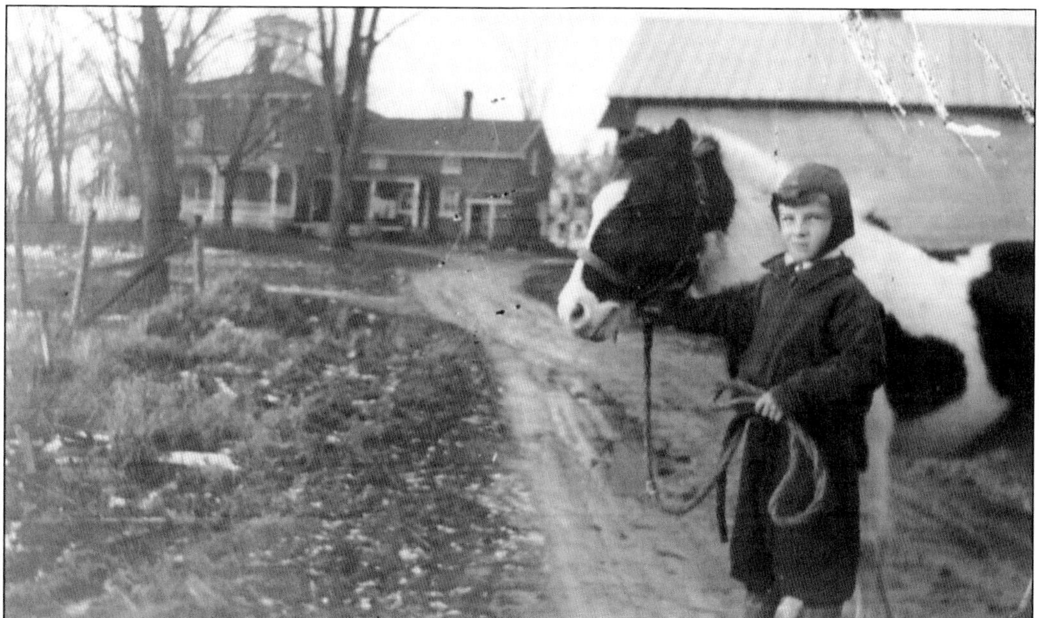

A young Winford Cheeseman stands with his pony in the yard of his family's Ellenburg Depot farm. Unlike many other Clinton County farmhouses, the Cheeseman farm—named Clover Crest Farm—used a hipped roof and ornamental bracings.

This photograph of Clover Crest Farm, which raised registered Ayrshires, shows a relatively standard Clinton County barnyard. Along with a cow barn (to the left), the farm boasts a barn to the right and two silos for grain storage. To get an idea of the scale of the buildings, look at the man standing atop the white silo.

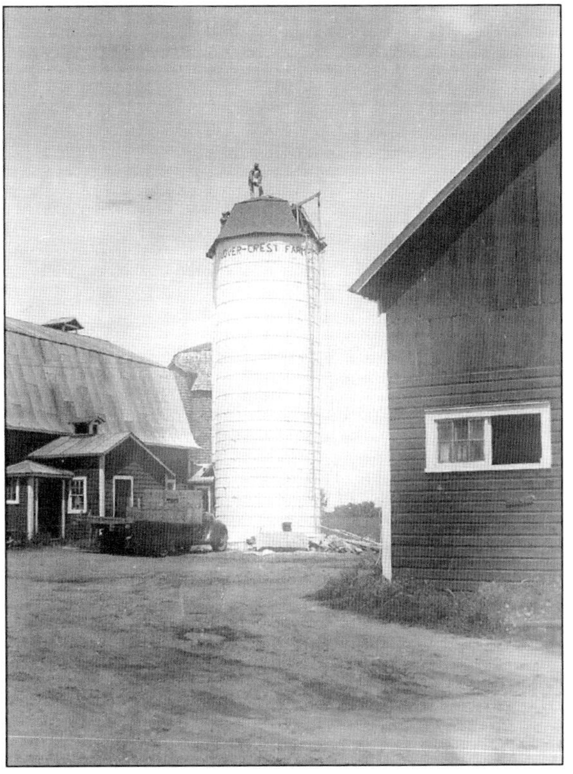

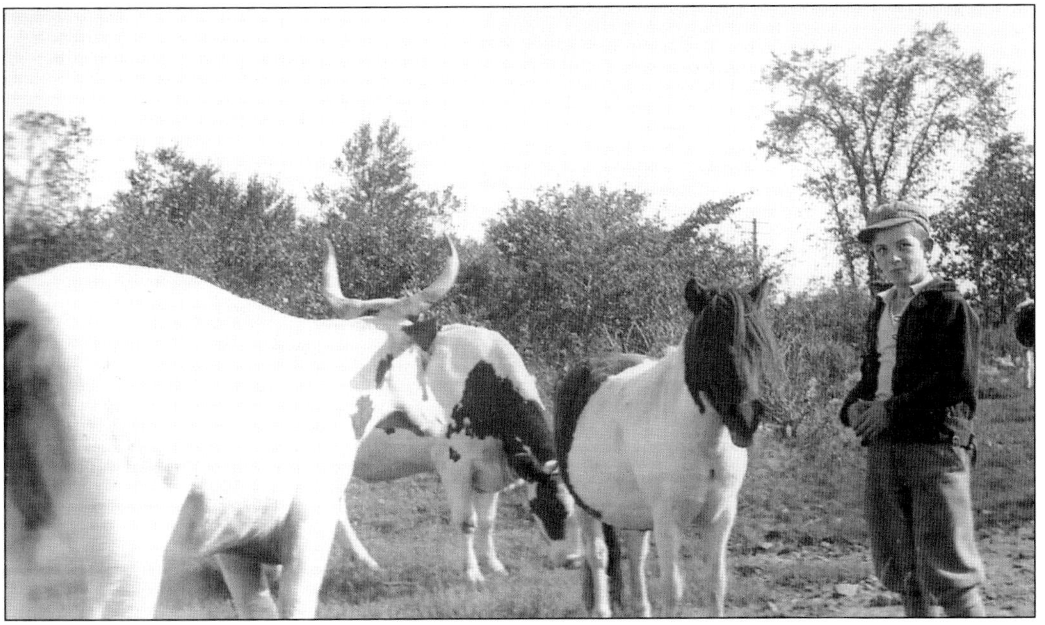

Winford Cheeseman, with his pony, stands in the field with some of his family's cows. Dairy farming has been the cornerstone of life in Clinton County, with family farms producing milk, butter, and cheese. In the latter half of the 19th century, more than 13,000 milch cows, on average, were kept. Those cows produced more than 52,000 gallons of milks, more than 28,000 pounds of cheese, and more than 1.1 million pounds of butter.

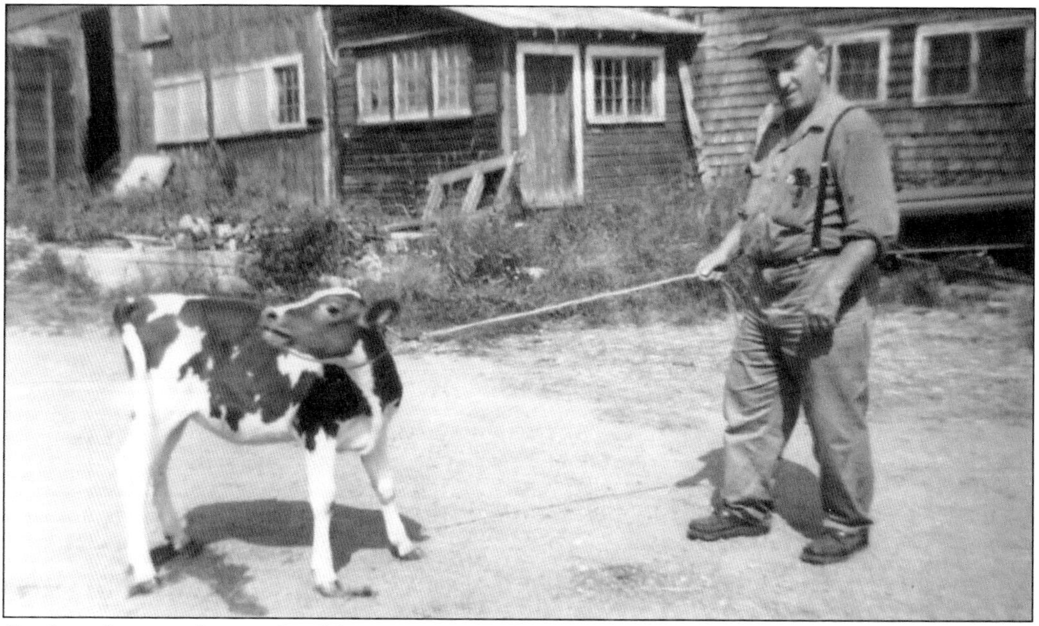

On dairy farms, calves are bred for maximum milk or beef production. Here Marshall Cheeseman works with Lucky Delight, a calf whose dame was CC Sun Myra and whose sire was Whitpain Man O'War. County-wide statistics show the presence of 3,493 two-year-old heifers, 4,028 yearling heifers, 4,316 calves, 1,951 bulls of all ages, and 1,959 working oxen and steers, in addition to 13,023 milch cows during the second half of the 19th century.

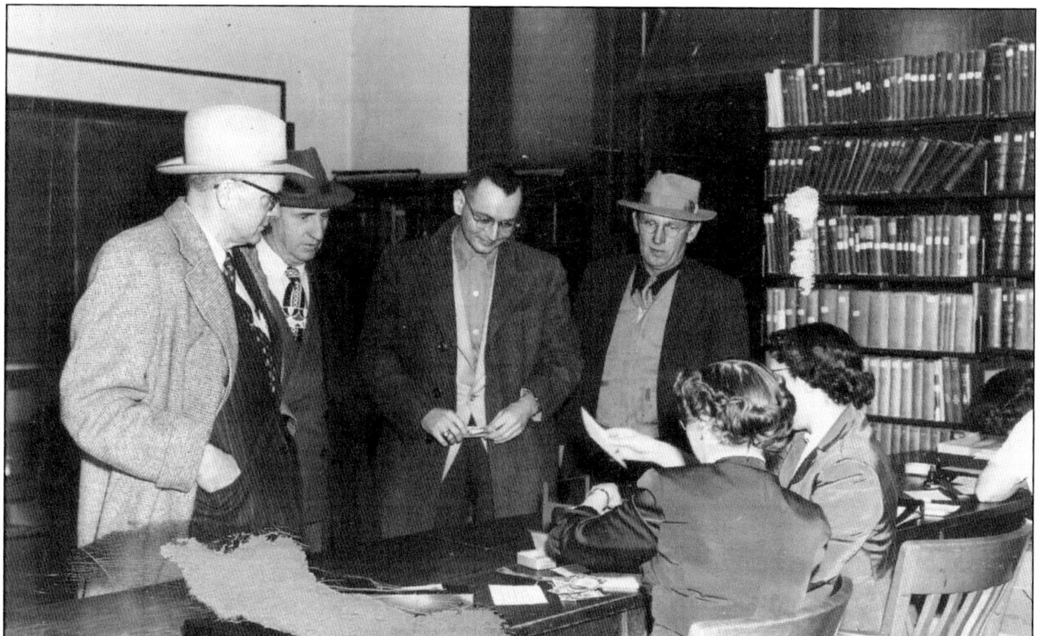

Marshall Cheeseman registers for the Beef Cattlemen's short course. From left to right, the men are Ralph Lewis of Mooers, Marshall Cheeseman of Ellenburg Depot, John Leveridge of Plattsburgh, and Floyd Grant of Cazenovia. Courses such as this, often offered by the Cooperative Extension, were designed to help farmers improve the productivity of their farms.

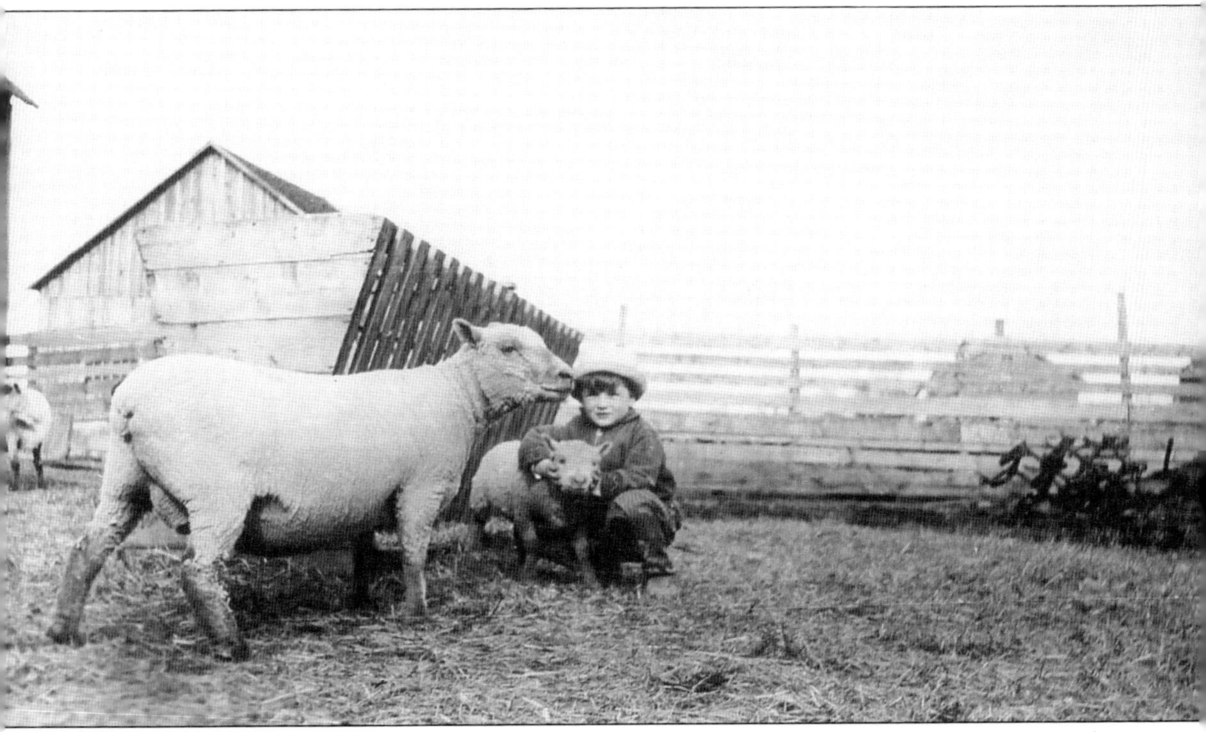

Along with cows, local farmers raised sheep for wool and meat. This photograph, taken around 1930, shows Winford Cheeseman holding a baby lamb while the lamb's mother looks on. Statistics from the second half of the 19th century show that more than 20,000 sheep were shorn, producing more than 95,000 pounds of wool. While more than 12,000 lambs were raised each year, about 2,500 sheep were slaughtered. Of raising sheep, Nettie Senecal recalled, "I helped raise the sheep we had, sheared them, washed the wool, picked the dirt out of the wool, and carded the wool. I made clothes from the wool on a large spinning wheel with a shuttle at the top. In order to knit the clothes—stockings, underwear, socks, dresses, mittens, everything we wore—I had to walk endlessly back and forth working the shuttle."

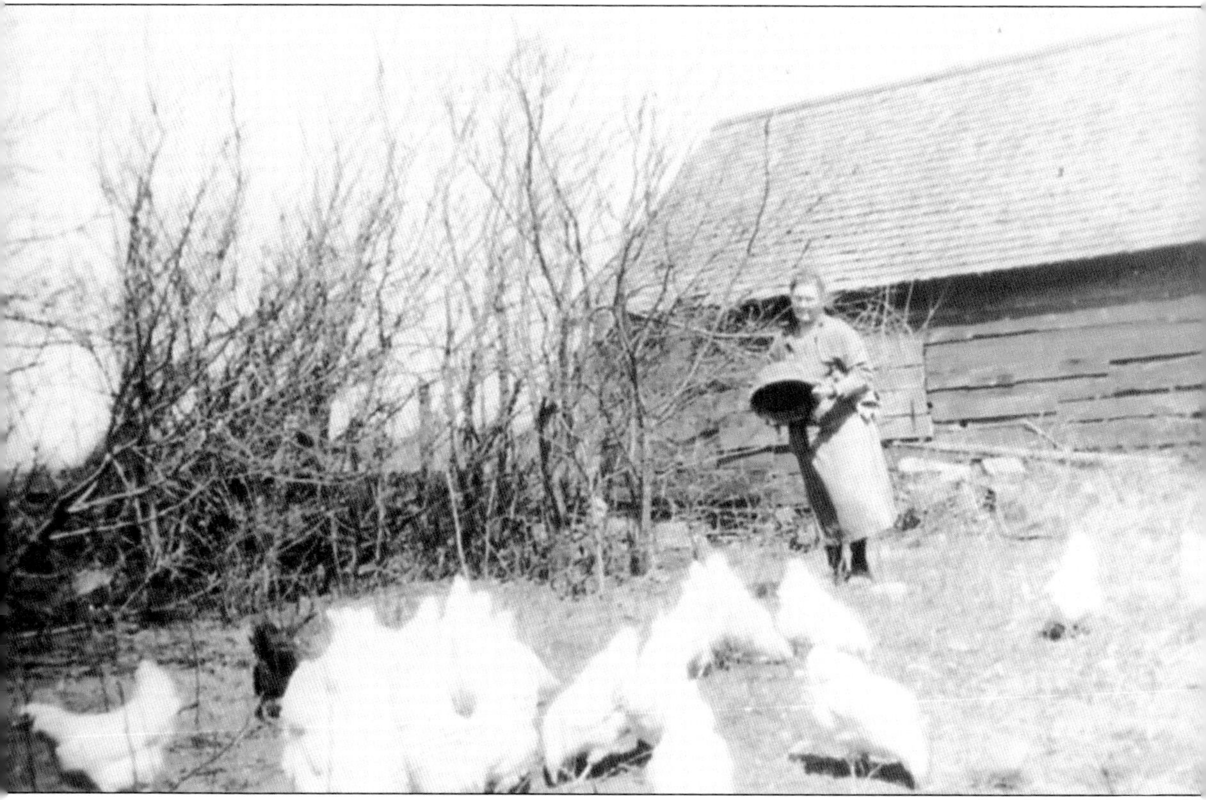

Edythe Corliss feeds the chickens in the barnyard of her family's Ellenburg Depot farm in 1931. Raising chickens and other poultry allowed farm families to have and sell eggs, which resulted in more than $17,000 a year in the second half of the 19th century. Local farms, like the Giroux Poultry Farm, continue to produce eggs, which earned $36.5 million throughout New York State in 2005, and broilers, which earned a statewide total of $7.61 million in the same year. Ducks, turkeys, and other chickens also earned a great deal of money, bringing in a statewide total $47.19 million in 2005.

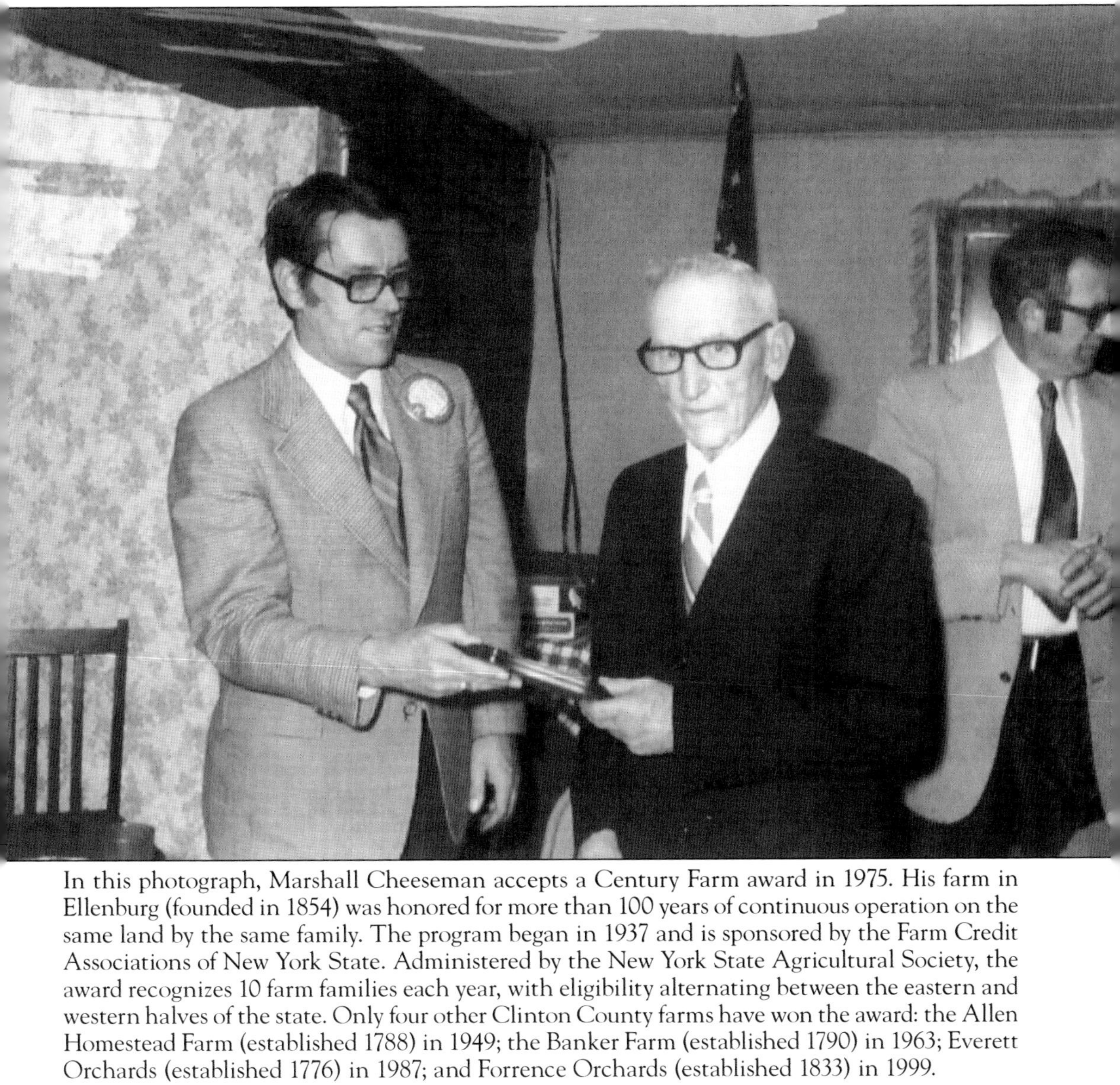

In this photograph, Marshall Cheeseman accepts a Century Farm award in 1975. His farm in Ellenburg (founded in 1854) was honored for more than 100 years of continuous operation on the same land by the same family. The program began in 1937 and is sponsored by the Farm Credit Associations of New York State. Administered by the New York State Agricultural Society, the award recognizes 10 farm families each year, with eligibility alternating between the eastern and western halves of the state. Only four other Clinton County farms have won the award: the Allen Homestead Farm (established 1788) in 1949; the Banker Farm (established 1790) in 1963; Everett Orchards (established 1776) in 1987; and Forrence Orchards (established 1833) in 1999.

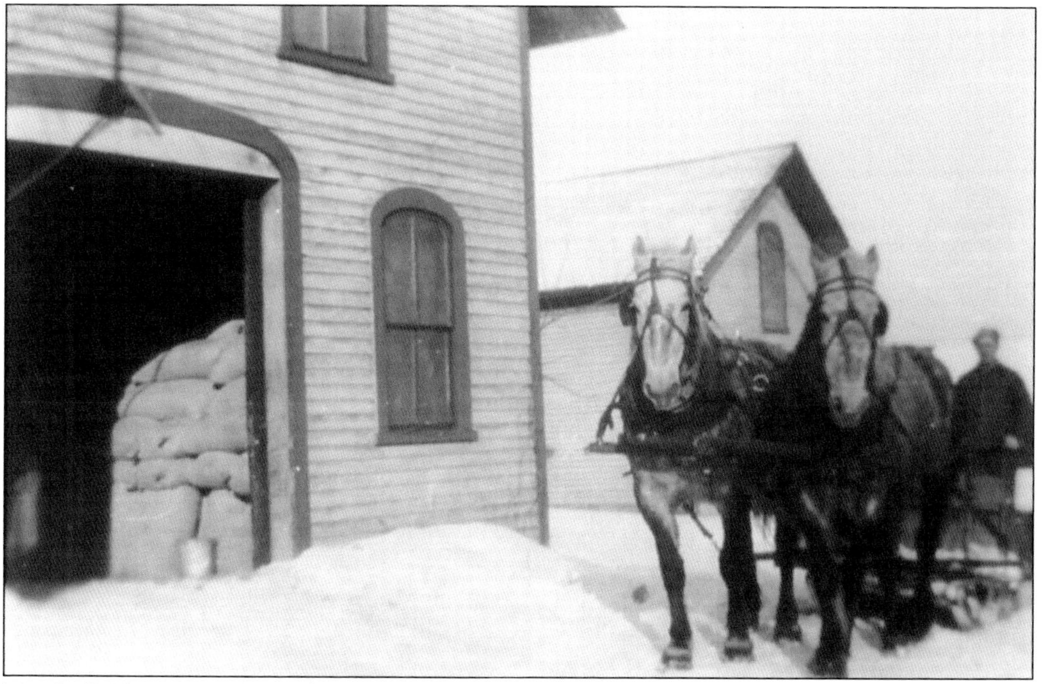

Marshall Cheeseman drives his team of horses near his Ellenburg Depot farm. More than 7,000 horses in the county were reported throughout the 19th century. Farmers fed some 590,000 bushels of oats a year to horses like these. Notice the feedbags—used to store oats—inside the barn.

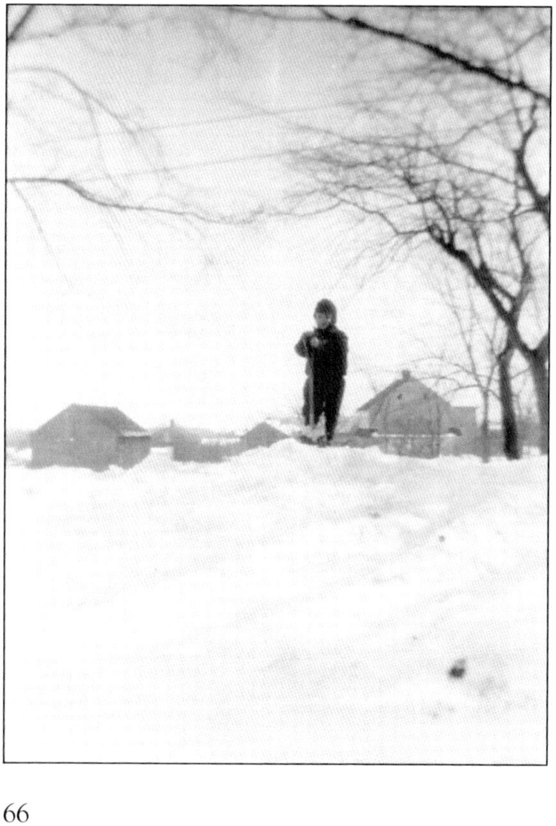

In the northern clime, snow removal is another significant portion of farm life. Here Winford Cheeseman shovels snow between his family's Ellenburg Depot farm (behind the photographer) and the neighboring farm, shown in the distance. Late winter and early spring also saw farmers cutting ice from local ponds and lakes. That ice, cut in large blocks, would be used in the farm's icehouse for storing cold food.

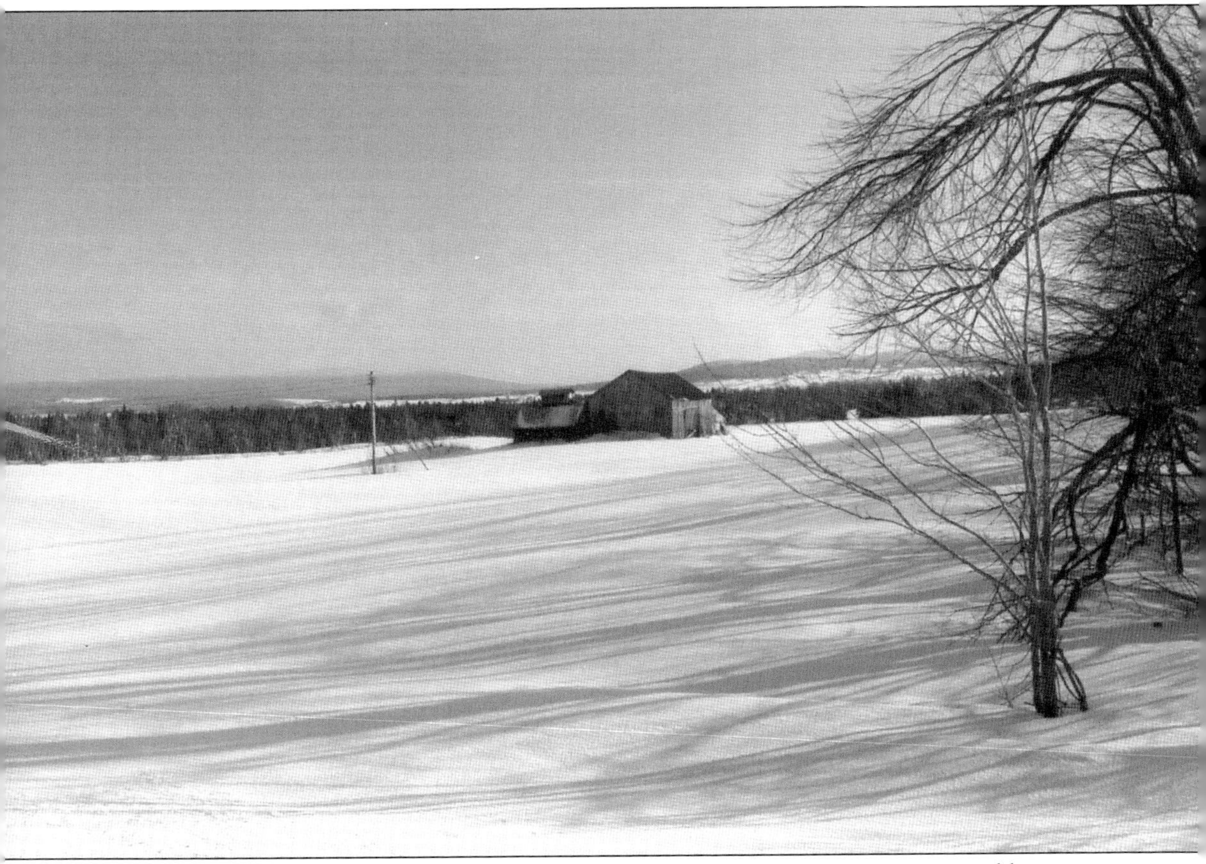

Thomas Hobbs's Ellenburg Center sugarhouse stands among the winter snow. In addition to potatoes and corn crops, local farmers have long relied on maple trees for their livelihood. Sap, taken from the trees in February and March, is boiled into maple syrup and sugar in small buildings like this one. Pearl Coryea describes her family's Altona farm: "We had a sugar orchard—tapped twenty-five hundred maple trees and gathered sap with horses on a sled with a tank to the top of the hill. From there we poured it in a big tank piped to the sugar house below. There we had a hired man to boil the sap into syrup. We would gather the sap in pails, carry it to the sled and empty in the tank. It was hard as we were small, trudging through the snow. Dad would take a yoke on his shoulders and carry two pails, one on each side."

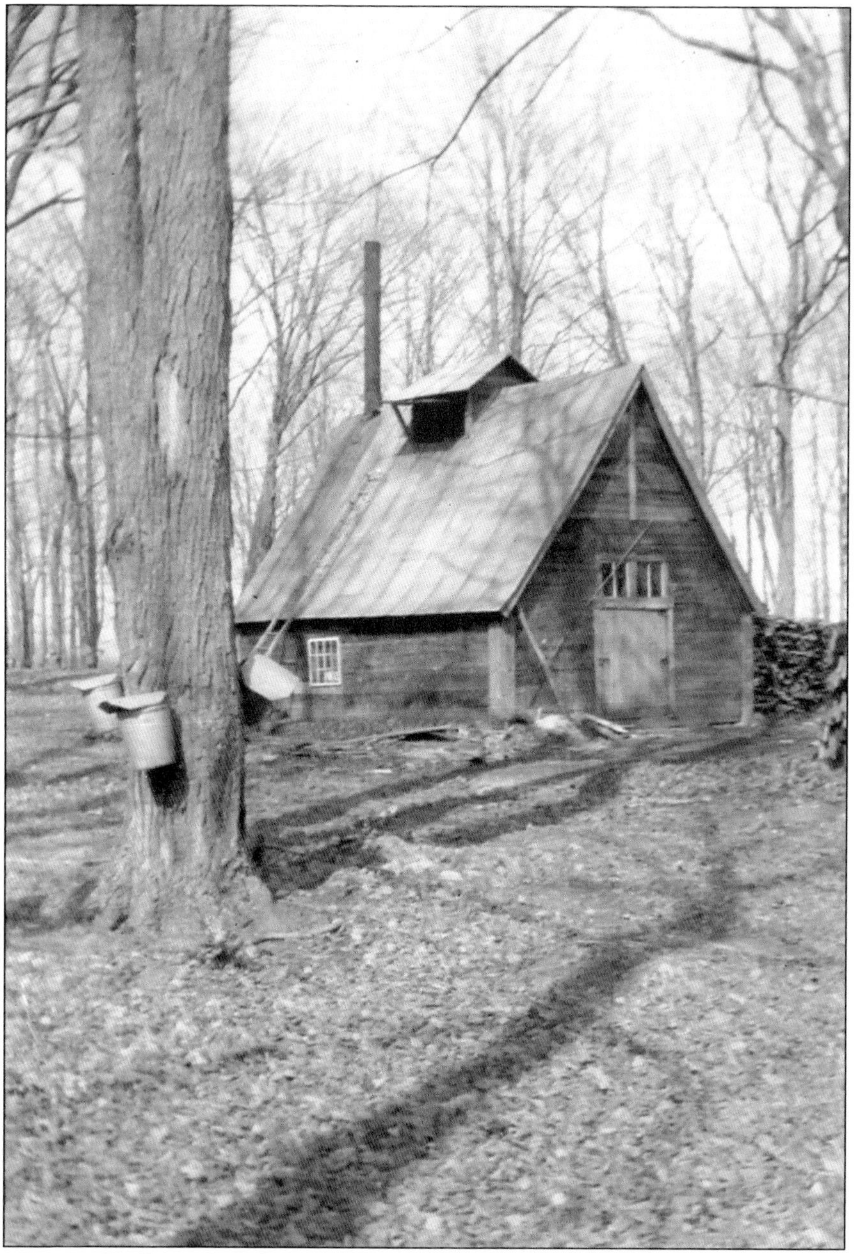

A sugarhouse on Spellman Road in Beekmantown offers an interesting glimpse of the buckets used to collect sap from the maple trees (foreground) and of the massive amounts of wood needed to fuel the boiling-down process (back right). In 1875, sugarhouses like this one produced 219,485 pounds of maple sugar and 5,348 gallons of maple syrup. Of sugaring in West Chazy, Yvonne Gonyo recalled, "The average yield was ten gallons of sap per tree. Then the long round of collecting the sap began. The sap was poured in gathering tanks, then to a huge vat from which the sap was strained and flowed to the evaporator. It was automatically controlled by a float and held two hundred gallons. The machine was gravity fed, wood fired, using about forty-five cords of wood during the season. It takes about thirty-five gallons of sap to make one gallon of syrup. Much of this syrup was used to make maple sugar and maple cream."

Five

Business and Industry

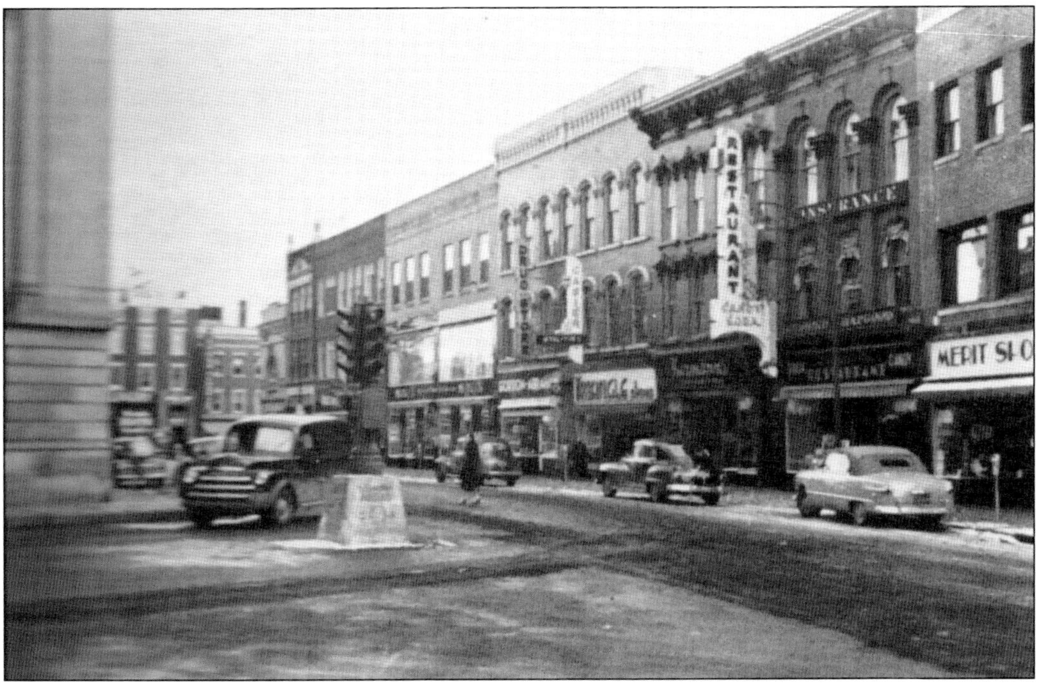

Prior to the 1970s, Margaret Street was the bustling center of Plattsburgh's consumer life, with a variety of banks and stores. This 1956 photograph shows one section of Margaret Street's storefronts. In this one image, a drugstore, two shoe stores, a restaurant, an insurance company, and a bank are visible. These establishments were joined by a host of other businesses, including Merkel's and Woolworth.

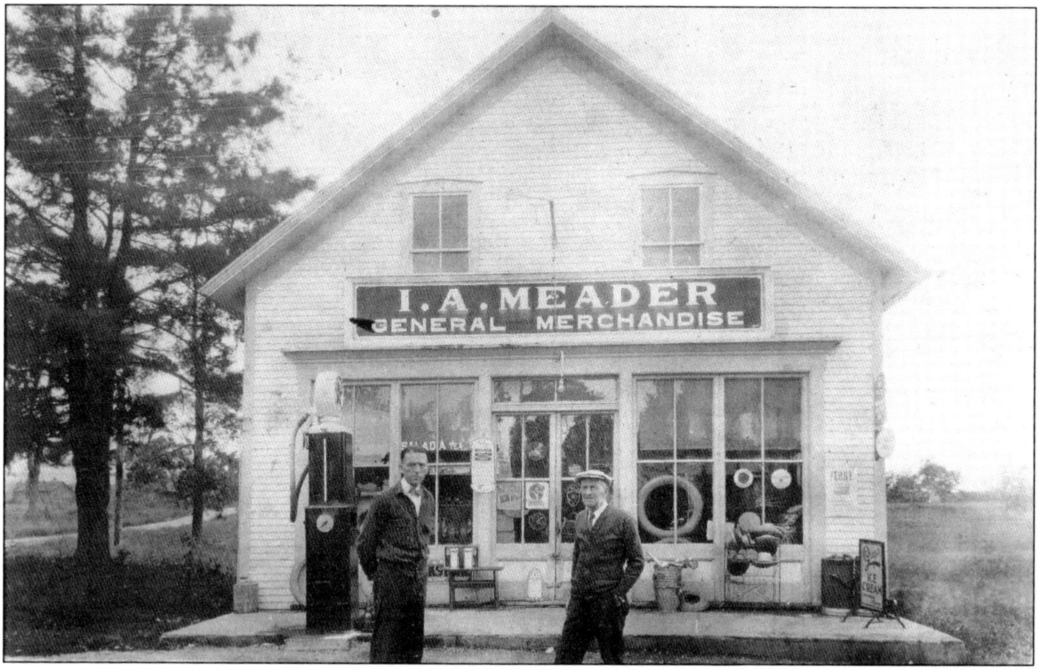

Located in West Plattsburgh, the Meader Store was accompanied by the Meader Hotel and the Meader Tavern. In addition, the Meaders operated a farm. After a fire destroyed their store and stock in 1937, Henry A. Riley and Frank J. Rugar, both of Morrisonville, secured this building, opening it on January 14, 1938, to sell general merchandise, groceries, and meat.

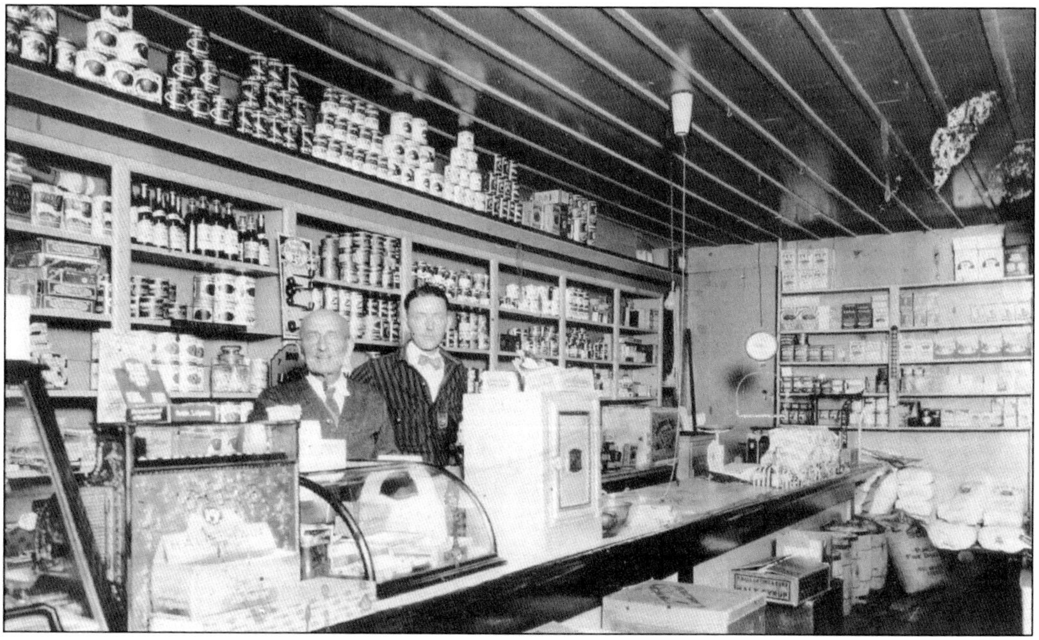

On September 13, 1934, the entire stock of the I.A. Meader store was sold at auction. Among the multitude of goods previously sold by the store were dry goods, hardware, notions, clothing, household furniture and equipment, and many types of canned goods. Some of those items are shown in this photograph from a more prosperous time.

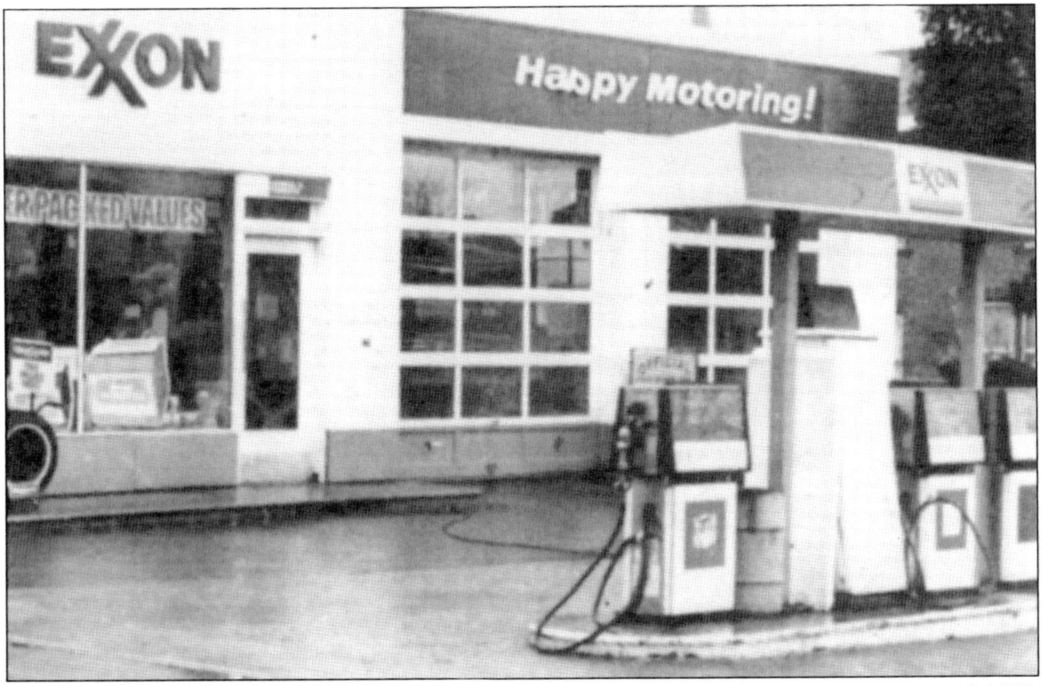

Located on the corner of Broad and South Catherine Streets, this Exxon station, around 1975, was one of a multitude of gas stations throughout the county. In recent years, the gas pumps have been removed from this site and the building used as Parrotte's garage.

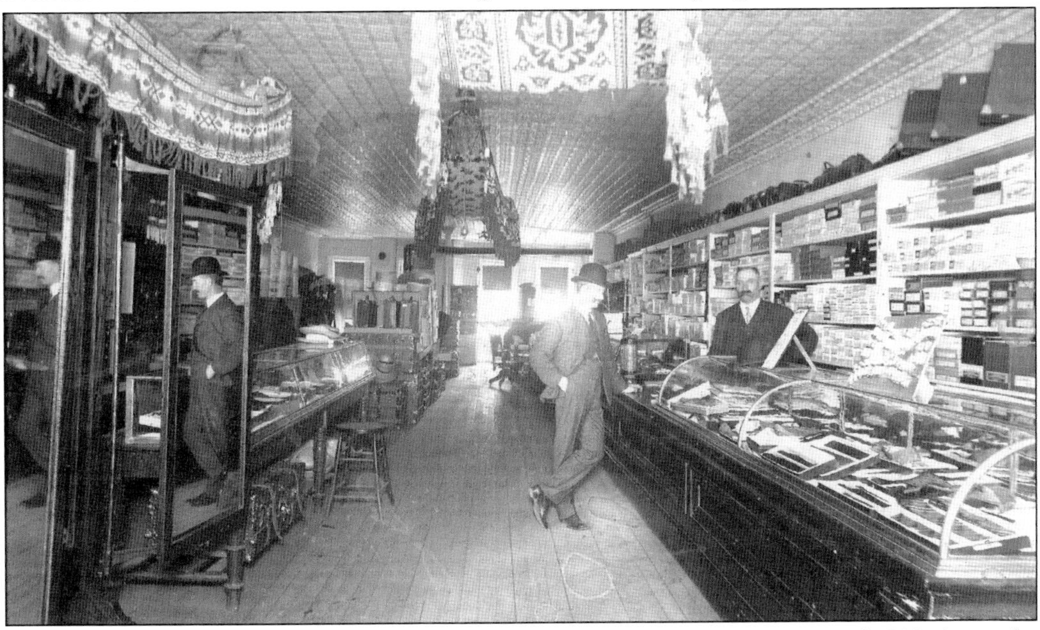

McGreore's Store was located at 7 Bridge Street, Plattsburgh. This image, around 1920, shows the variety of wares sold in local general merchandise stores. Until the 1960s and 1970s, Plattsburgh's downtown was the vibrant home to many locally owned businesses. A concerted local effort since the late 1990s has returned many stores and restaurants to the downtown, though the heyday era of the 1920s has not been replicated.

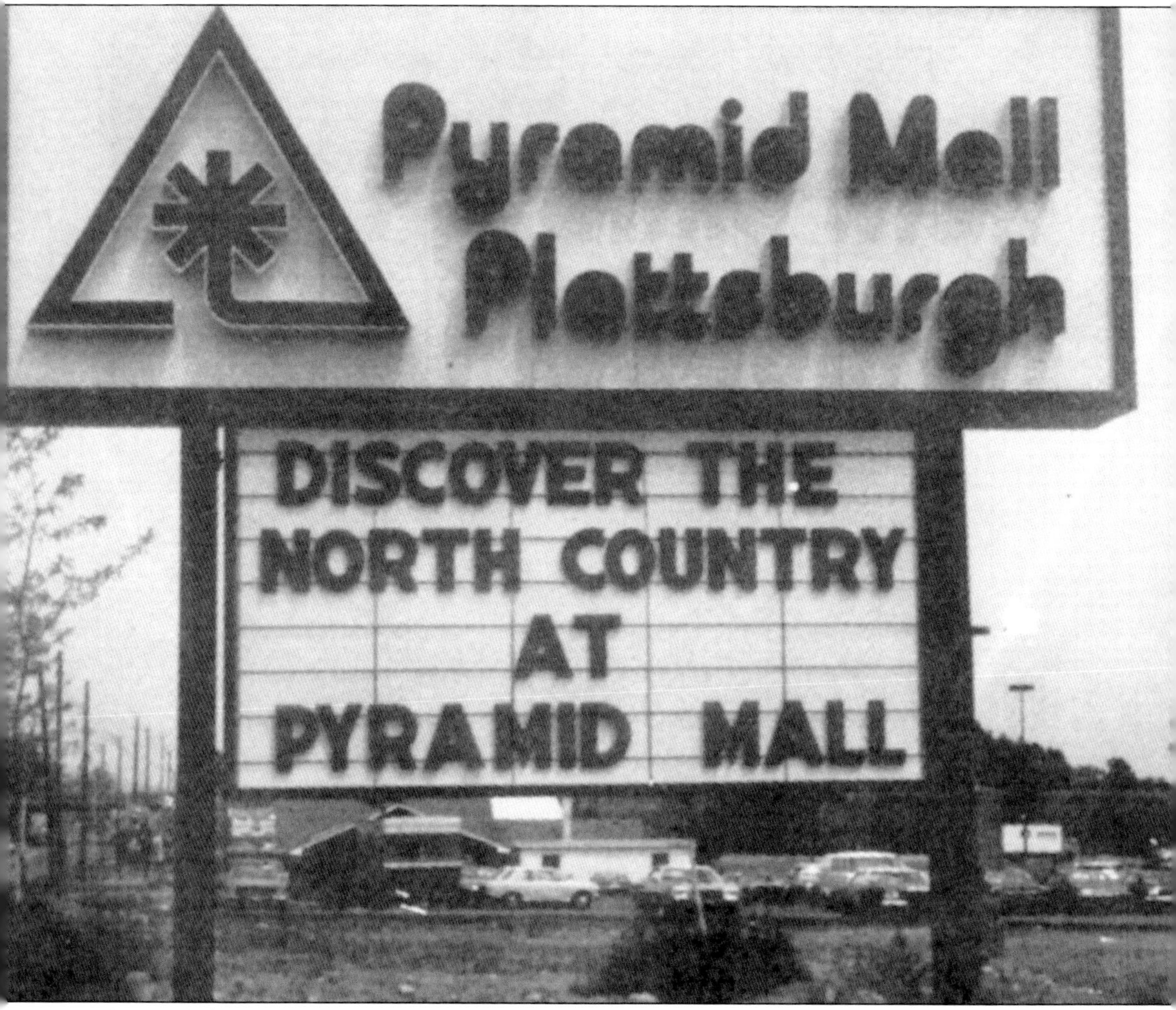

In 1975, the Pyramid Mall was completed. Located conveniently at Interstate 87's exit 37, the Cornelia Street complex held a variety of stores, including Montgomery Ward and J. C. Penney, both of which moved from the downtown area. By 1986, the company that owned the mall was ready to expand and named the new, two-mall venture the Champlain Centres (north and south). When the new mall proved more lucrative, the Pyramid Corporation tore down the majority of the original mall, leaving a K-Mart behind. Eventually Price Chopper, Lowes, and Bed Bath and Beyond built structures on the same lot. The newer mall continues to operate, offering a variety of chain stores.

Bonanza was one of the many restaurants located on Plattsburgh's Cornelia Street. Since the 1970s, Cornelia Street has been the commercial heart of the city and the county, with grocery and retail stores, restaurants, car dealerships, banks, and malls. The growth of consumer traffic on Cornelia Street, which becomes Route 3 and extends from the city to the town of Plattsburgh, has hindered the revitalization of Plattsburgh's downtown.

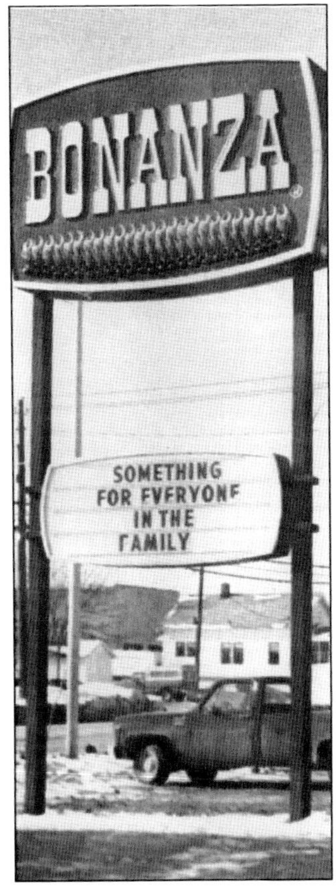

The M/V *Juniper*, shown here, operated as an excursion vessel on the lake into the 21st century. Promotional literature explained the boat as a place to "explore historic Lake Champlain from the deck of the enclosed all steel, twin diesel powered Juniper. See historic Valcour Island with its scenic shoreline, marvel at the majestic Adirondack and Green Mountains, and most of all enjoy yourself."

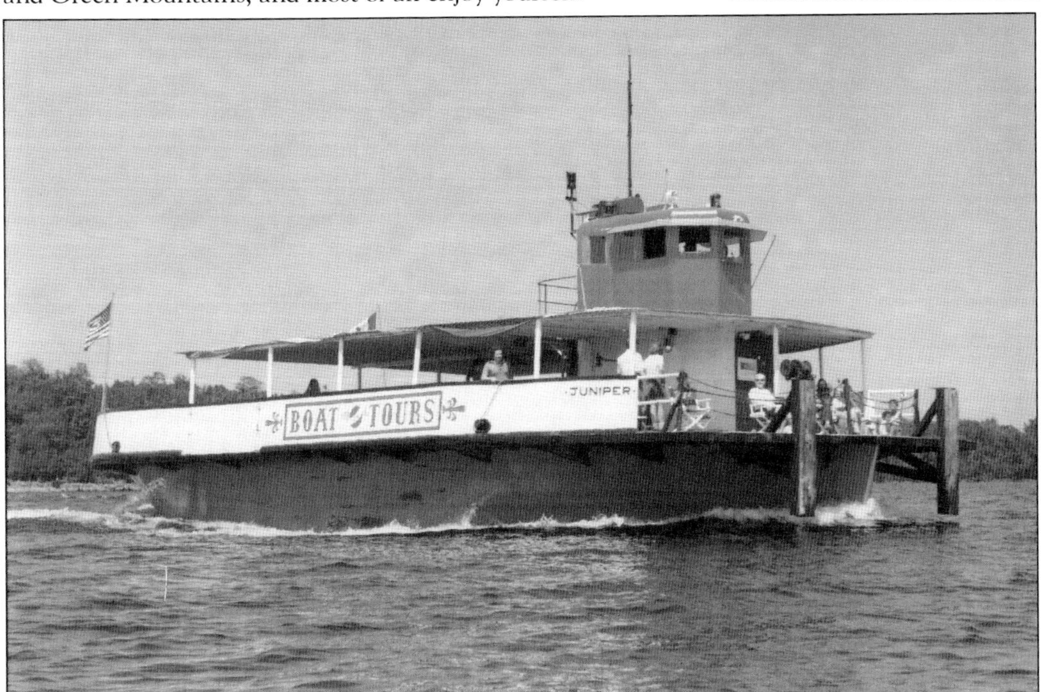

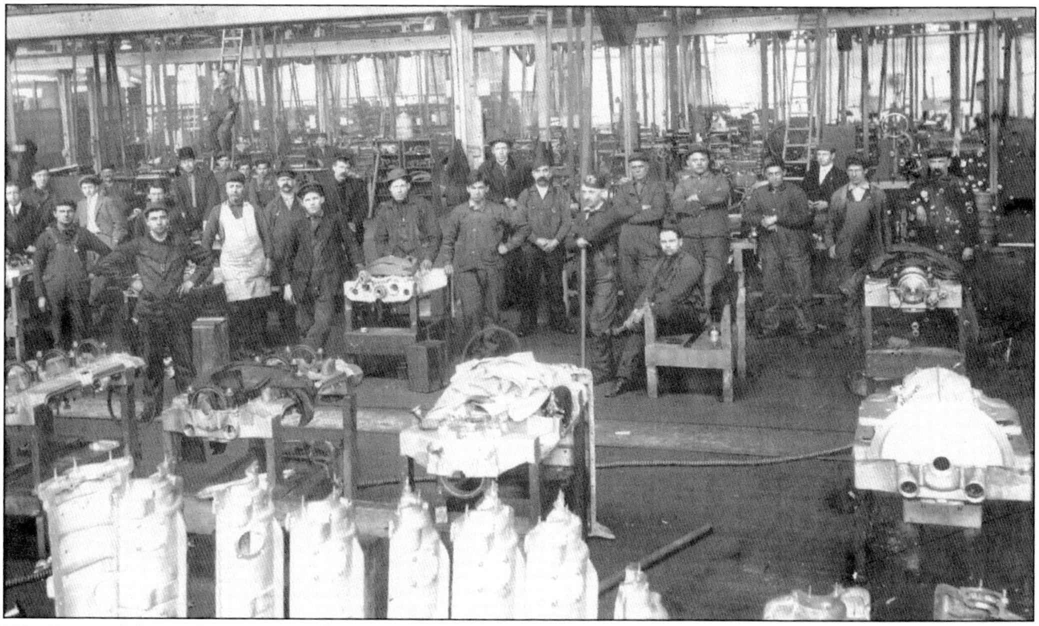

The Lozier Motor Company, whose unidentified employees are pictured here, began building boats in Plattsburgh in 1900 and luxury cars in 1904. Employing 400 men, the company's products—luxury cars that cost $5,000 by 1912—were in high demand until lower priced cars put the Lozier Company into bankruptcy in 1914. The legacy of the Lozier Motor Company lives on through the Champlain Valley Transportation Museum and car enthusiasts around the world.

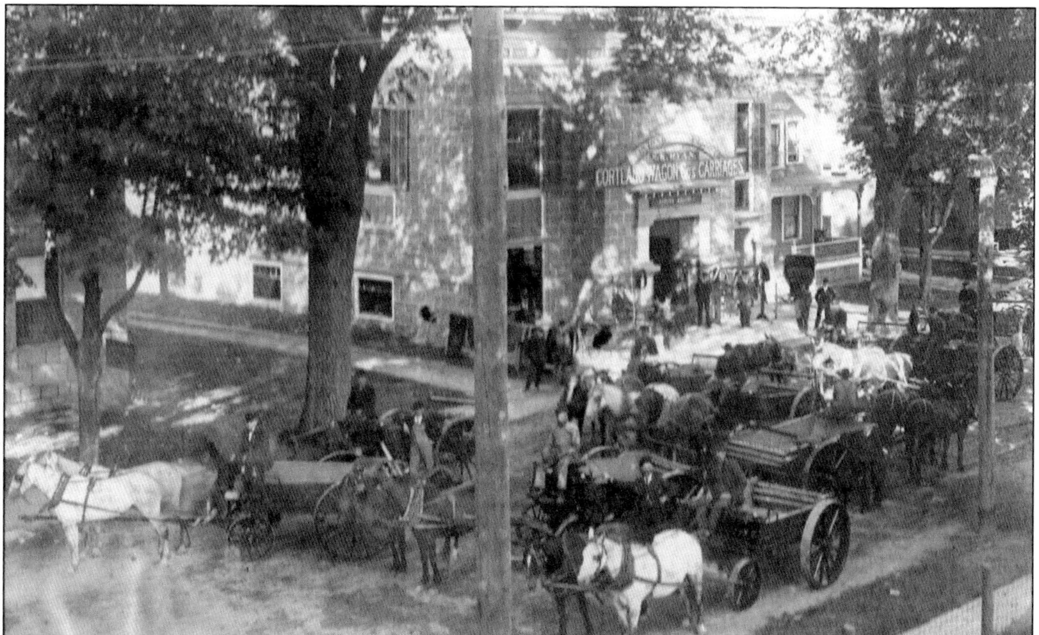

This image, taken around 1908, shows the S. K. Ryan Carriage House in Plattsburgh. The Ryan family, which has included various lawyers and judges, is shown here: Andrew (the youngest) is the child on the wagon; S. K. is the man with the mustache; James (the oldest) stands left of the door; from left to right, John, Stephen, Dr. Frank, and George stand to the right of the door.

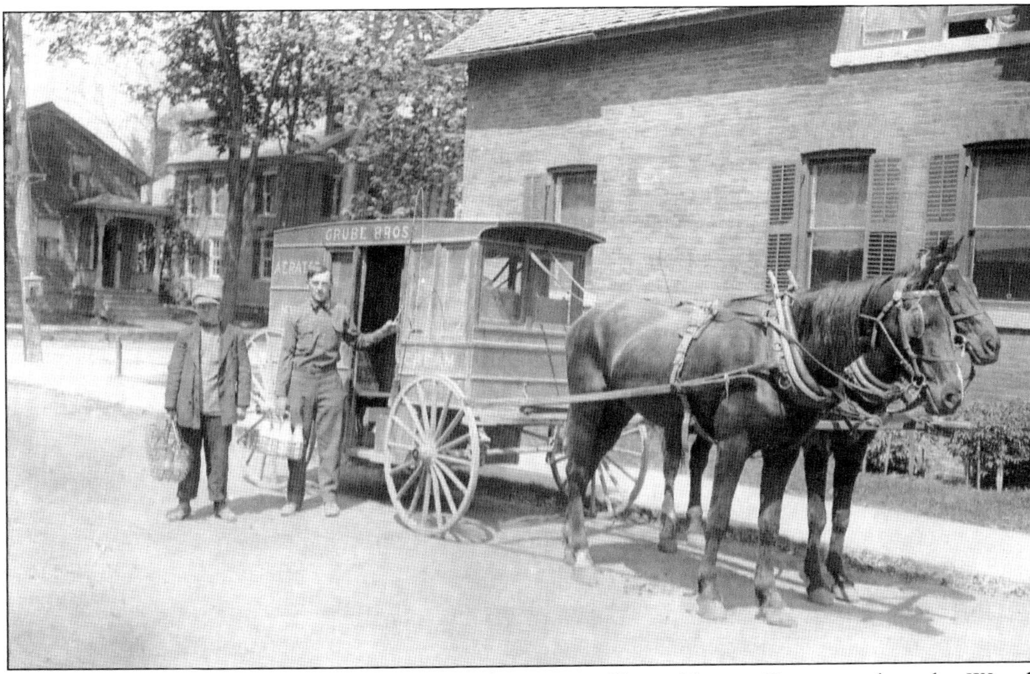

In 1913, George Grube sent this photograph to one of his siblings. Connected to the Wood, Wright, and Stafford families, the Grubes owned and operated a milk route. Notice that the wagon—in which milk and cream were stored—is aerated. A 1919 *Plattsburgh Daily Press* article indicates that George and Paul Grube were among 14 retailers selling the milk they had produced on their farms door to door.

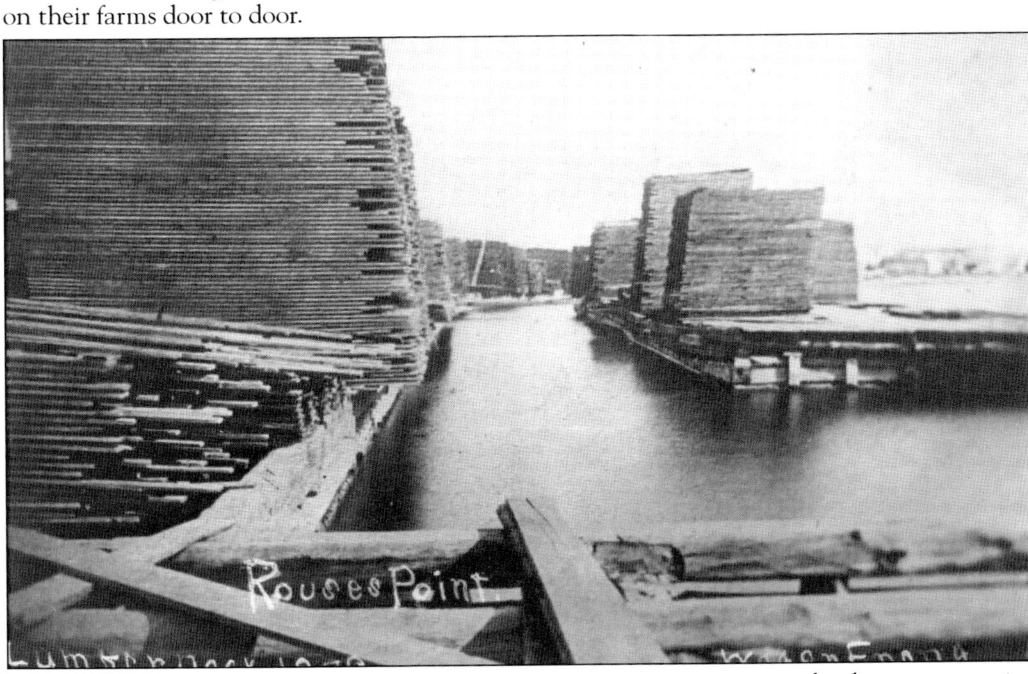

Situated very close to the Canadian border, Rouses Point was a major port for the transportation of logs and lumber. Shown here in 1870, the lumber dock in the village offered a point from which to load, store, and sell wood.

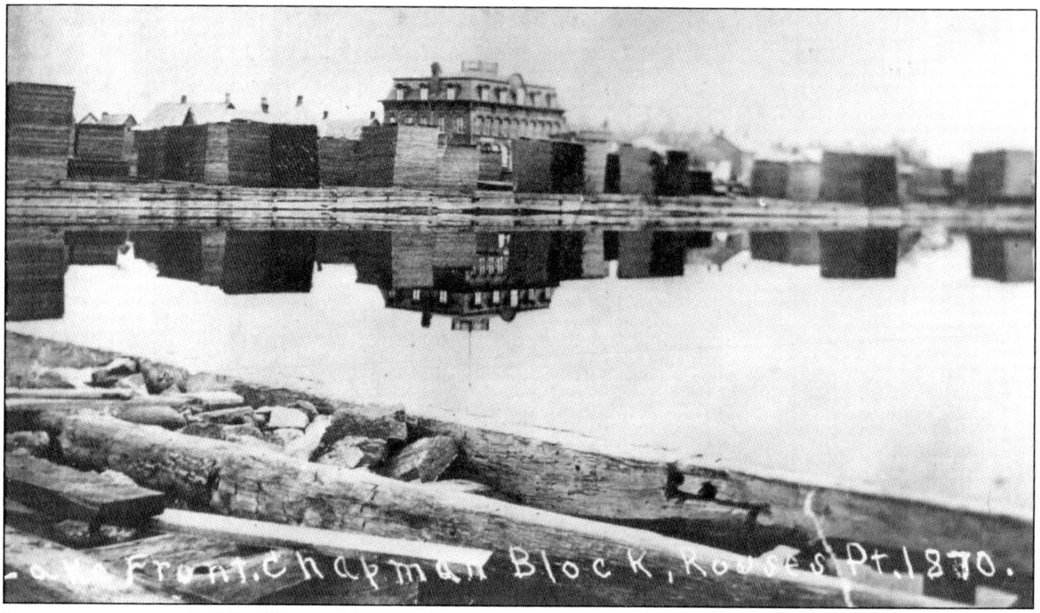

Logging was a profitable Clinton County business. Not only could the logs be used in the production of potash, but they could be milled into usable lumber, with millions of feet of pine board being produced by local sawmills in 1820. This image of the Chapman Block in Rouses Point shows the village's role in the lumbering industry.

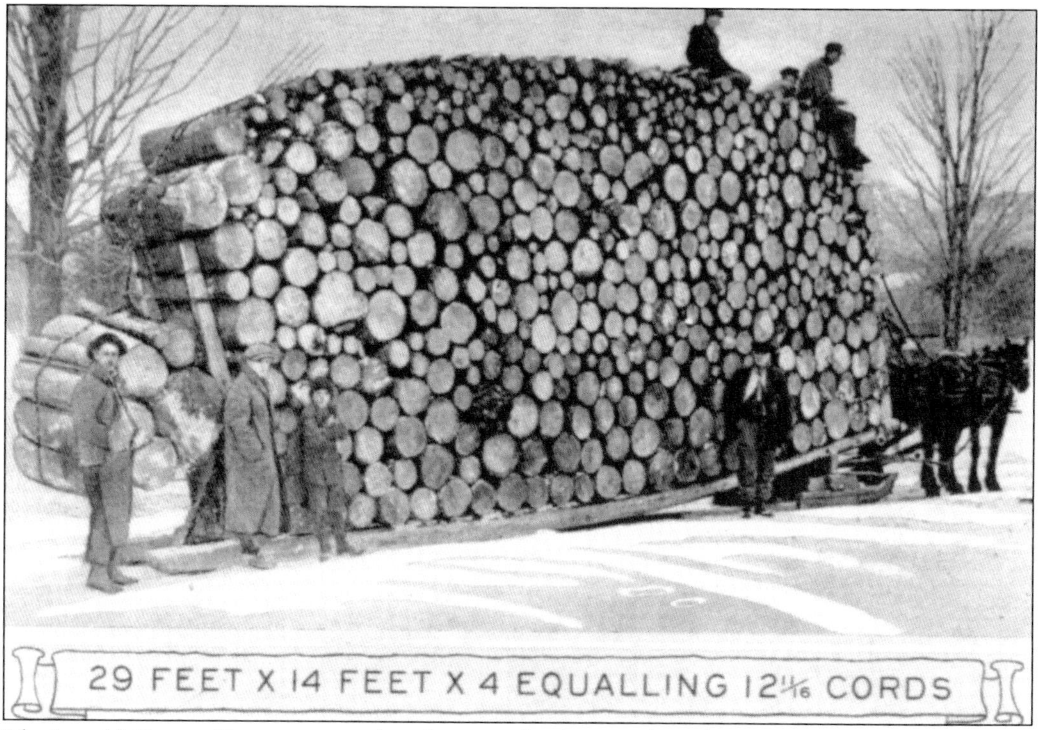

The J. and J. Rogers Company sent this photograph, along with a Christmas card, to its employees. While the accompanying card read, "Christmas Greetings and best wishes for your happiness in the New Year," the *c.* 1900 image emphasizes the importance of logging for the company.

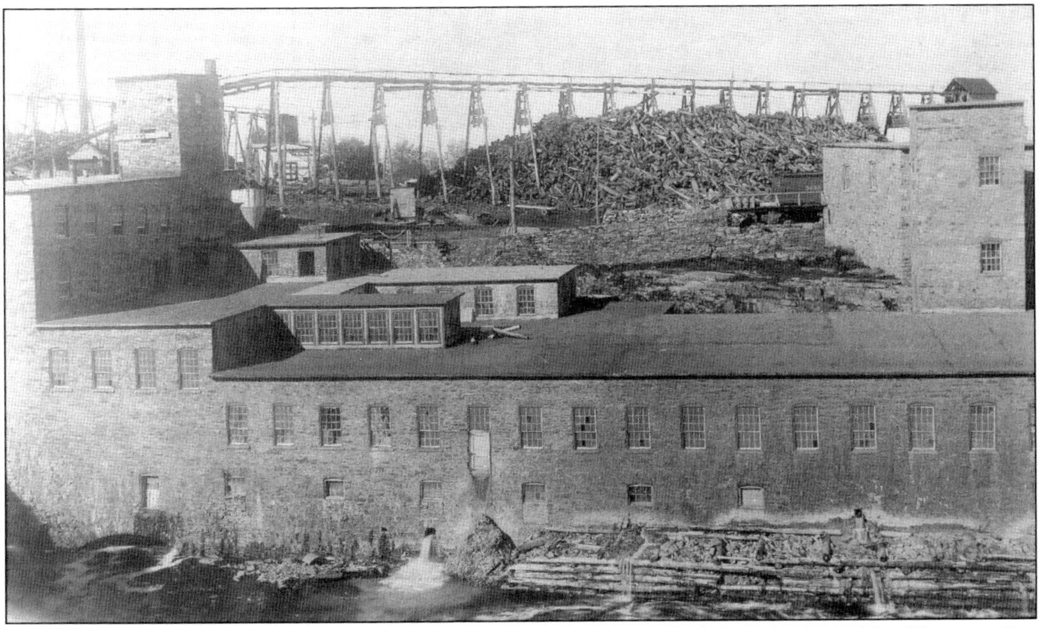

The J. and J. Rogers Company, which originally mined iron in Black Brook, Au Sable, Clintonville, and the surrounding towns, started to make paper and pulp in the early 20th century. To produce pulp, the conveyor belt seen in the background moved wood to a cooker. After it was no longer possible to use wood from its own property, the Rogers Company bought wood in Canada and transported it to Clinton County by train.

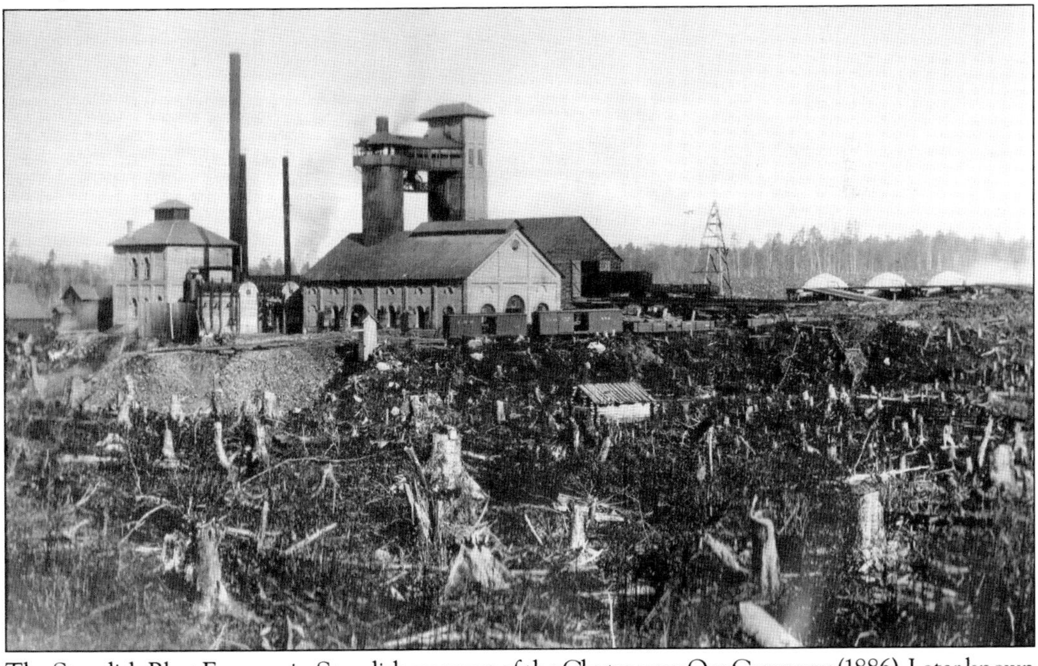

The Standish Blast Furnace in Standish was part of the Chateaugay Ore Company (1886). Later known as the Chateaugay Ore and Iron Company, this iron-mining operation created the villages of Lyon Mountain and Standish and owned more than 60,000 acres of land that included a 2,600-foot vein of iron and a 40,000-foot work surface. More than 600 men were employed by the company.

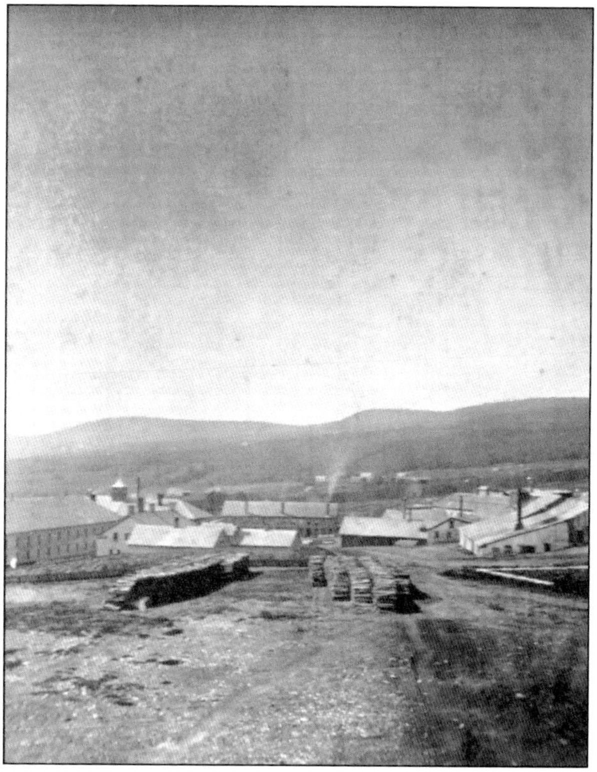

Dannemora Prison was built in 1844. The third prison in New York State, it has survived as a maximum-security facility famous for housing criminals like Charles "Lucky" Luciano, Tupac Shakur, and Joel Rifkin. Officially known as the Clinton Correctional Facility, the prison houses about 3,000 inmates. "Little Siberia," nicknamed for its remote location and harsh winters, continues to be a principal employer in the county.

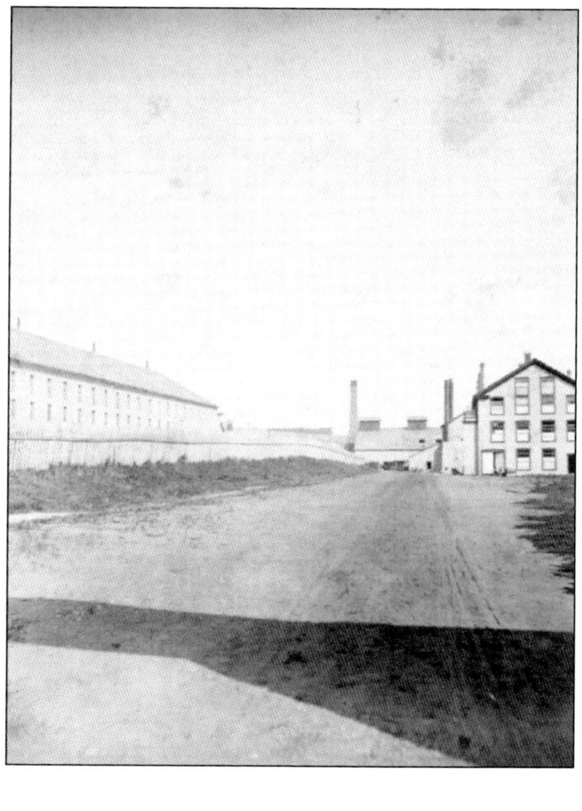

Ransom Cook, the man appointed to find the location for a third prison, chose Dannemora because of its rich iron ore deposits. After being appointed warden of the prison, Cook oversaw the construction of the facility and the production of iron ore. That quickly proved unprofitable, though, and the prison switched to creating textiles (including hats) and the production of food on the prison farm. This image shows the hat factory at Dannemora Prison.

Six

Government and Civic Organizations

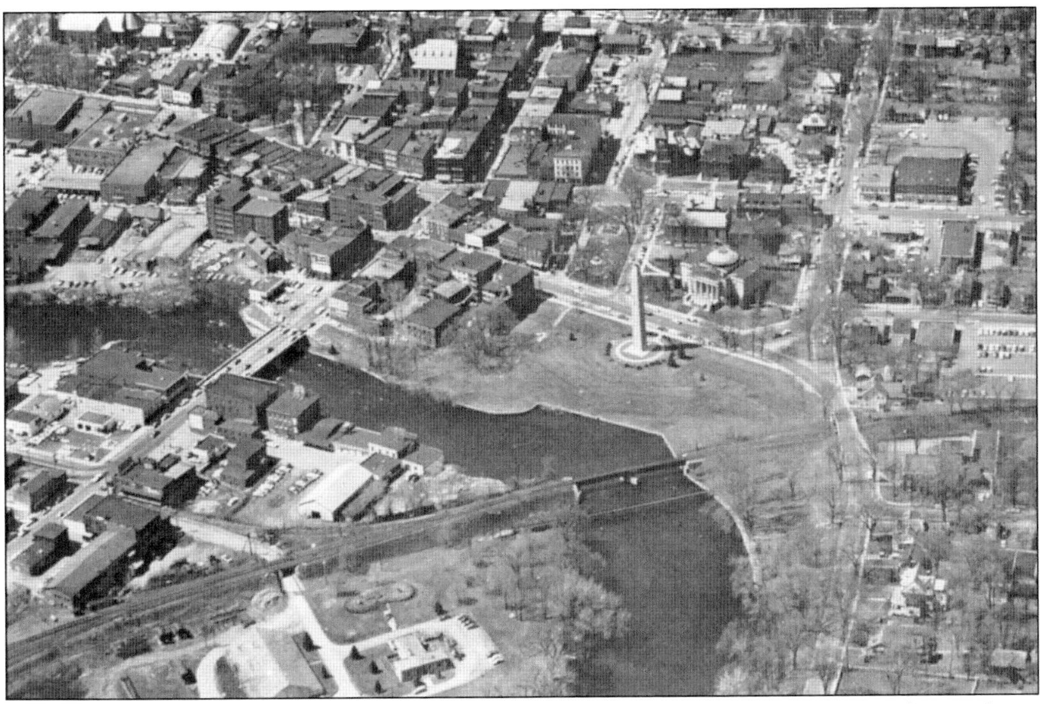

Taken from the vantage point of a Plattsburgh Air Force Base plane, this 1961 aerial view shows the Saranac River as it winds through the city of Plattsburgh. The Macdonough Monument, dedicated in 1926, stands near the center of the image and recalls the county's role in the War of 1812, when Lt. Thomas Macdonough led his fleet to victory at the Battle of Plattsburgh.

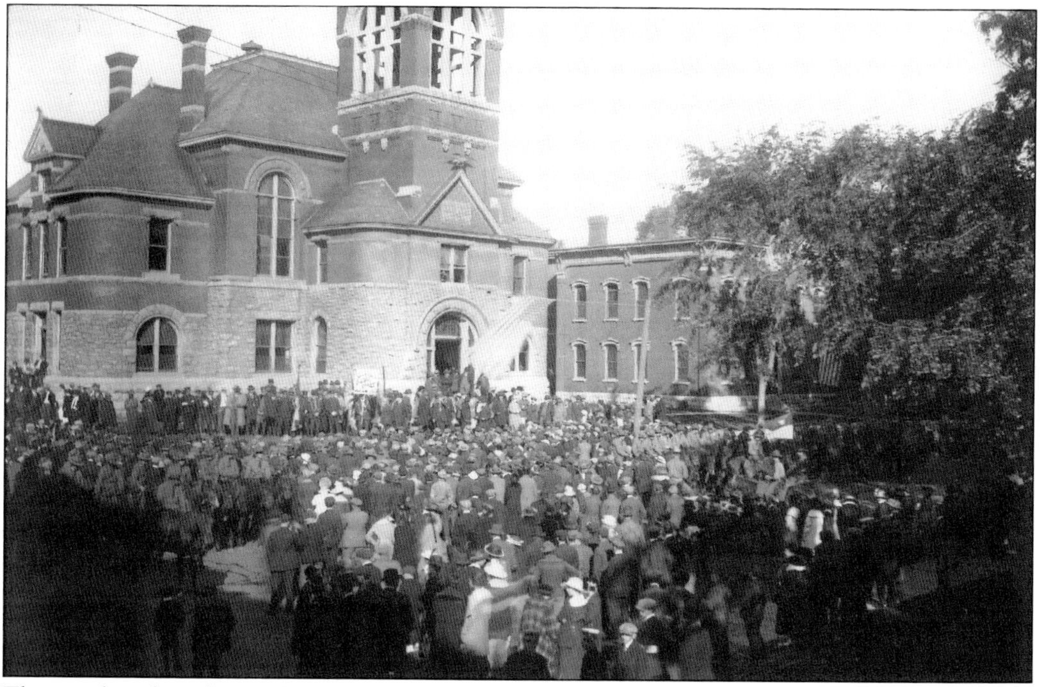

The crowds said goodbye and wished luck to World War I soldiers in front of the county court on Margaret Street in Plattsburgh. In addition to sending troops, Clinton County contributed to the war effort by training citizens for service to the country during wartime. The "Plattsburgh Idea," which originated with Maj. Gen. Leonard Wood, called for military training in anticipation of wartime service.

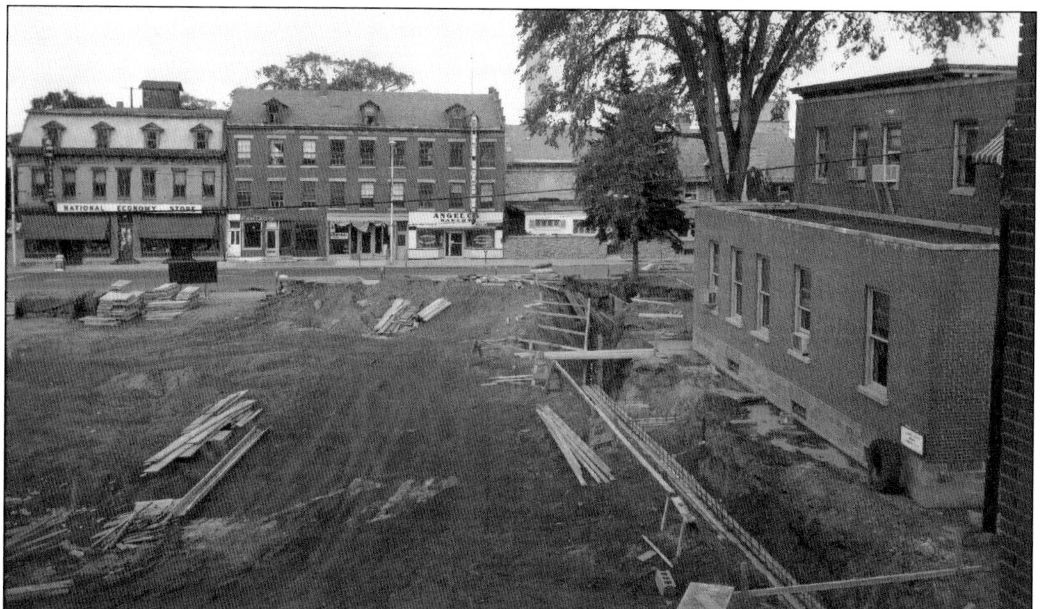

The Clinton County Government Center was built in 1974. This photograph, by Robin Brown, looks across Margaret Street. To the right stands the Clinton County Courthouse, now used by various county offices. The Government Center changed the landscape of downtown Plattsburgh with the creation of a governmental complex in the area between Cornelia, Margaret, Court, and Oak Streets.

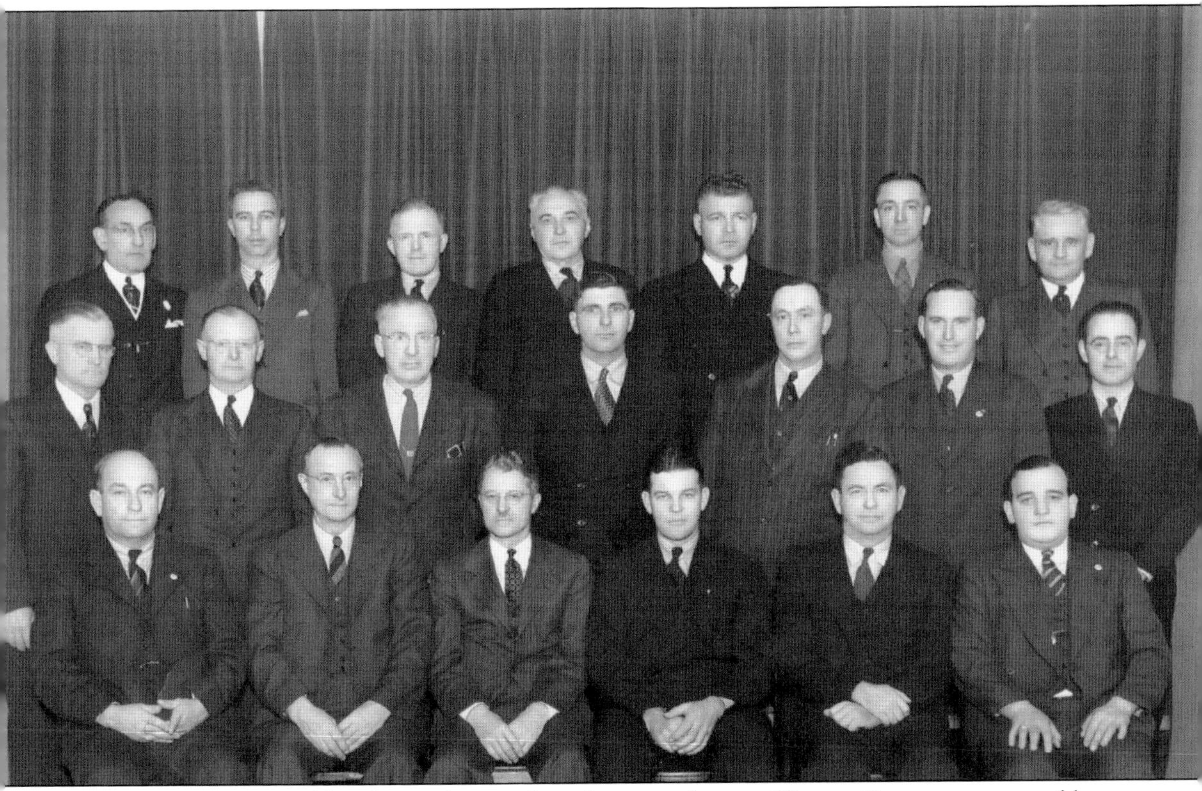

Prior to the creation of legislative districts based on population, Clinton County was served by a board of supervisors. Each supervisor was elected by a county municipality. The 1941 board of supervisors is shown here, from left to right: (first row) Eber Stackpole of Black Brook, William Broderick (clerk), Harold Jerry (attorney), Ralph Sanger of Beekmantown (chairman), John C. Coffey (highway superintendent), and Donald Breyette of Dannemora; (second row) Ralph Lamberton of Mooers, Ross Clark of Peru, Grant Frederick of the city of Plattsburgh, Robert Napper of Saranac, Schuyler Ormsby of Schuyler Falls, Dewey McCormick of Ausable, and Floyd Jenkins; (third row) Edward Gallant of the city of Plattsburgh, Archie Bordeau of the town of Plattsburgh, Elisha McPherson of Ellenburg, Willis Stone of Chazy, Elmer Caron of Clinton, Walter Averill of Altona, and W. W. Cooper of Champlain.

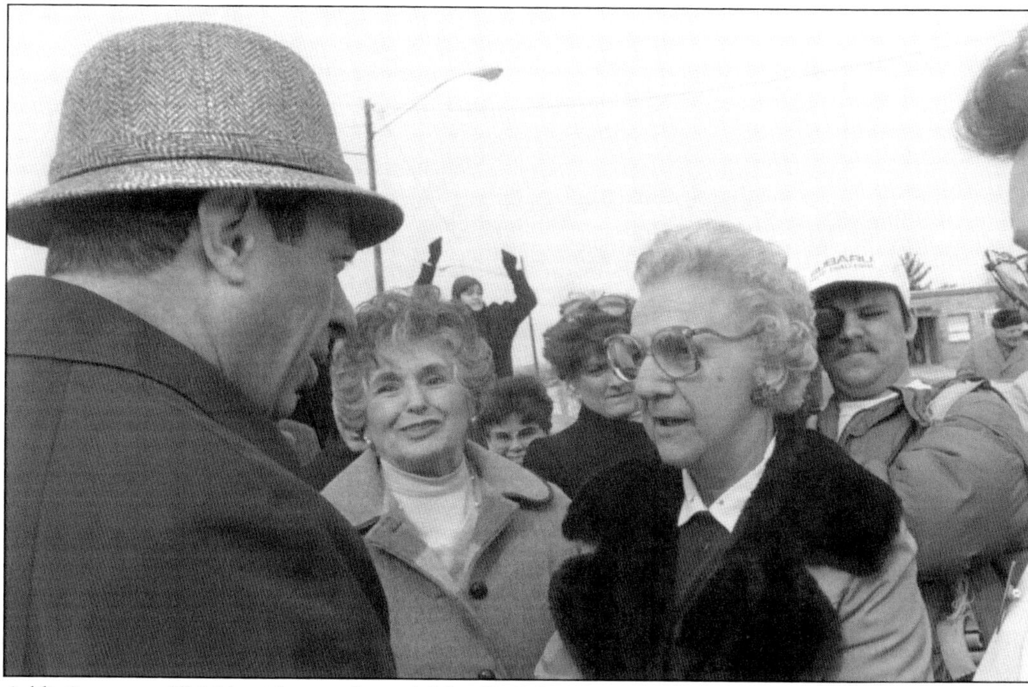

Addie Lawrence Shields, right, speaks with New York State governor Mario Cuomo during his 1987 visit to Plattsburgh. Mrs. Shields, who graduated from the Plattsburgh Normal School and who, with her husband, ran a farm in Beekmantown, was the Clinton County historian for almost 30 years.

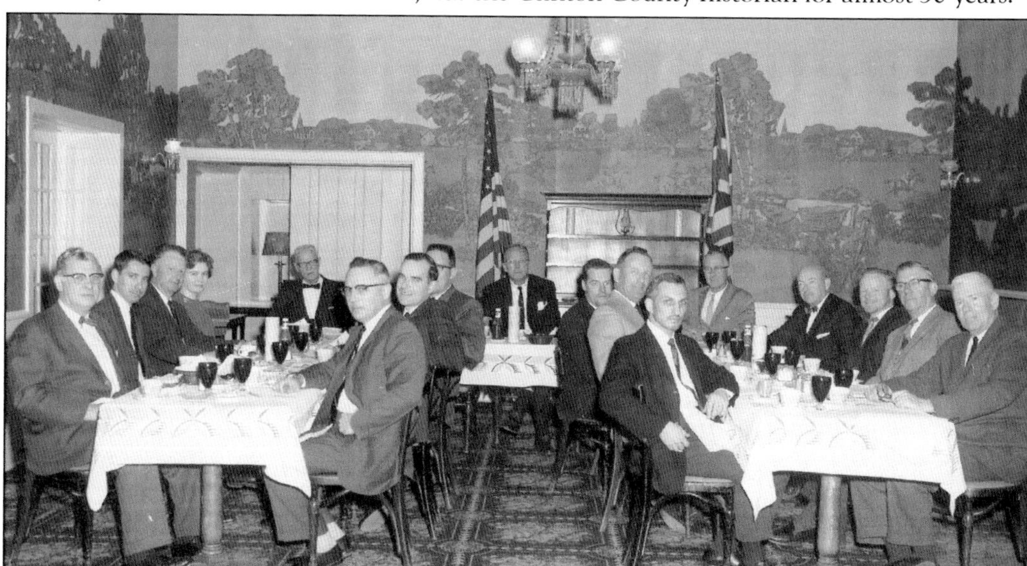

The Board of Governors of the Plattsburgh Area Chamber of Commerce is shown in this image. Included are, from left to right, S. I. GiamBruno, Roderick G. Giltz, George A. Barnett, Patricia Graupp, M. Aspinall, E. Roger Thomas, Arthur F. Young, Donald Green Jr., J. R. Slattery, Leo J. Pearl, Robert P. Marcus, M. J. Gordon, Philip E. Fitzpatrick, Dr. Edward Siegel, Larence House, Emil J. Zitek, and Daniel M. Shea. Dr. Franklin F. Conversa, William E. Field Jr., Col. James A. Brantner, Henry D. Hendee Jr., and Paul H. Gordon are not pictured.

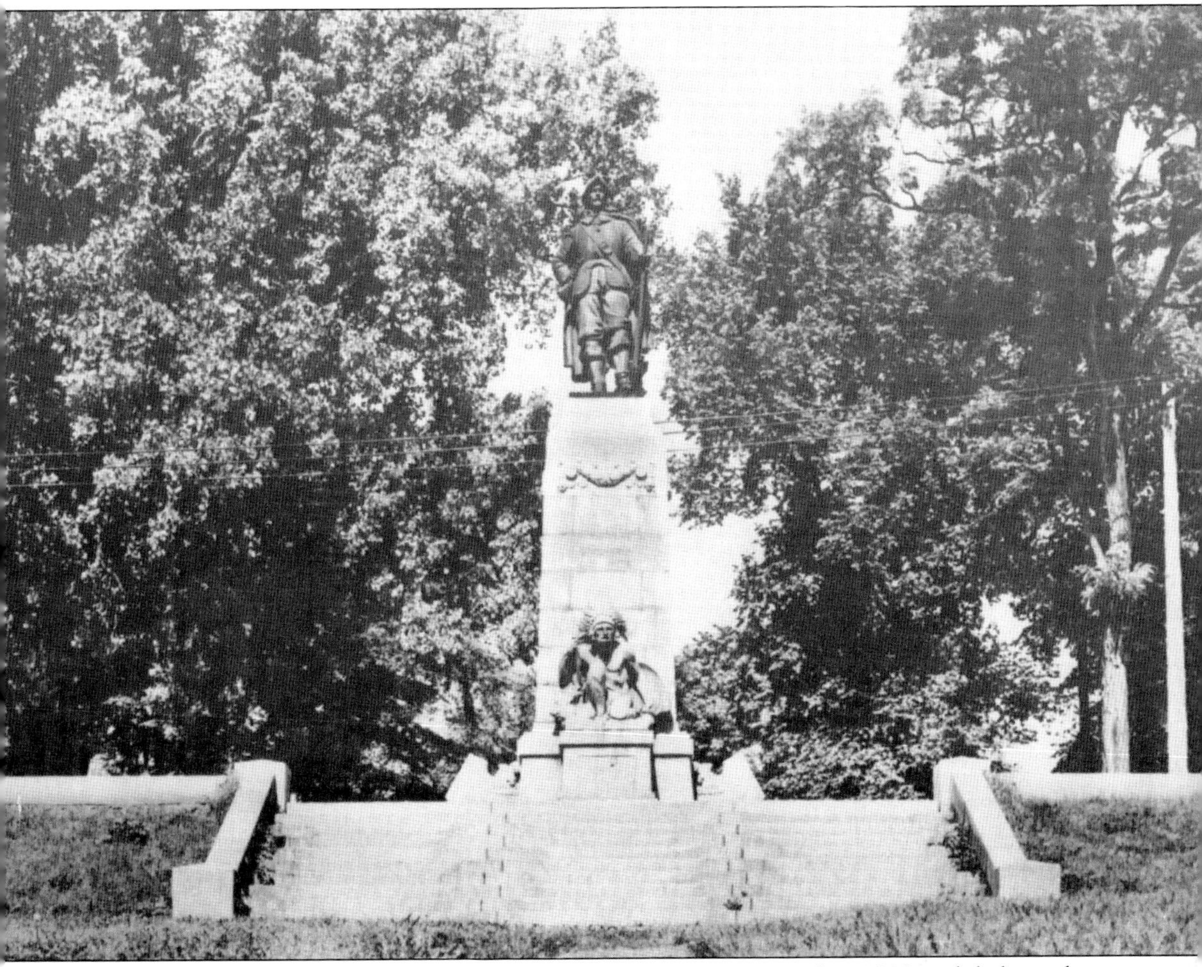

Designed by Hugh McLellan, the Champlain Monument was erected in 1908 and dedicated in 1912 as part of the 300th anniversary of Samuel de Champlain's arrival in this region. The base of the Champlain Monument includes a carved Native American and birch bark canoe. McLellan was an architect in New York City, though he later moved to Champlain and established the Moorsfield Press. Interested in history, McLellan published historical materials related to his ancestors, who were among the founders of both the village and town of Champlain. Since its original construction, McLellan's Champlain Monument, which sits in the city of Plattsburgh opposite the Kent-Delord House and overlooking the Saranac River, has become a major point on the city's river walk, which also passes the Macdonough Monument.

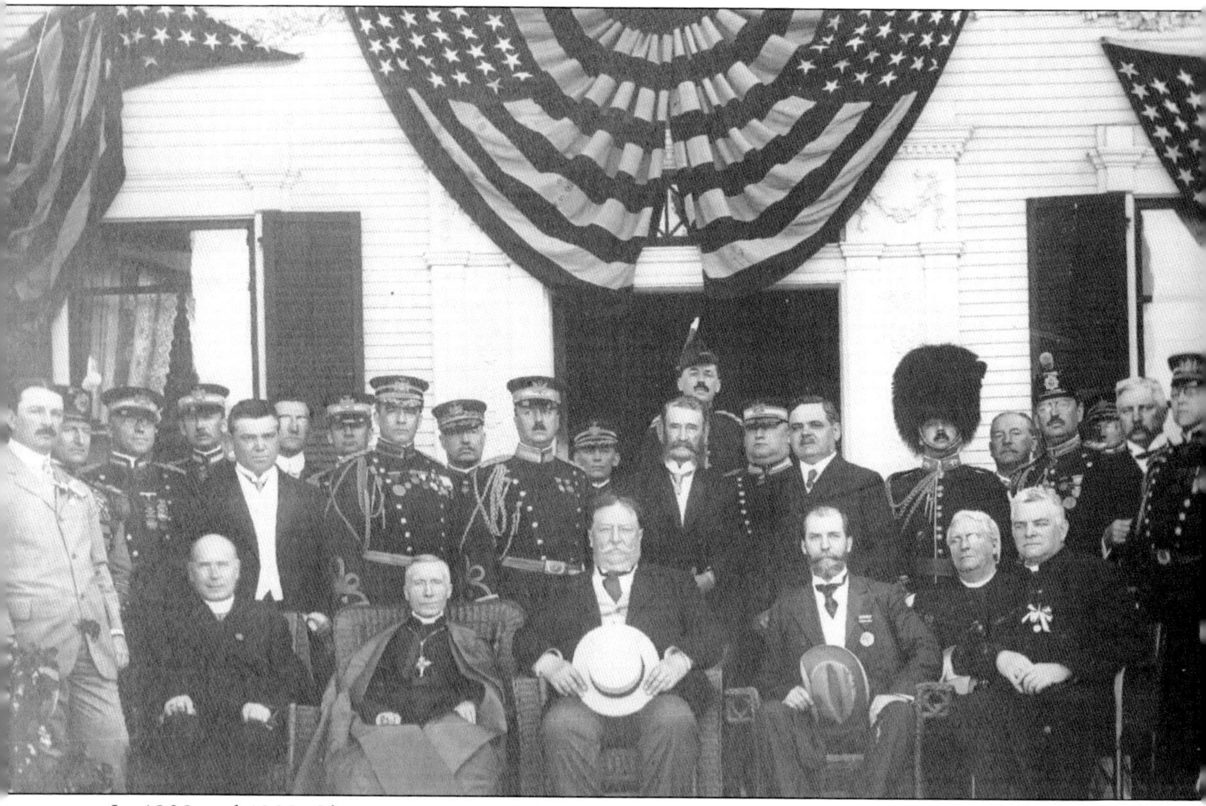

In 1908 and 1909, Clinton County celebrated the 300th anniversary of Samuel de Champlain's journeys through the region. President Taft visited on that occasion and participated in a number of local events, including a review of troops at the Plattsburgh barracks. This photograph shows the president in Cliff Haven, at the Catholic Summer School. In his remarks, which focused more on U.S. involvement in the Philippines, Taft said, "And now, my dear friends, I ought to talk about Champlain, and I could talk somewhat about him, because I appreciate as highly as anyone can, those motives that governed him and his high character as a man and the obstacles that he had to overcome."

Mayor John Tyrell and an unidentified air force colonel display the wooden nickels produced for the 1964 celebration of the Battle of Plattsburgh. In addition to the wooden nickel campaign, the region celebrated with graveside services, performances by local bands, and volleys from the Plattsburgh Air Force Base firing squad.

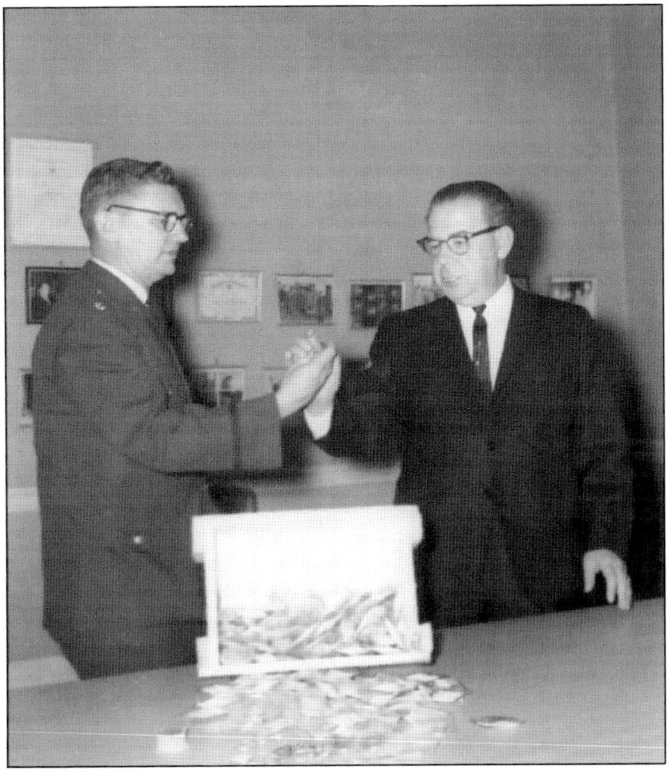

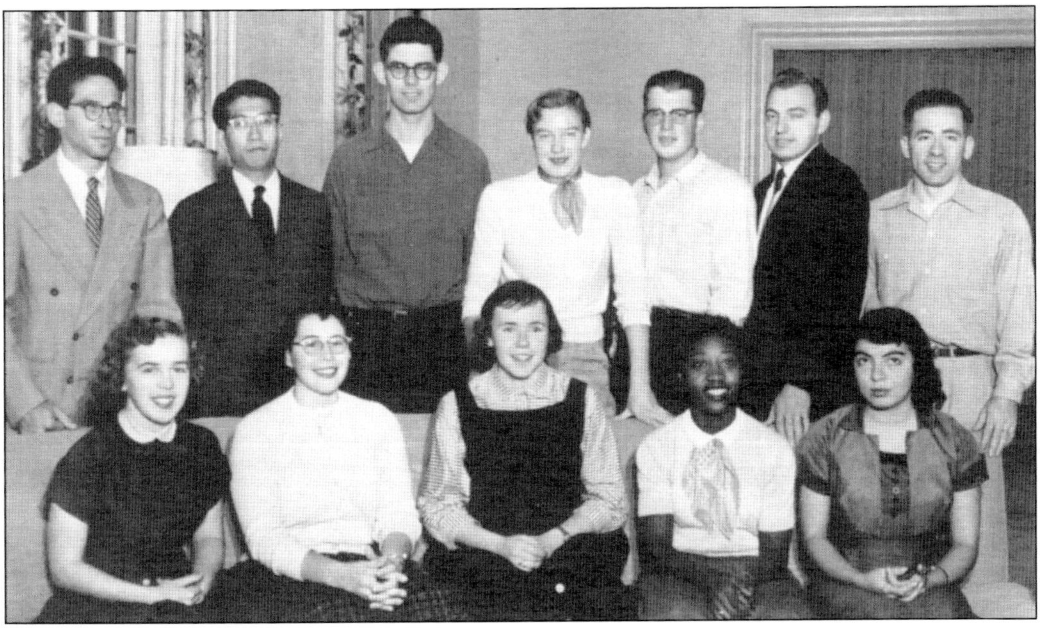

Clinton County's close historical ties and geographic proximity to Canada have long fostered an interest in international trade relations and tourism. Students at Plattsburgh State University take the interest one step further by participating in an International Relations Club, shown here in 1956. Members of the student association-sponsored group learn about other cultures, build ties between international and American students, and promote global respect.

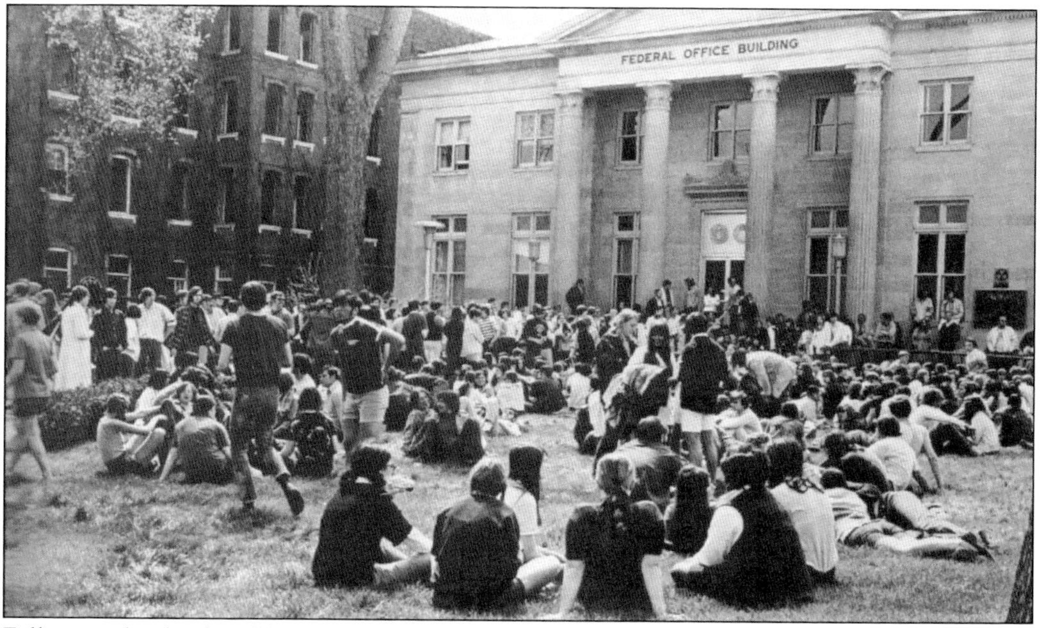

Following the deaths of four students at Kent State University, Plattsburgh State's campus took part in a week of protest activities that ranged from a candlelight march on the Plattsburgh Air Force Base to open forums, teach-ins, and the peaceful occupation of the U.S. Federal Building in Plattsburgh, shown here. Importantly, Pres. Charles Angell joined in these protests, helping to foster a sense of respectful and responsible protest.

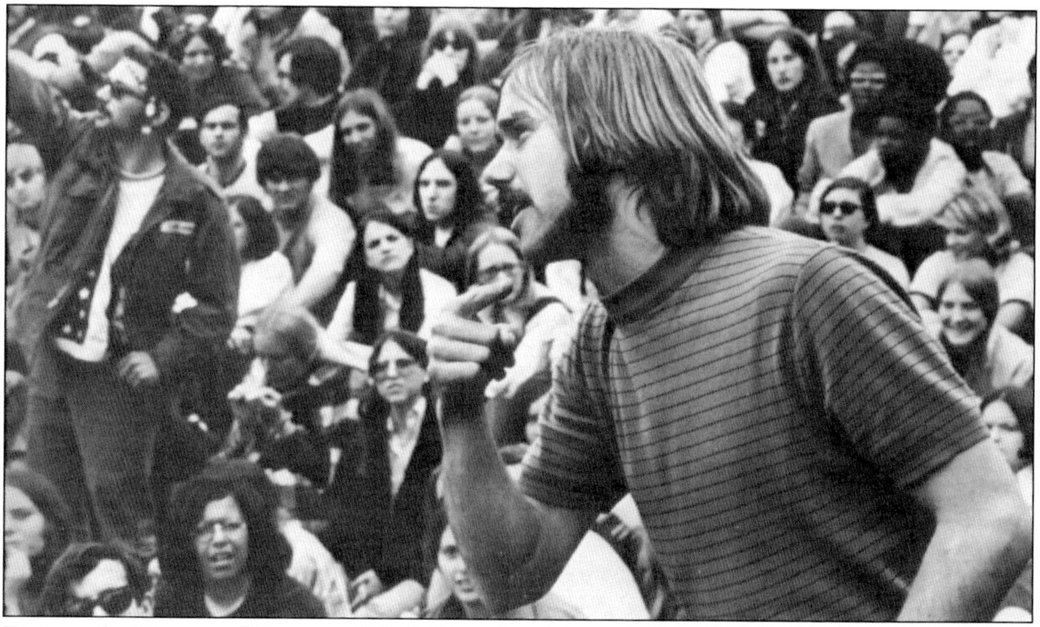
During the Vietnam War era, SUNY Plattsburgh's students, like their counterparts across the country, protested the war. This May 1970 rally included prominent faculty members and administrators. The legacy of these protests—which occurred throughout the 1960s—is still felt on campus, as every year students and faculty remember the students who fell at Kent State in 1970 by rededicating the stone monument in front of the Kehoe Administration Building.

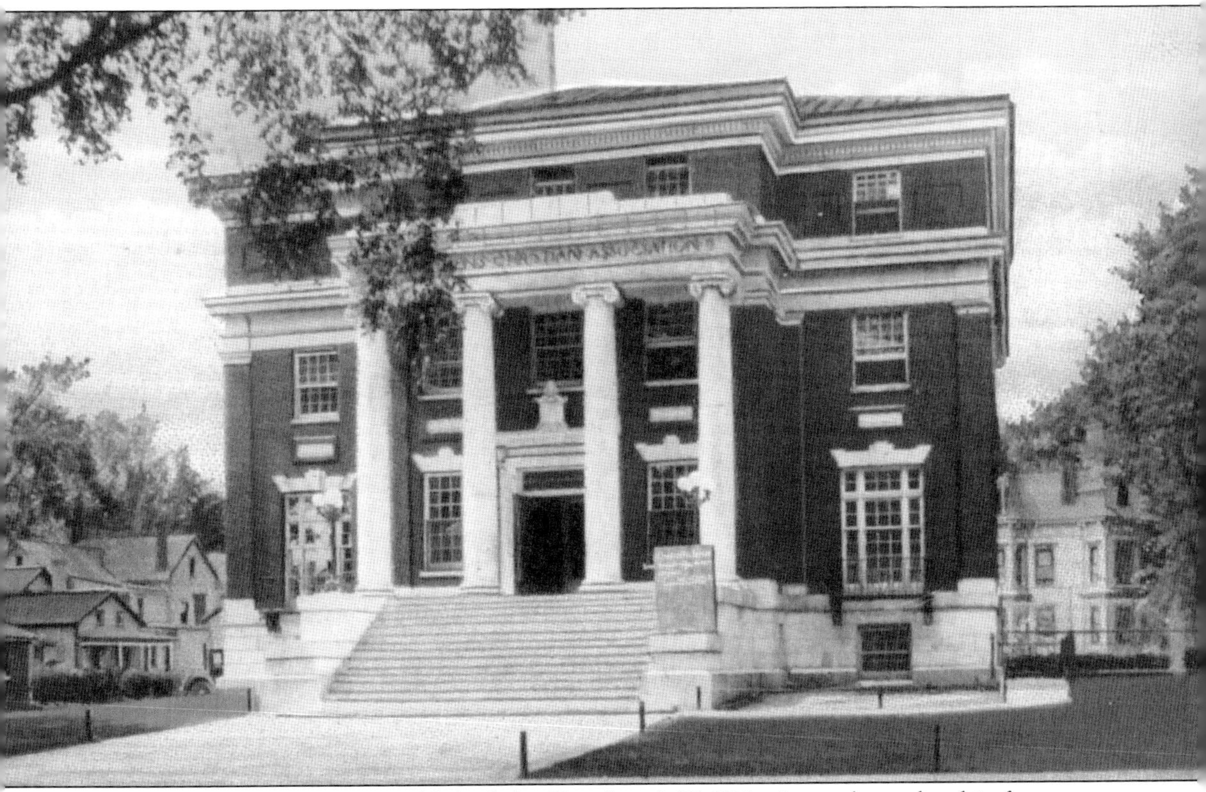

In 1895, C. A. H. Carson Jr. established the Plattsburgh YMCA. Annual membership fees were $5 for men and $3 for boys. After a fire destroyed the organization's original Margaret Street building, this structure was erected in 1908. Plattsburgh businessman and politician Loyal Smith donated generously to the project so that the Low mansion on Oak and Brinkerhoff Streets could be purchased and torn down. In its place, this three-story stone and brick building was established. Although the building no longer resembles this structure, the YMCA continues to serve the people of Clinton County, offering classes, emergency shelter, Camp Jericho, and a wealth of other activities.

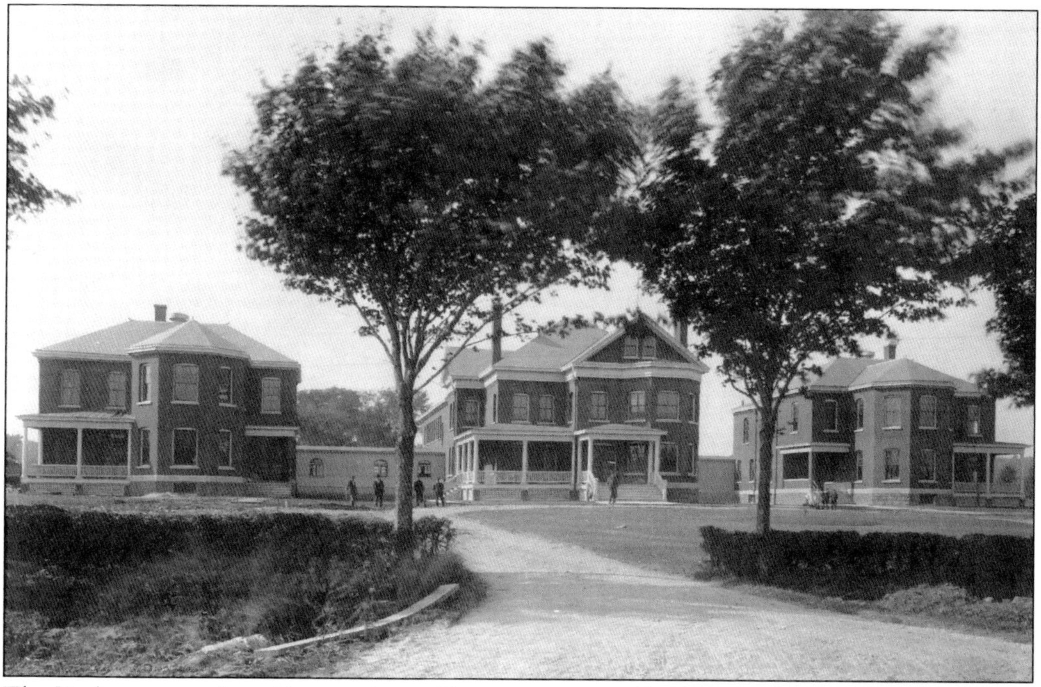

The Beekmantown Poor House, pictured here, was originally the site of the County Home and the County Farm. From the late 19th century, the home offered respite for those down on their luck and economically disadvantaged. Residents were required to work for their keep and to find other work and accommodations as soon as possible.

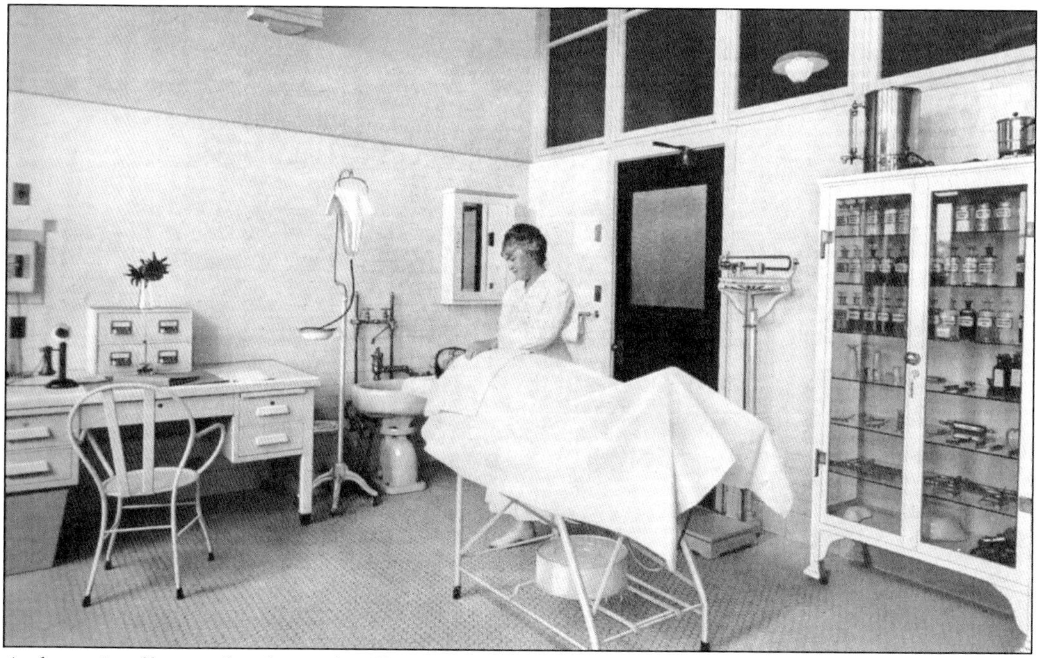

A doctor's office and a dentist's office were part of the Chazy Central Rural School District. Here a nurse assists a student. Later, William and Alice Miner would contribute heavily to the Physician's Hospital in Plattsburgh.

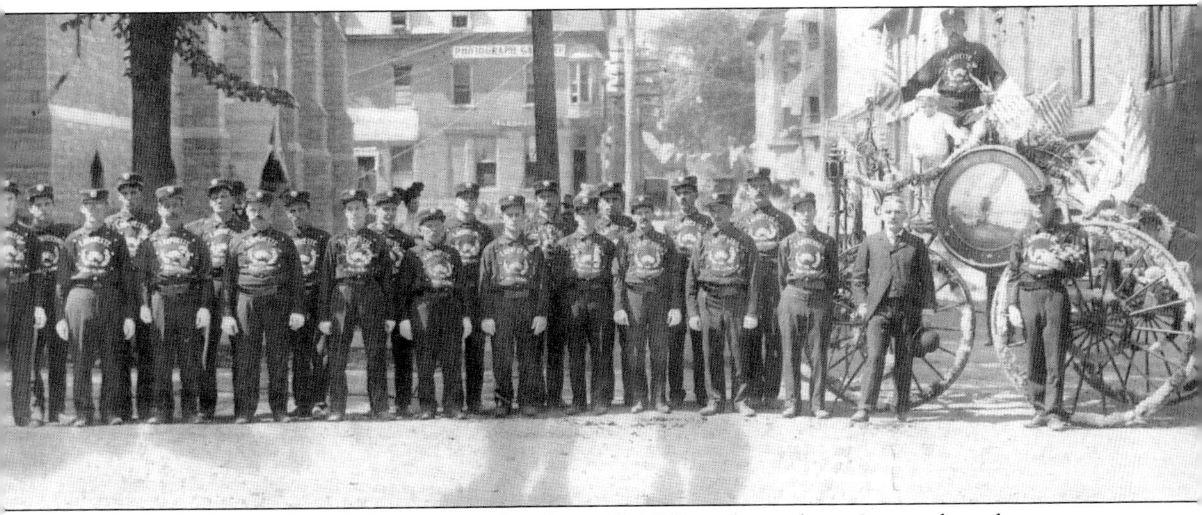

The Lafayette Hose Company, organized on June 17, 1872, is shown here. Located on the corner of Brinkerhoff and Marion Streets, this division of the Plattsburgh Volunteer Fire Department included 40 men as permanent members. In this image, honorary fire chief William T. Burleigh is second from the right. Notice the barrel on a wheeled cart that carried water to a fire scene. In 1902, the City of Plattsburgh resolved to appoint 12 firemen who would be paid $1 for each call to a fire and $2 for services at the fire. This formation of the fire department allowed the city to move away from the volunteer fire companies that formed throughout Clinton County beginning in the late 19th century.

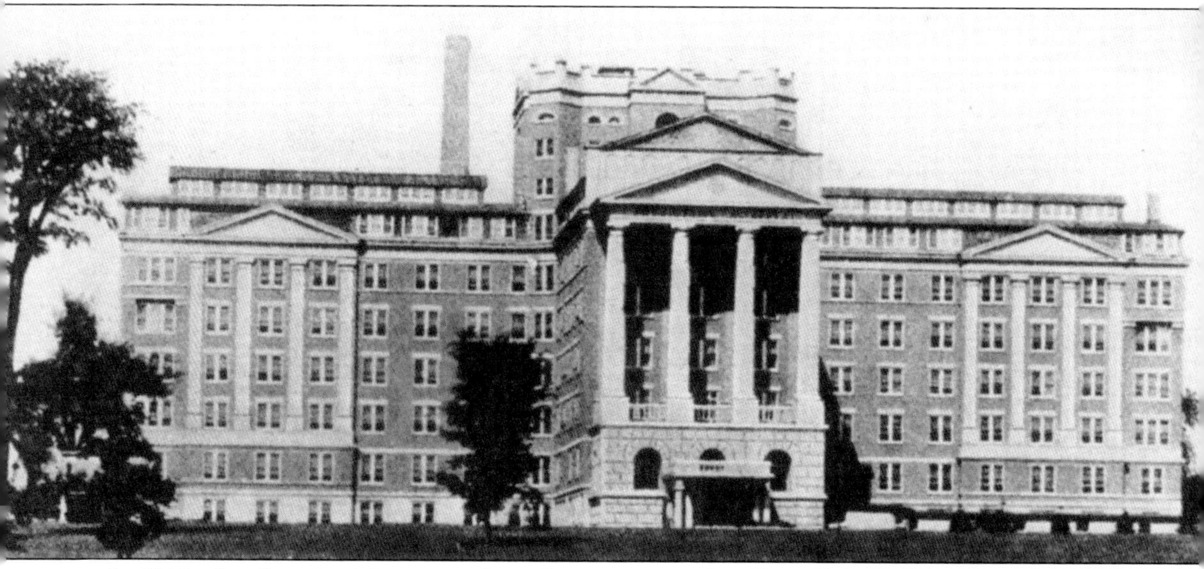

In 1911, after five physicians were denied positions on the Champlain Valley Hospital Board of Trustees, the Physicians Hospital, along with its own nursing school, opened on Court Street. After the hospital—which had been built in an existing mansion—experienced financial difficulties, William H. Miner agreed to build a new Physicians Hospital, with 212 beds (shown here). In 1972, the Physicians Hospital united with the Champlain Valley Hospital to become the Champlain Valley Physicians Hospital Medical Center. Subsequent years have seen the addition of the James A. Fitzpatrick Cancer Center (1990), the Emergency Care Center (1997), and the Alice T. Miner Center for Women and Children (1999). The CVPH has also built outpatient, surgical, and laboratory facilities at various remote sites.

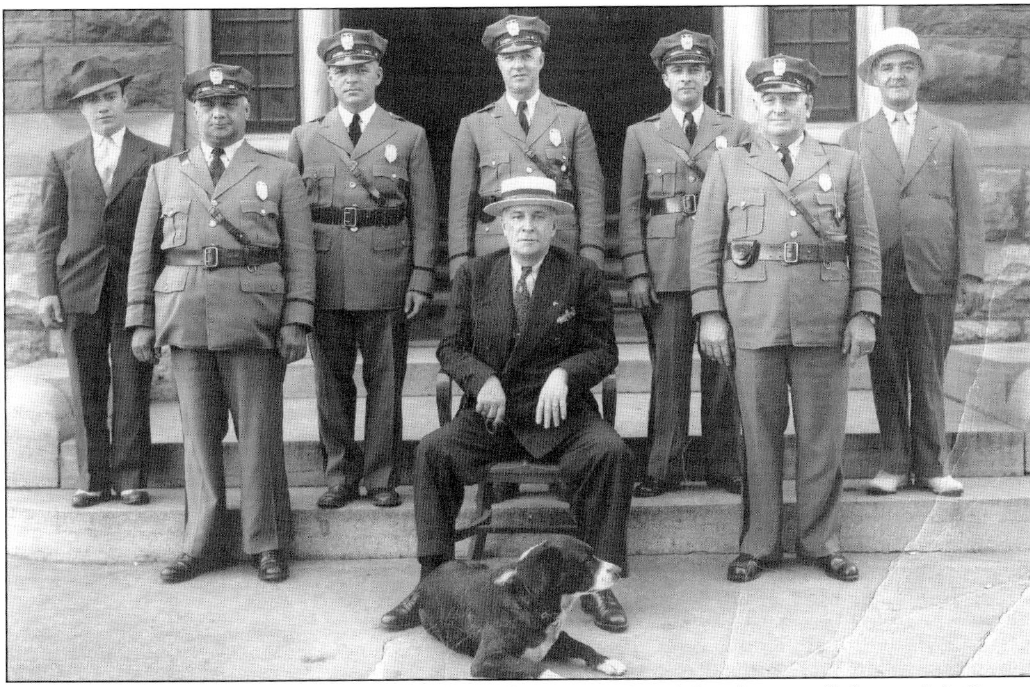

Sheriff Rudolph L. LaChapelle (seated) is shown here in 1940 with his deputies (left to right): George Moriarty, Peter A. Fessette, Emile J. La Fountaine, Charles Jandreau, William Mandigo, Herbert F. Sorrell, and Raymond R. Cashman. The first sheriff in the county, Benjamin Mooers was appointed in 1788. Later, Caleb Luther became the first elected county sheriff, winning the position in 1822.

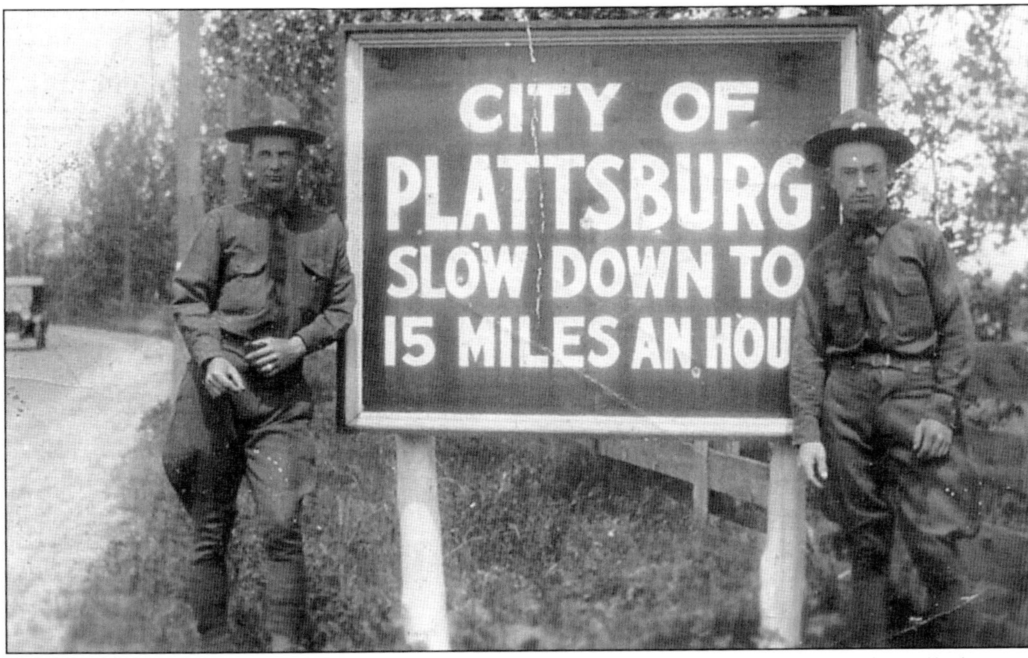

Two city of Plattsburgh policemen stand near a speed limit sign in 1919. As automobile traffic became more common, speed limits were determined and posted. Within the county, the City of Plattsburgh Police, the county Sheriff's department, and the New York State Troop B all patrol the streets.

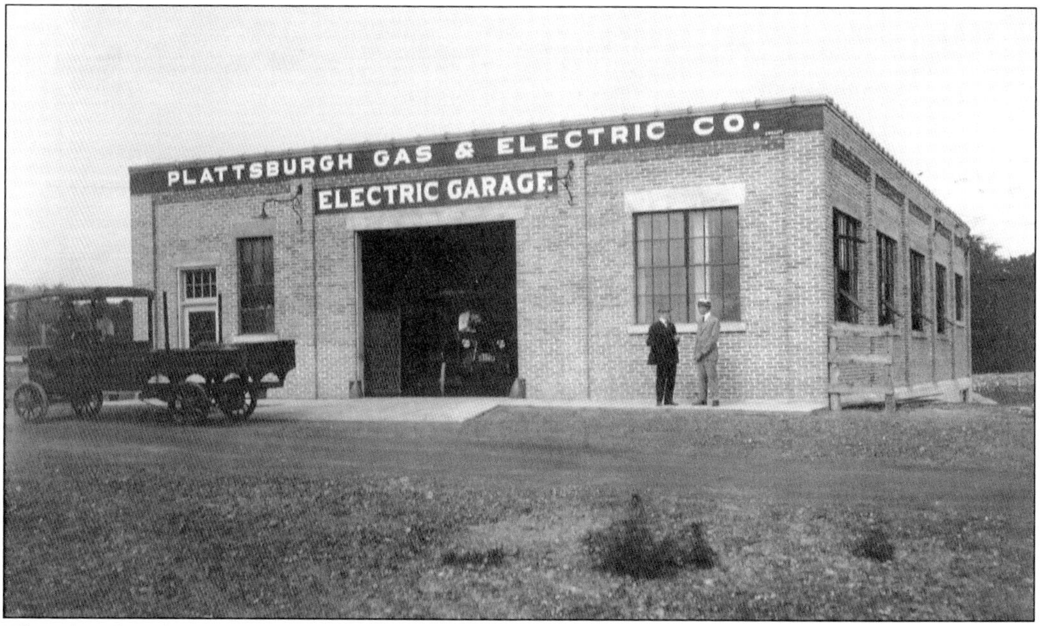

The Plattsburgh Gas and Electric Company, which eventually became part of New York State Electric and Gas, was situated on Saranac Street in Plattsburgh. This building, which is still standing, remained in use as a transit station and office until 1980. This image shows the building in 1914 (note the license plate designation).

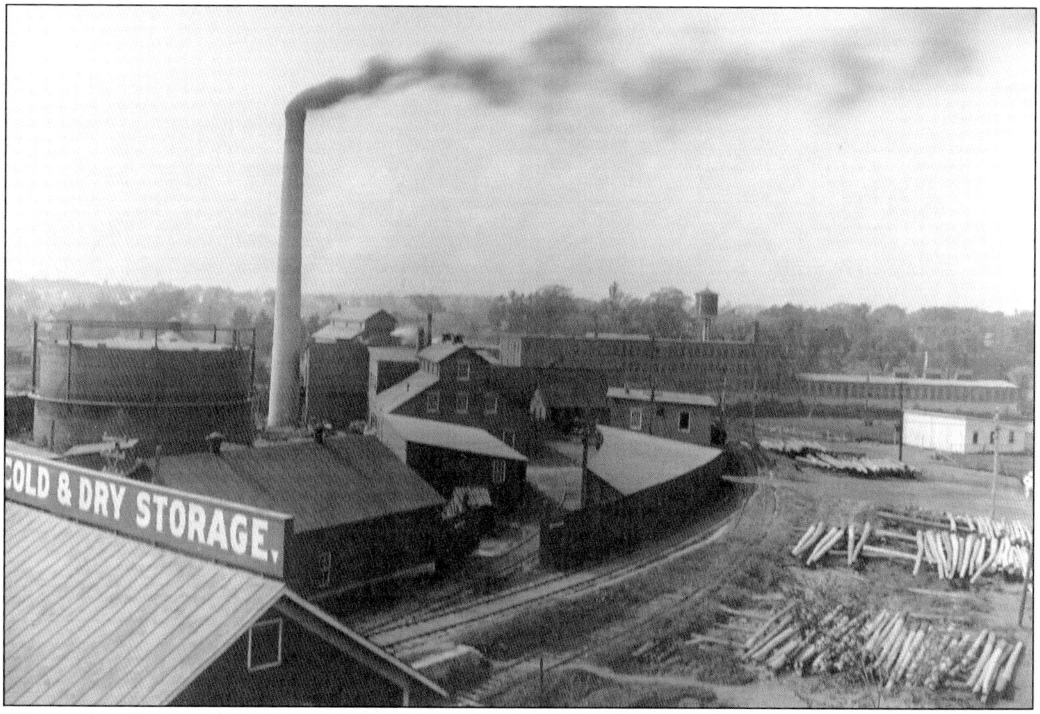

This undated image shows the gas plant of the New York State Electric and Gas Corporation. NYSEG and its predecessors operated the plant, located on Saranac Street in the city of Plattsburgh, from 1896 until 1960. After the gas plant closed, NYSEG continued to use the facility as a service center.

Seven

MILITARY

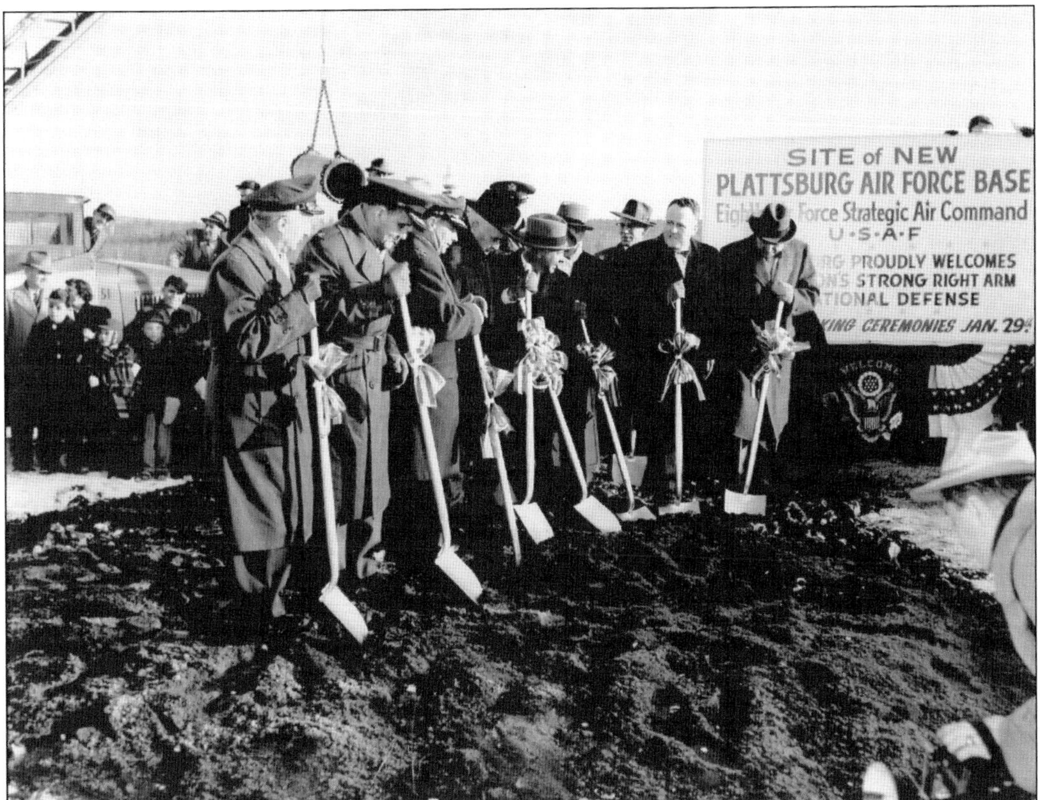

This 1953 photograph shows the official ground breaking for the Plattsburgh Air Force Base, one of the Strategic Air Command bases. While it was open, the base flew FB111s, B52s, B24s, B47s, and KC135s. Although the base survived several realignment and closure committees, it was closed in 1995.

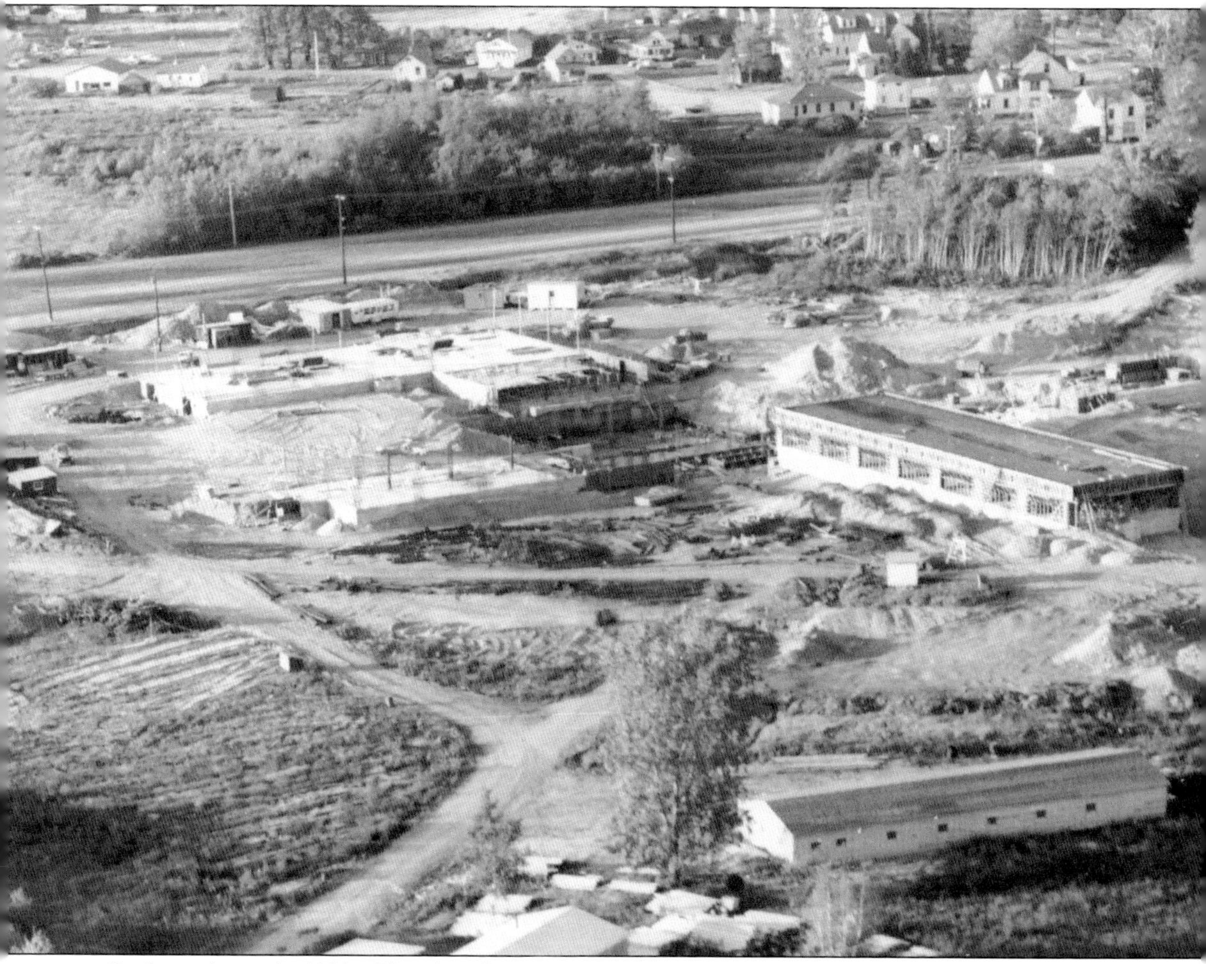

Built in the early 1950s, Plattsburgh Air Force Base (PAFB) was developed to house the 380th Bombardment Wing, which arrived in Plattsburgh in 1955. The new base was built around the existing barracks sites, known to generations of Clinton County residents as the old base. This image shows the construction of the base hospital, located between the old and new bases. PAFB was a Strategic Air Command base and, as such, fell under the mission to "be prepared to conduct long-range offensive operations in any part of the world, either independently or in cooperation with land and naval forces; to conduct maximum-range reconnaissance over land or sea, either independently or in cooperation with land and naval forces; to provide combat units capable of intense and sustained combat operations employing the latest and most advanced weapons; to train units and personnel of the maintenance of the Strategic Forces in all parts of the world; to perform such special missions as the Commanding General Army Air forces may direct."

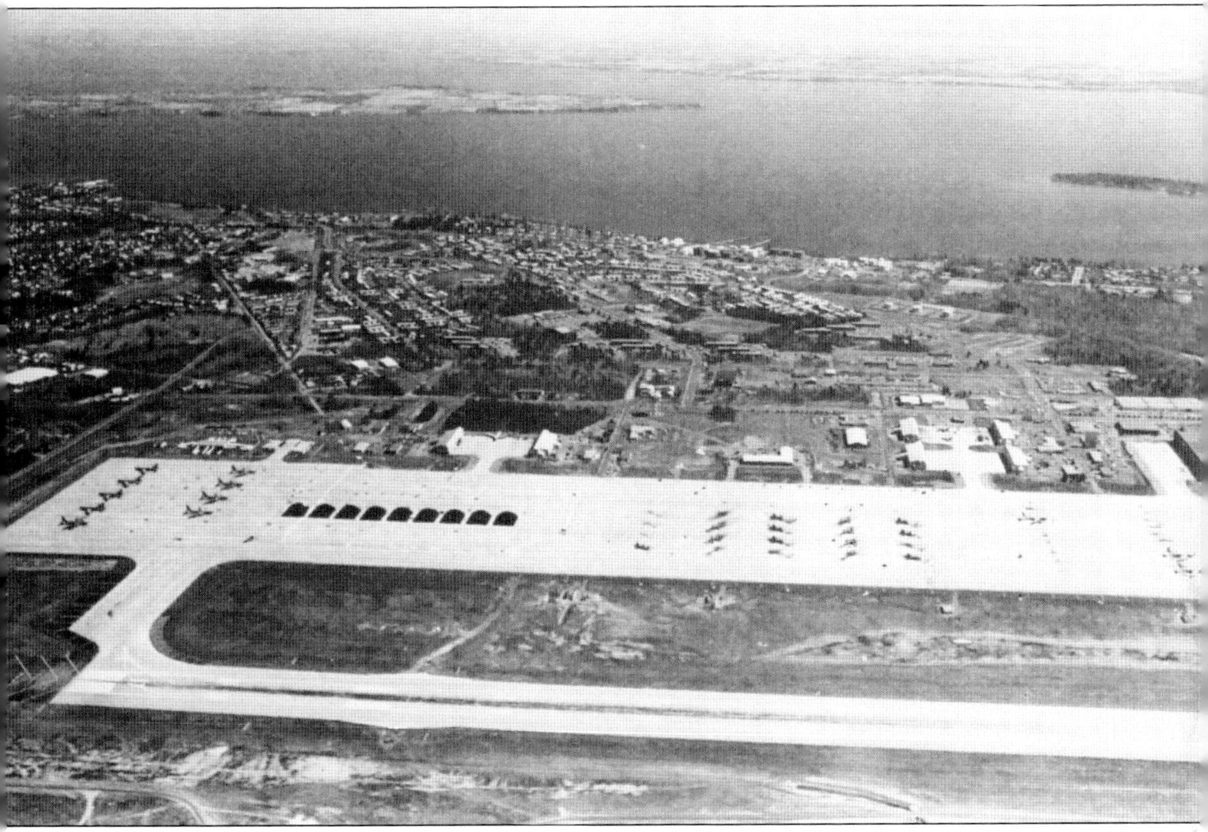

This 1981 aerial view of the Plattsburgh Air Force Base shows the runway and flight line complex of the base, as well as portions of the city and town of Plattsburgh. Specially fortified for the B-52s, Plattsburgh's runway was a backup landing site for the space shuttles. B-52s were actively involved in the U.S. cold war activities. Besides offering the capability of carrying nuclear weapons, the planes were used to fly missions throughout the world. Most famously, under Gen. Curtis LeMay, the planes were used to bomb acres of land in Japan and Korea by flying virtually wing to wing.

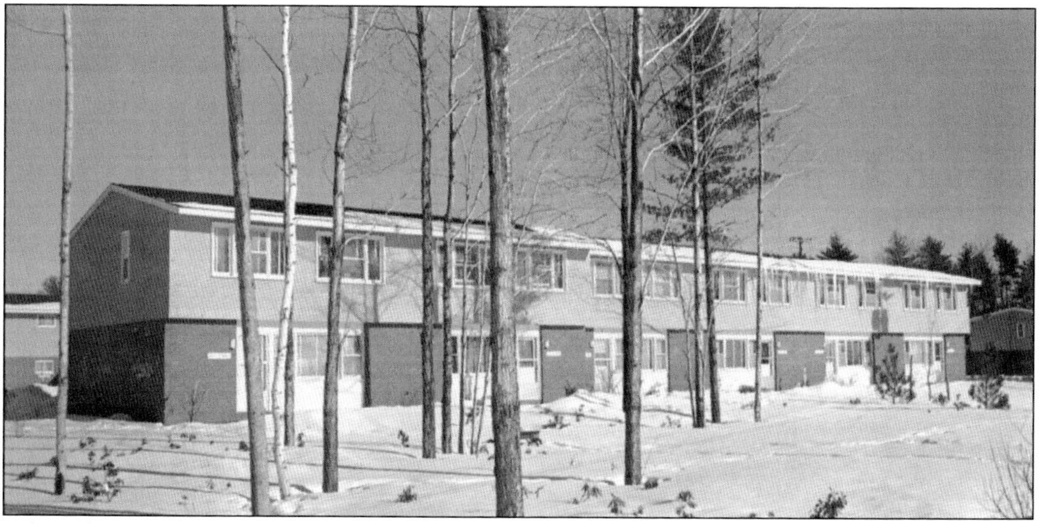

When the new base was constructed in the 1950s, multiple-family dwellings, like this structure, were erected. Each house was a duplex, and each duplex stood in a cul-de-sac full of duplexes. After the 1995 closure of the Air Force Base, all of these structures were torn down and new housing developments created.

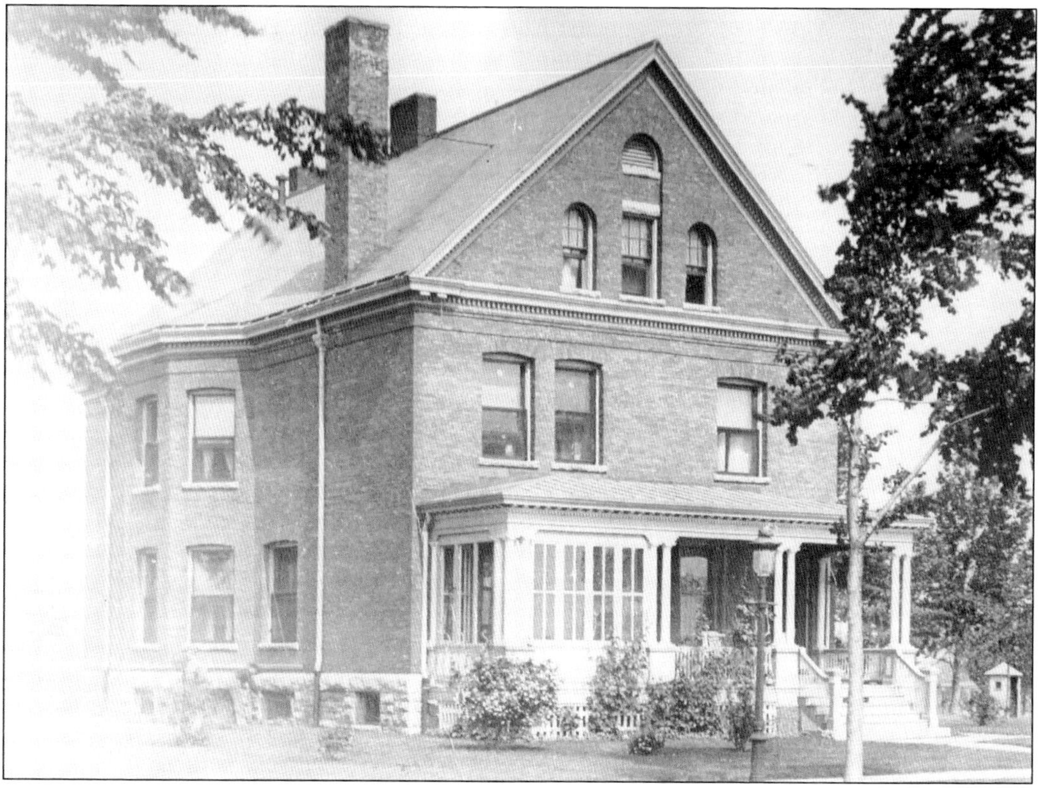

Houses like this two-and-a-half-story brick structure were built along the Oval at the Plattsburgh barracks. Circling the parade grounds, the houses were used to house officers' families while the Plattsburgh Air Force Base was in operation. Between use as residences for military families, the houses were part of the Champlain College campus.

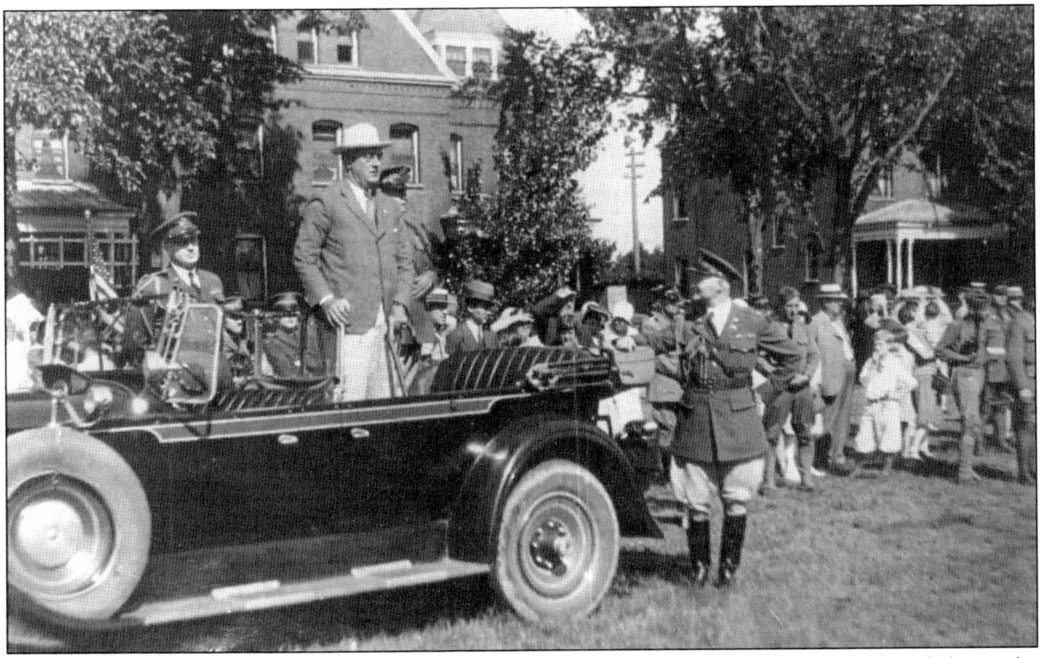

Franklin Delano Roosevelt, then governor of New York State, visited the Plattsburgh barracks in 1926. He stands in the back of his car, addressing the troops and civilians gathered along the Oval, more commonly known as Officers' Row. The buildings in the background were used by Champlain College, after World War II, when the barracks were abandoned.

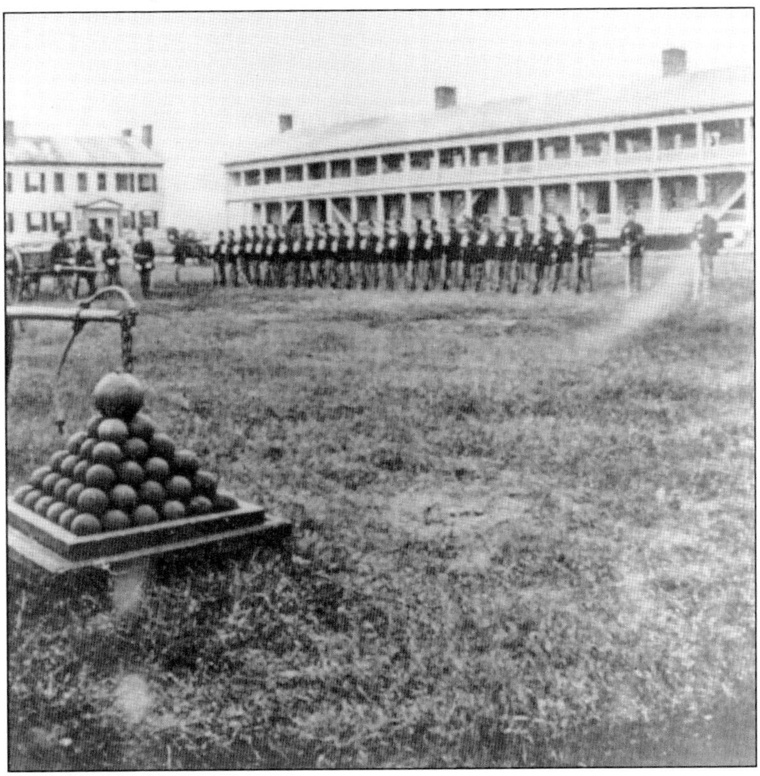

Troops line up in front of the old stone barracks on the campus of the Plattsburgh barracks. During the Civil War, the Plattsburgh barracks served as the organizing point for the 96th Regiment, which later served in Virginia and North Carolina.

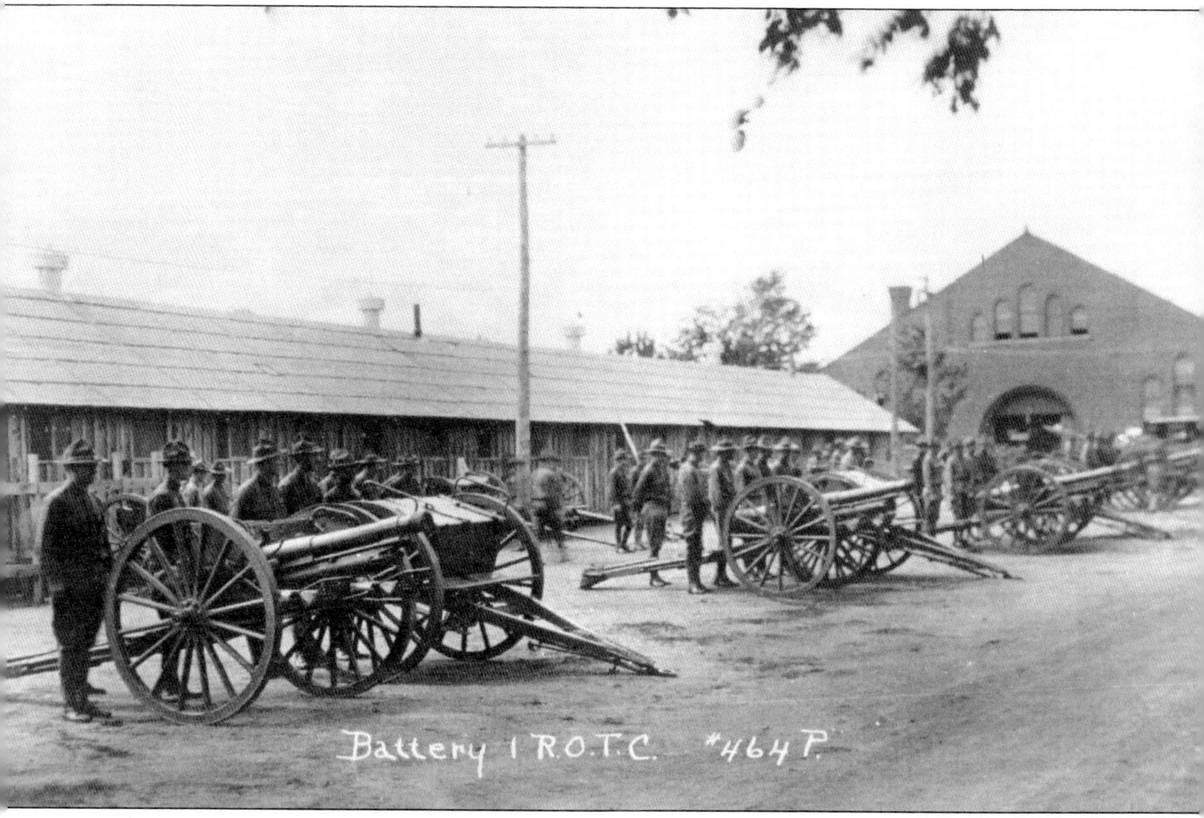

The Battery 1 Reserve Officers' Training Corps poses at the Plattsburgh barracks. These men trained at the Civilian Military Training Camp. After the National Defense Act of 1916 was passed, the U.S. Army developed a Junior Reserve Officers' Training Corps "to instill in students in United States secondary educational institutions the value of citizenship, service to the United States, personal responsibility, and a sense of accomplishment." The 1964 Vitalization Act changed the parameters of the JROTC to include all branches of the armed forces. JROTC programs still exist on college campuses across the country and spring from the Plattsburgh Idea developed by Maj. Gen. Leonard Wood.

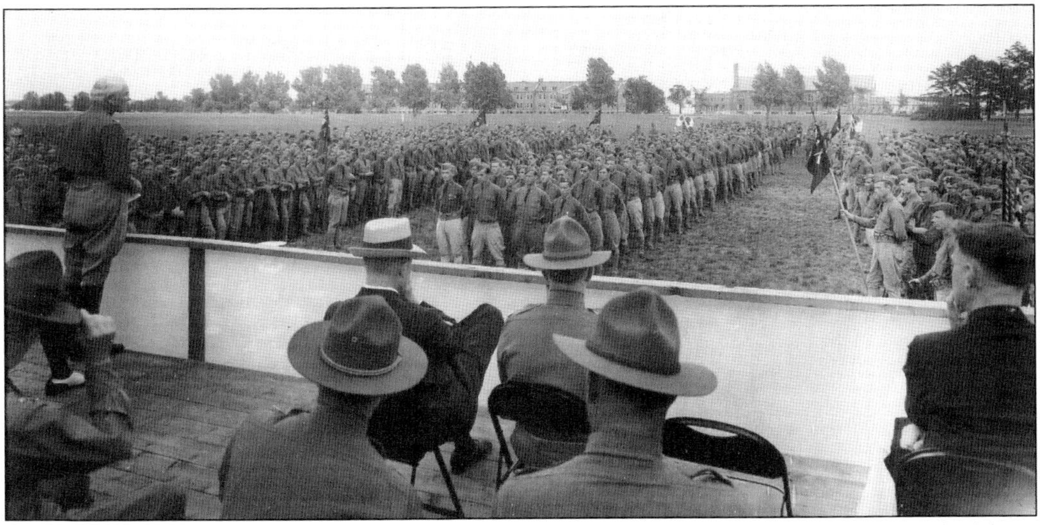

Troops are reviewed on the parade grounds of the Plattsburgh barracks prior to 1936. The buildings in the distance were later used as offices by the Plattsburgh Air Force Base. Located out of the shot, behind the speaker, are the brick officers' quarters.

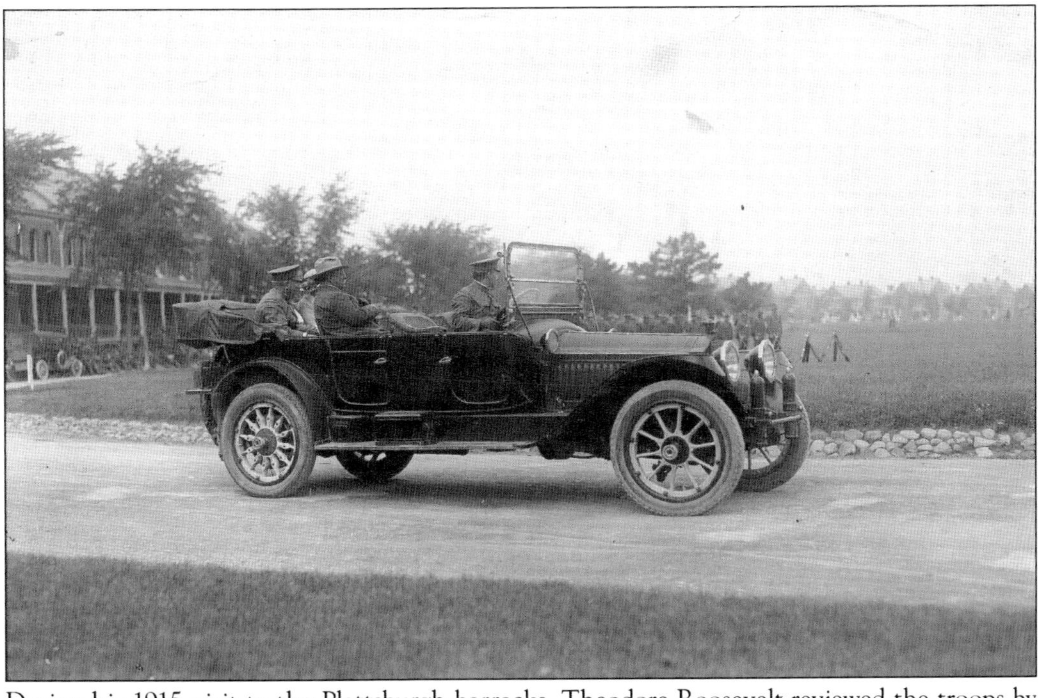

During his 1915 visit to the Plattsburgh barracks, Theodore Roosevelt reviewed the troops by driving around the Oval, a road that encircles the parade grounds and borders on the houses of Officers' Row and the administrative buildings of the barracks.

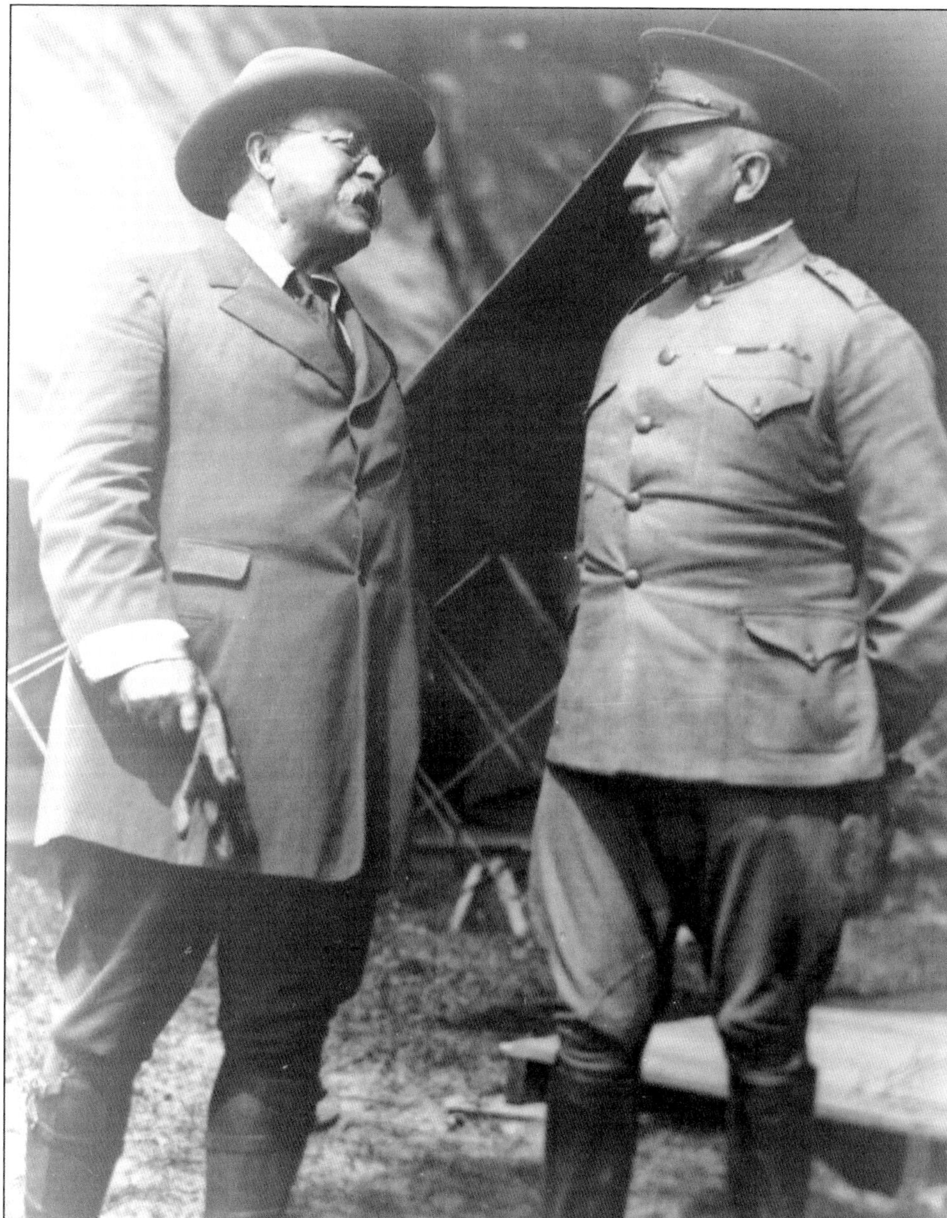

Former president Theodore Roosevelt (left) talked with Maj. Gen. Leonard Wood at Plattsburgh's Citizen Camp in 1915. Before the creation of the Plattsburgh Air Force Base, the barracks at Plattsburgh were used to train soldiers and citizen soldiers. The camp and parade grounds were the sites of military maneuvers, historic ceremonies, and various exercises. This photograph was taken on the occasion of Roosevelt's August 22nd visit to address the troops. Toward the end of his life, General Wood wrote: "We built better than we knew at the time, and the 'Plattsburgh Idea' . . . has come to stay. The training camps gave up many thousands of officers for the War, and an outstanding feature in their preparation was that it was made before the War came upon us. The growth of the Plattsburgh Idea and its standing at the present time are most encouraging. The Movement is the basis on which our present system of citizens' training rests."

The Atlas Missile, shown here, came to Clinton County in the 1960s. Twelve missile sites were built within a 30-mile radius of Plattsburgh Air Force Base. Each site housed a missile designed to burn liquid oxygen and hydrocarbon fuel and to carry a thermonuclear warhead. Designed to reach targets up to 5,000 miles away, the missiles were part of the Intercontinental Ballistic Missile Program.

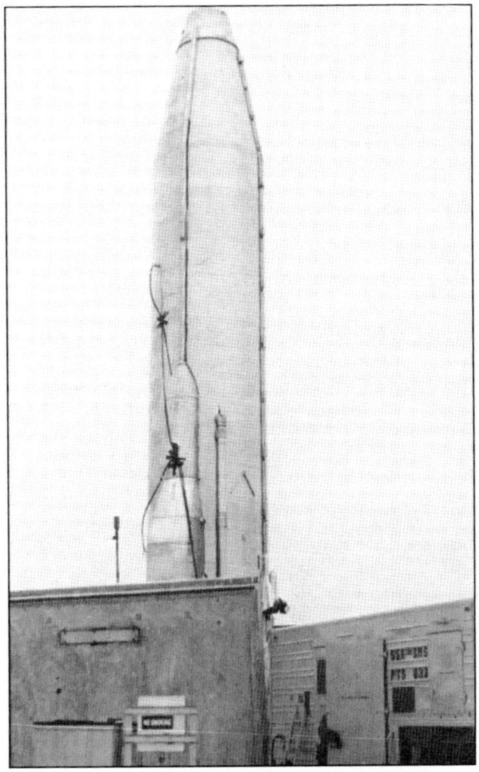

Shown here in 1961, the guardhouses at the Plattsburgh Air Force Base evolved to outposts at which guards could check two lanes of traffic. Although the original 50-foot-by-15-foot wooden, three-room and two-cell guardhouses were used to hold prisoners sentenced to solitary confinement, the newer version, shown here, was much smaller (at most 36 square feet) and designed for the sole purpose of allowing guards some protection from the weather.

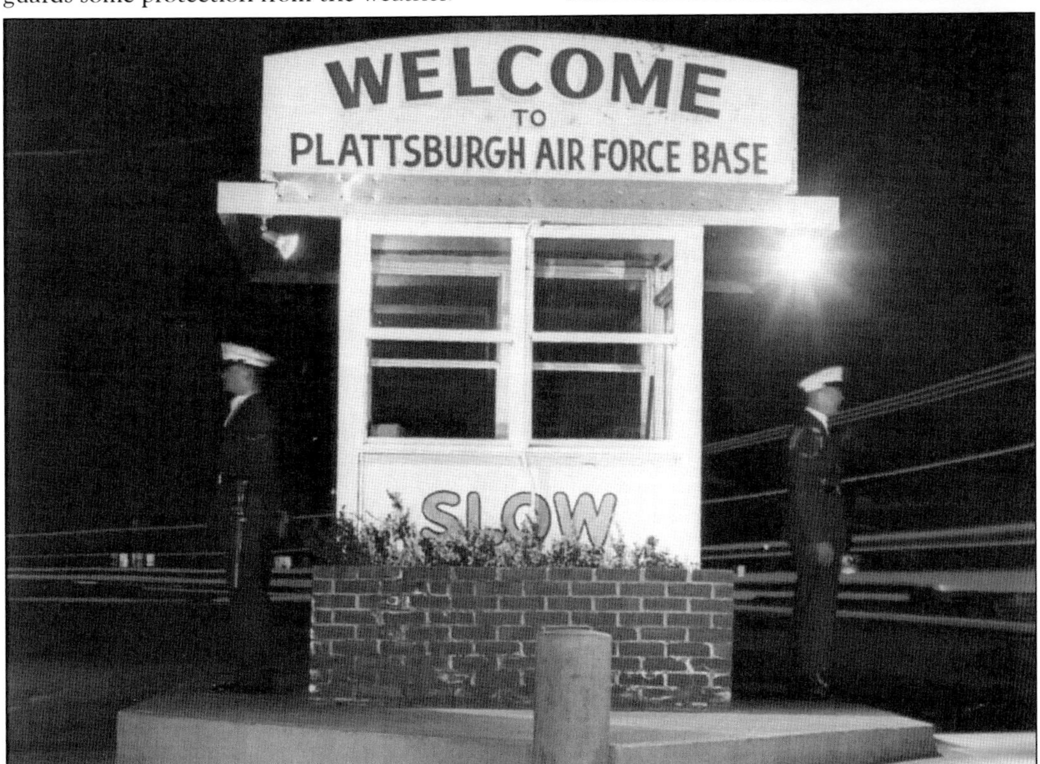

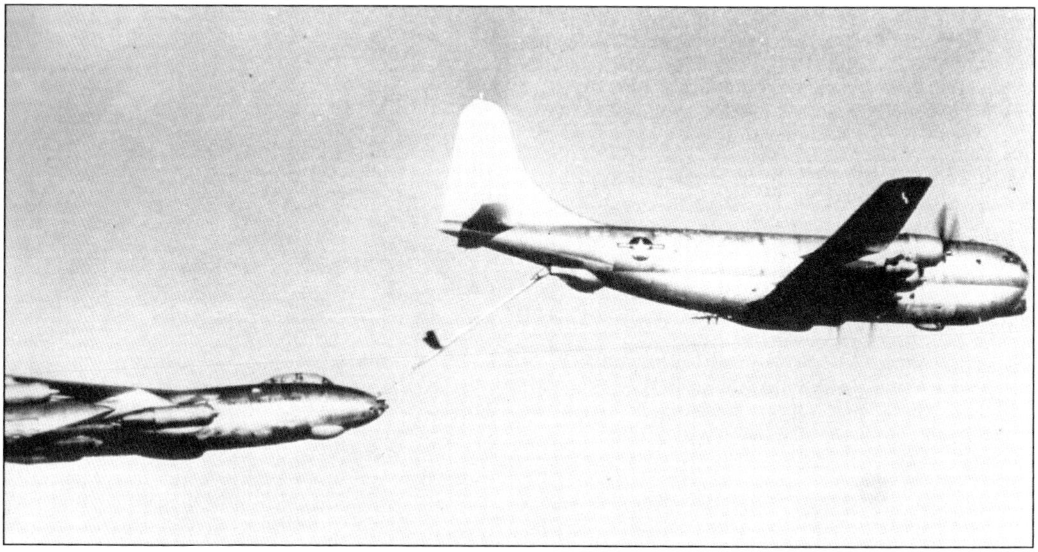

This photograph shows the 380th Bombardment Wing's first aircraft. On July 1, 1955, the 380th was sent to Plattsburgh Air Force Base. Later, on February 1, 1956, the 380th was accepted into the 820th Air Division.

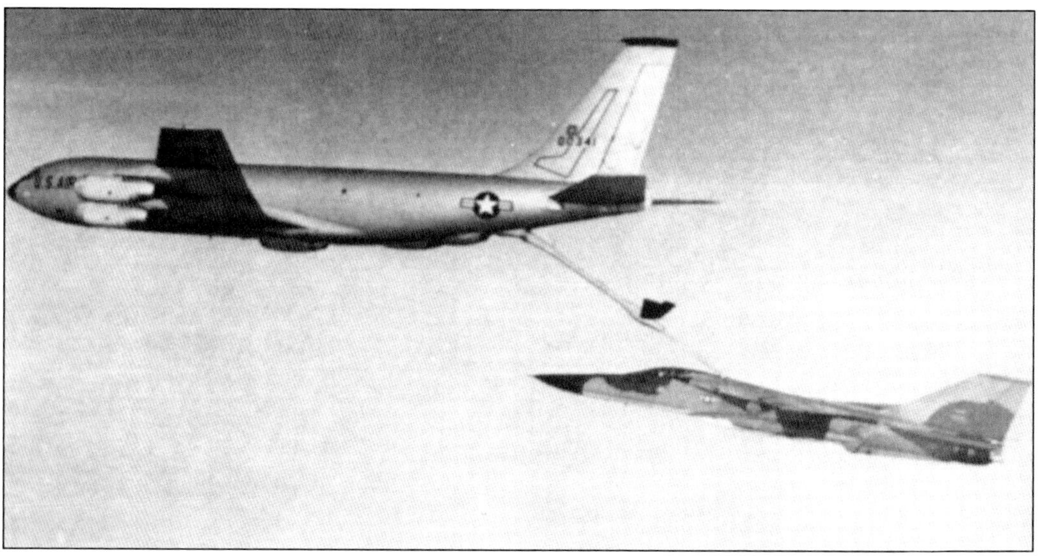

A KC-135 Stratotanker refuels an FB-111 bomber. Training and support for refueling missions occurred at the Plattsburgh Air Force Base from its 1954 opening until its closure in 1995.

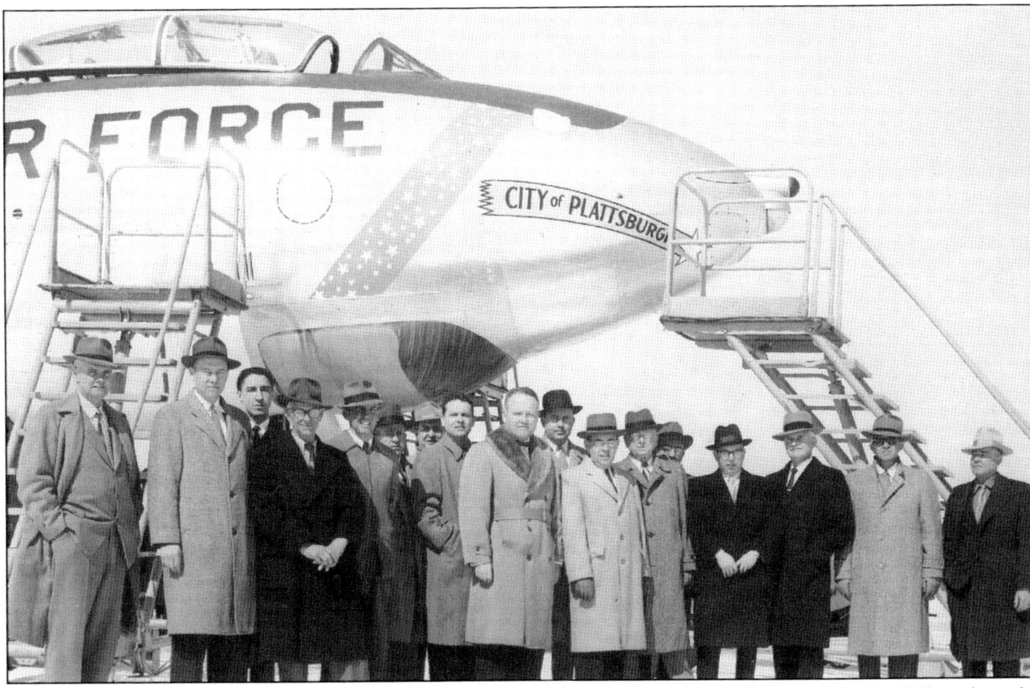

An unidentified group of men stand around an air force plane named for the city of Plattsburgh. That name underscores the ties between the military and the community. During construction, $135,000 a week was earned by the 1,353 local union members contracted to develop the base.

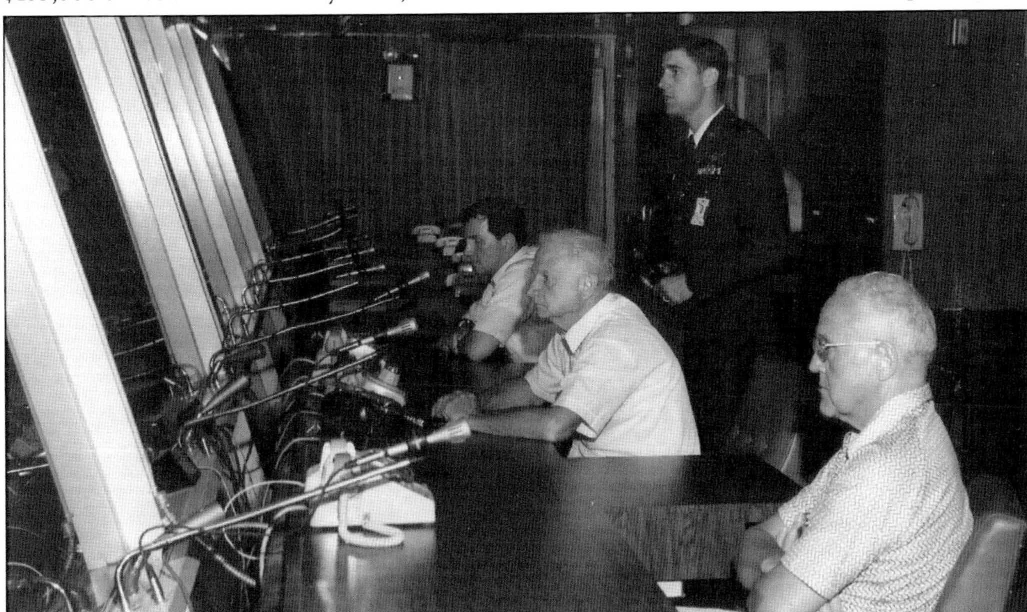

As a Strategic Air Command base, Plattsburgh maintained an extensive complex of flight line buildings. Here Capt. Thomas L. Aslakson, Chief of the Data Display Section, shows visitors the command balcony of the underground command post that overlooked the runway. Clyde Lewis, who was instrumental in bringing the air force base to Plattsburgh, sits to the right with his arms crossed.

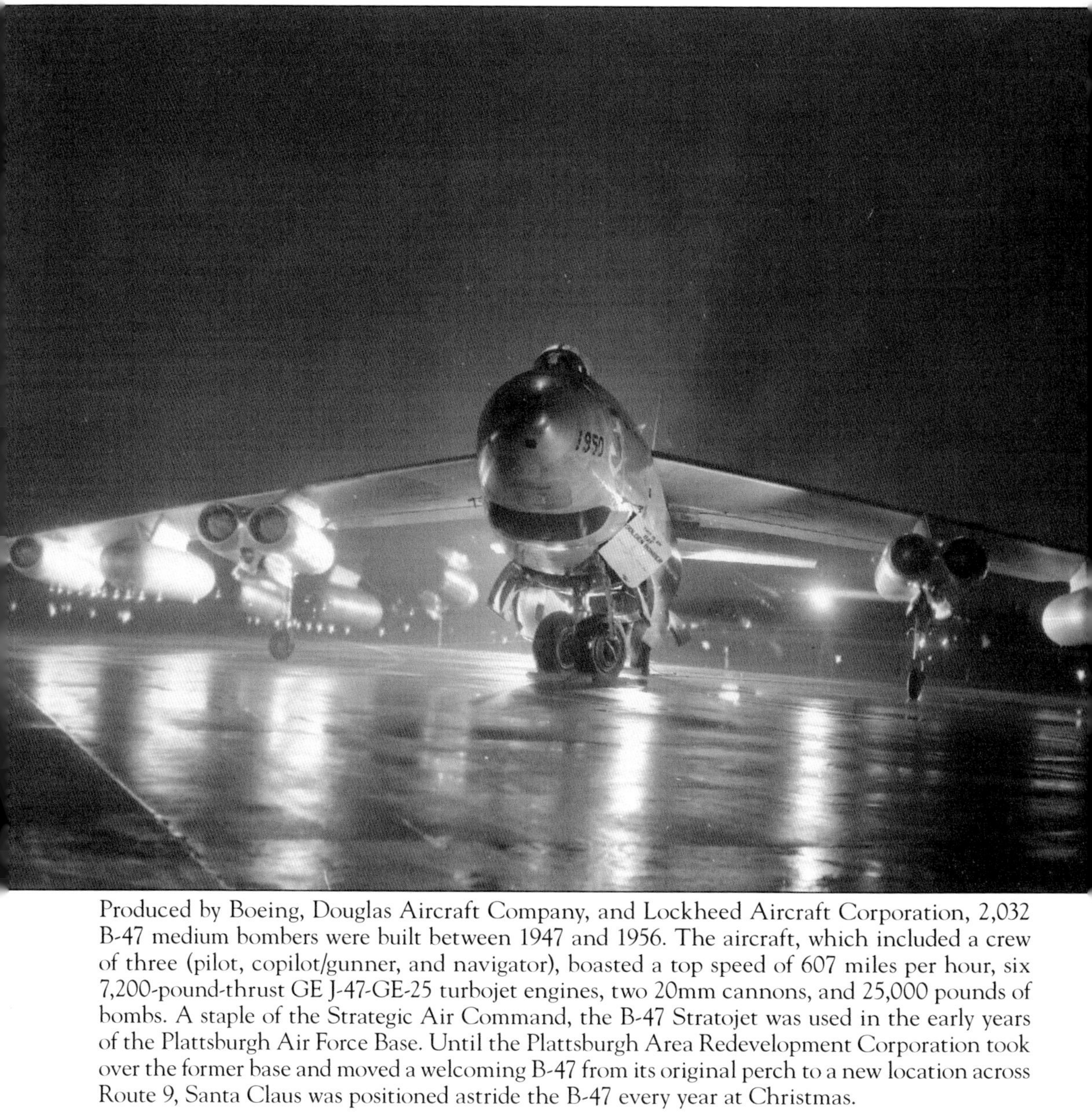

Produced by Boeing, Douglas Aircraft Company, and Lockheed Aircraft Corporation, 2,032 B-47 medium bombers were built between 1947 and 1956. The aircraft, which included a crew of three (pilot, copilot/gunner, and navigator), boasted a top speed of 607 miles per hour, six 7,200-pound-thrust GE J-47-GE-25 turbojet engines, two 20mm cannons, and 25,000 pounds of bombs. A staple of the Strategic Air Command, the B-47 Stratojet was used in the early years of the Plattsburgh Air Force Base. Until the Plattsburgh Area Redevelopment Corporation took over the former base and moved a welcoming B-47 from its original perch to a new location across Route 9, Santa Claus was positioned astride the B-47 every year at Christmas.

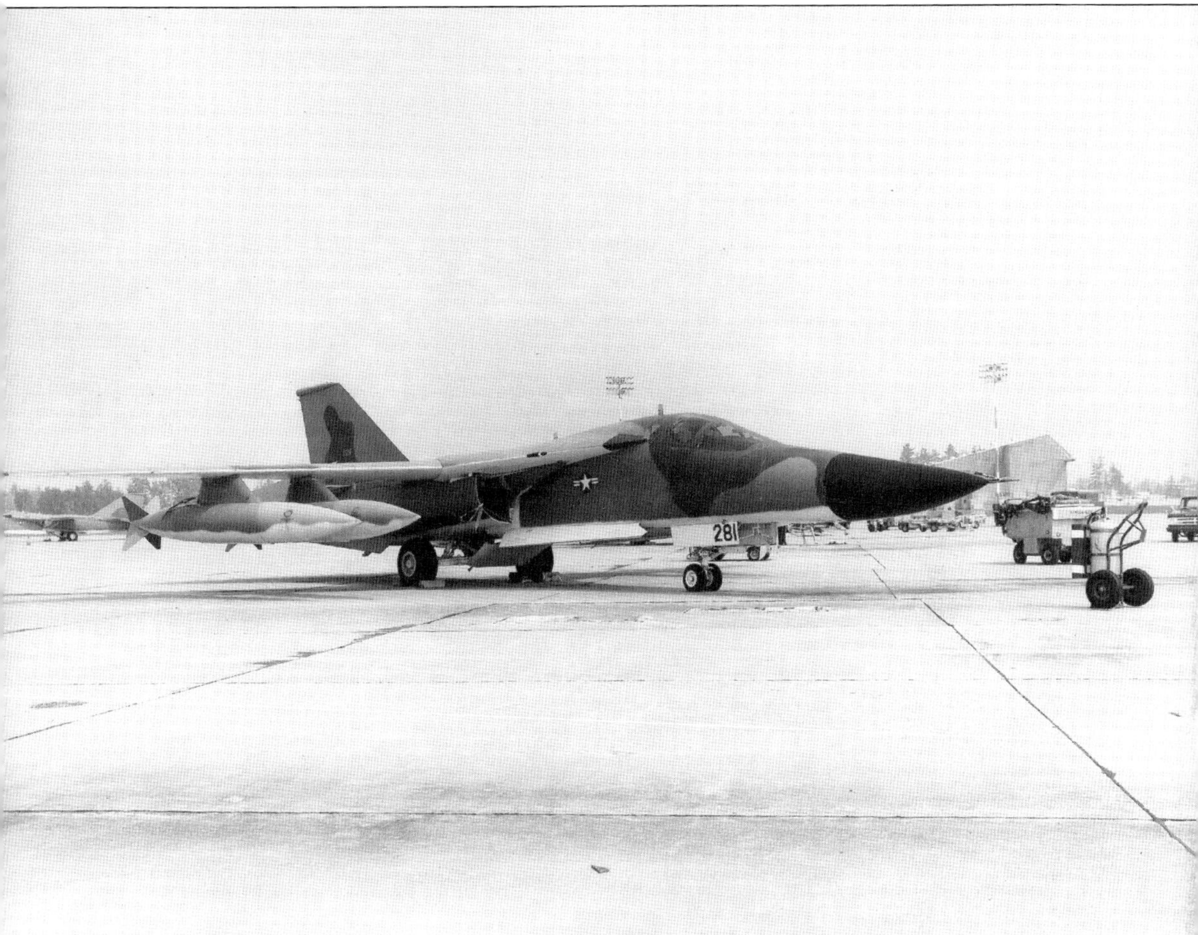

The FB-111, a medium-range bomber produced by General Dynamics, was used by the United States Air Force from 1967 until 1998. Despite a limited range and a variety of production and maintenance difficulties, the FB-111s could function at both high and low altitudes while carrying up to 24 conventional bombs or 2 internal SRAM/gravity bombs and up to 4 external pylon-mounted weapons (all nuclear weapons). Moreover, the FB-111's quick take-off capability was useful in allowing the plane to penetrate low altitudes and to escape from ground alert locations.

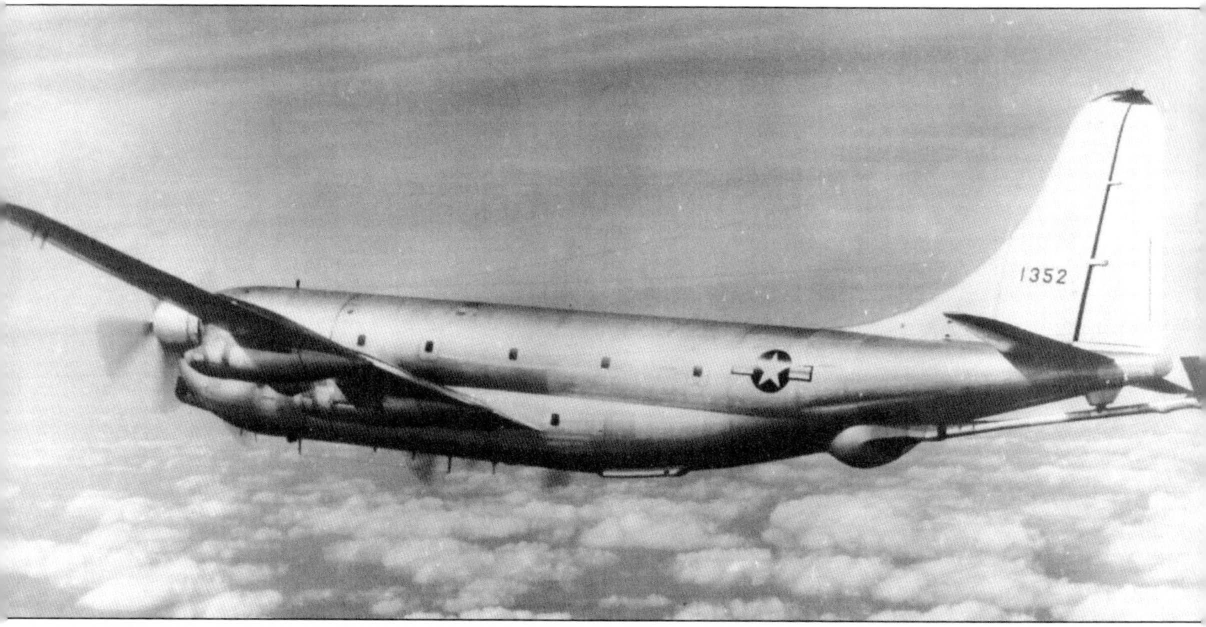

The KC-97 Stratotanker was one of the earliest planes stationed at the Plattsburgh Air Force Base. Built by Boeing, the planes could carry 9,190 gallons of fuel and reach a cruising speed of more than 300 miles per hour. Designed to refuel planes, the KC-97 supported the Strategic Air Command and its B-47 bomber wing by refueling planes mid-air. The major benefit of mid-air refueling, of course, is that it allowed planes to carry out longer missions with fewer landings.

Pictured on the Plattsburgh Air Force Base runway (notice the Adirondacks in silhouette behind the plane), the B-52 Bomber required fortified and extended runways. Between 1952 and 1962, 744 were built. With a top speed of 650 miles per hour, a range of more than 10,000 miles, and a ceiling of more than 50,000 feet, the B-52 Stratofortress remains in use today. Although the B-52 was designed to carry nuclear weapons, it has only ever dropped conventional munitions in combat. The planes were officially assigned to SAC units from 1957 until 1992 and then to the Air Mobility Command after the 1992 SAC realignment.

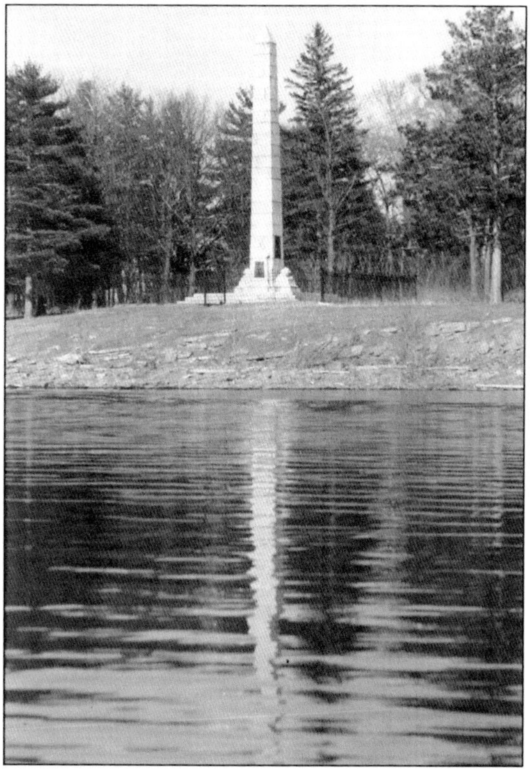

Dedicated in 1908, the Crab Island Monument marks the grave site of British and American soldiers who died during the Battle of Plattsburgh. Crab Island was also the site of a military hospital during the War of 1812.

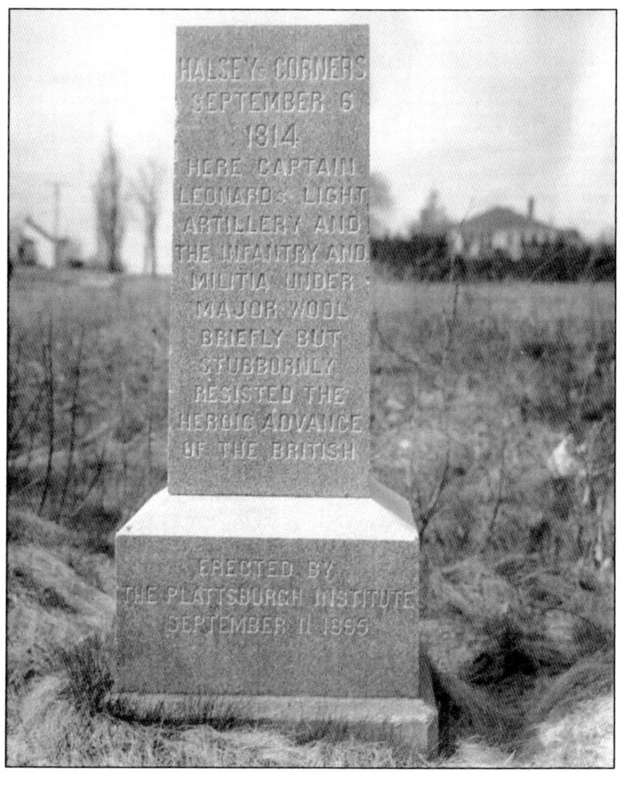

Halsey's Corners, memorialized by this granite marker, was the site of one of the skirmishes of the War of 1812. The Battles at Plattsburgh—on land and on the lake—allowed American forces to defeat the British and end the war. Clinton County residents commemorate the Battle of Plattsburgh each year in a weeklong celebration.

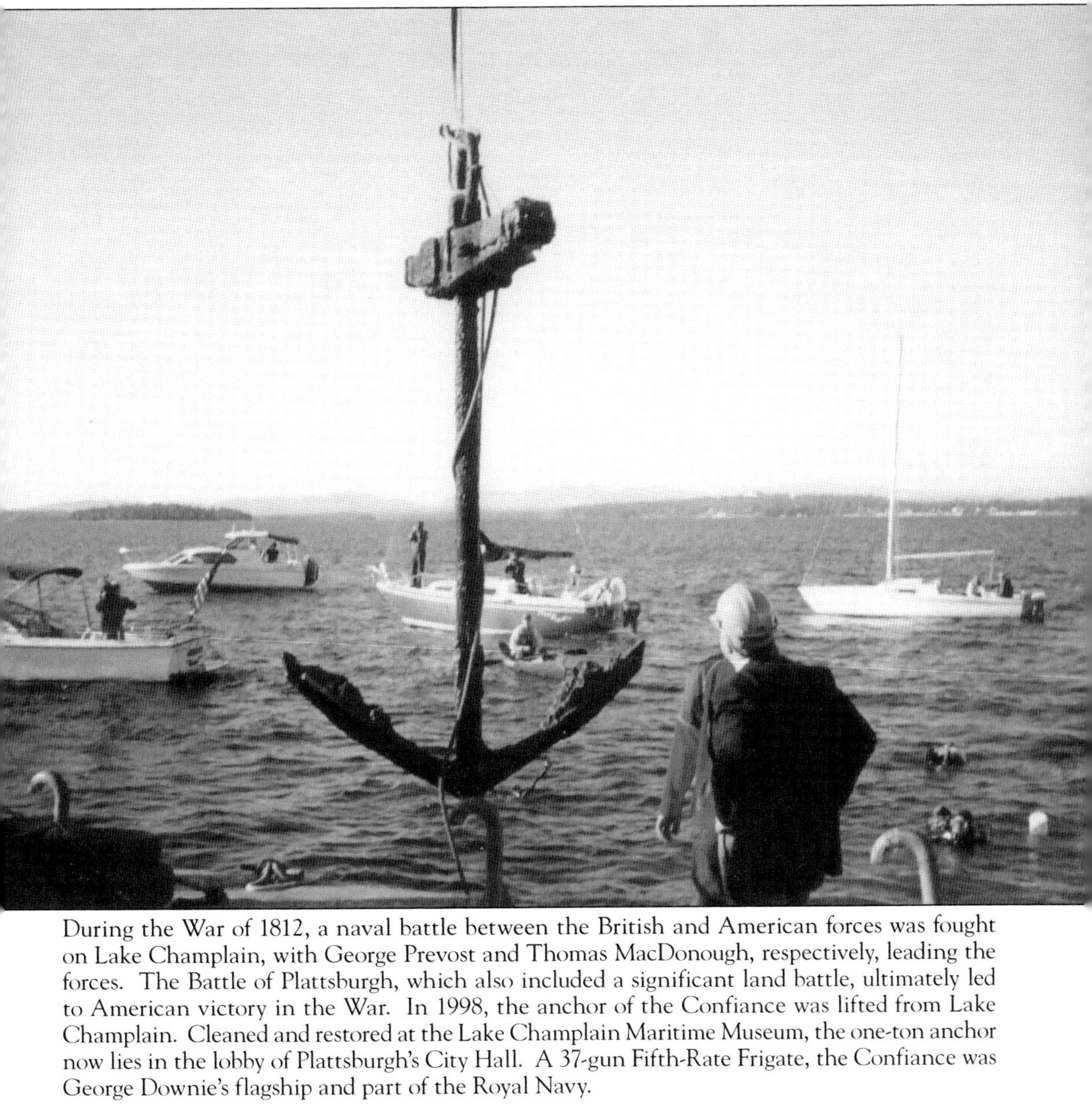

During the War of 1812, a naval battle between the British and American forces was fought on Lake Champlain, with George Prevost and Thomas MacDonough, respectively, leading the forces. The Battle of Plattsburgh, which also included a significant land battle, ultimately led to American victory in the War. In 1998, the anchor of the Confiance was lifted from Lake Champlain. Cleaned and restored at the Lake Champlain Maritime Museum, the one-ton anchor now lies in the lobby of Plattsburgh's City Hall. A 37-gun Fifth-Rate Frigate, the Confiance was George Downie's flagship and part of the Royal Navy.

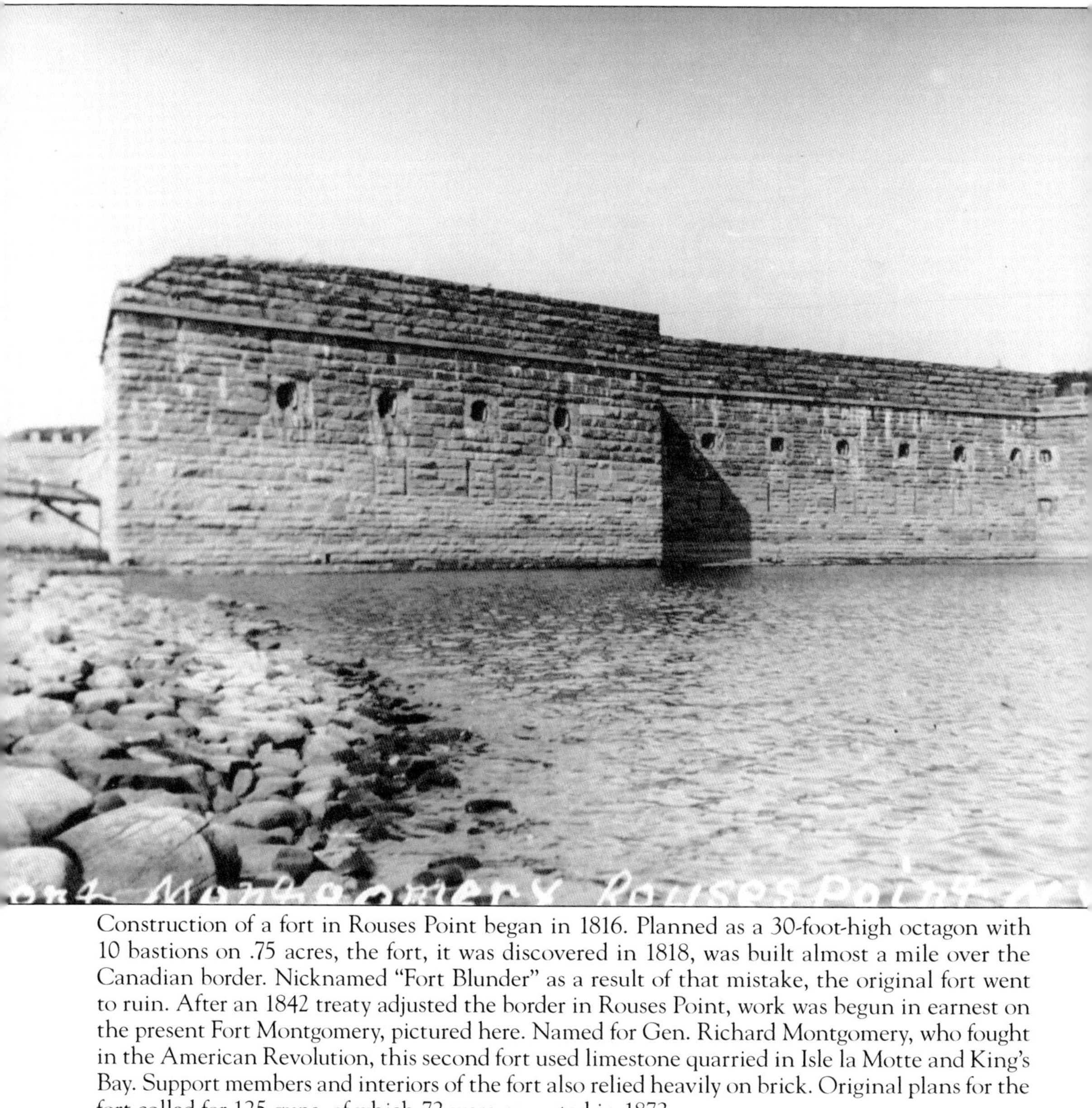

Construction of a fort in Rouses Point began in 1816. Planned as a 30-foot-high octagon with 10 bastions on .75 acres, the fort, it was discovered in 1818, was built almost a mile over the Canadian border. Nicknamed "Fort Blunder" as a result of that mistake, the original fort went to ruin. After an 1842 treaty adjusted the border in Rouses Point, work was begun in earnest on the present Fort Montgomery, pictured here. Named for Gen. Richard Montgomery, who fought in the American Revolution, this second fort used limestone quarried in Isle la Motte and King's Bay. Support members and interiors of the fort also relied heavily on brick. Original plans for the fort called for 125 guns, of which 72 were mounted in 1872.

Eight
LEISURE

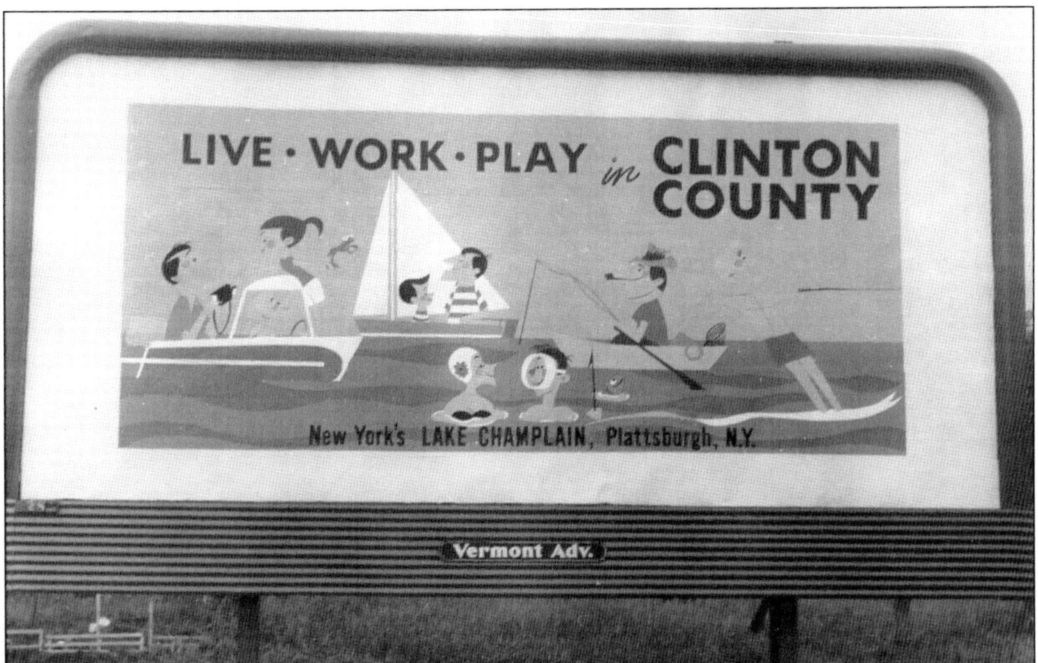

"Live, Work, Play in Clinton County." These words, featured on a mid-20th-century billboard, offer a vision of the northeastern-most county of New York State. Although the advertisement features Clinton County's water activities—fishing, boating, swimming, and water skiing—the county also enjoys a wide array of land activities, including hiking, automobile racing, snowshoeing, and skiing.

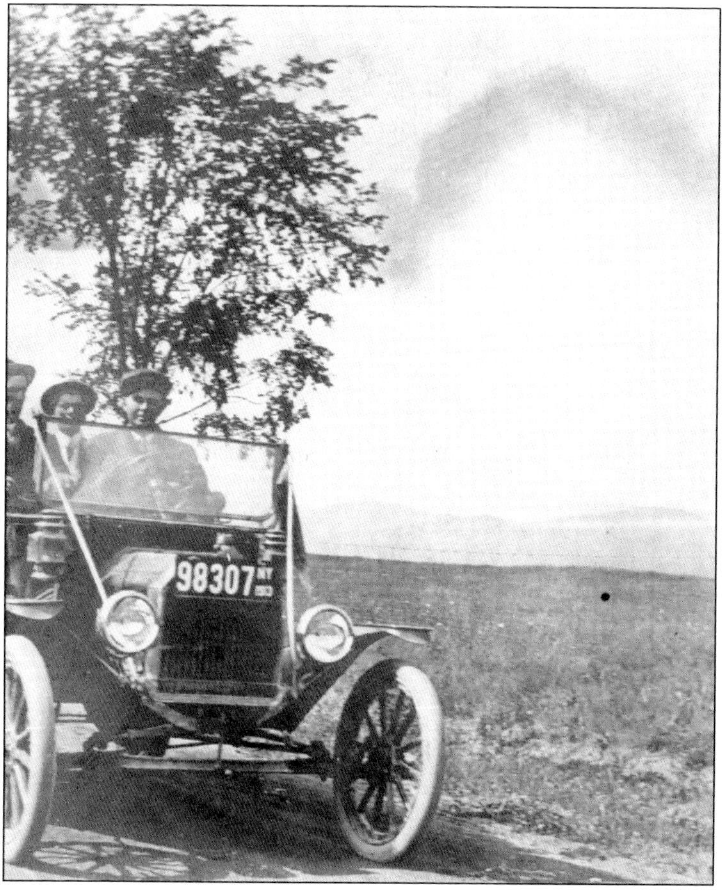

Travel became increasingly possible as county residents bought automobiles. This photograph shows a group traveling through the northern part of Clinton County in 1913. The mountains in the distance are the Green Mountains of Vermont.

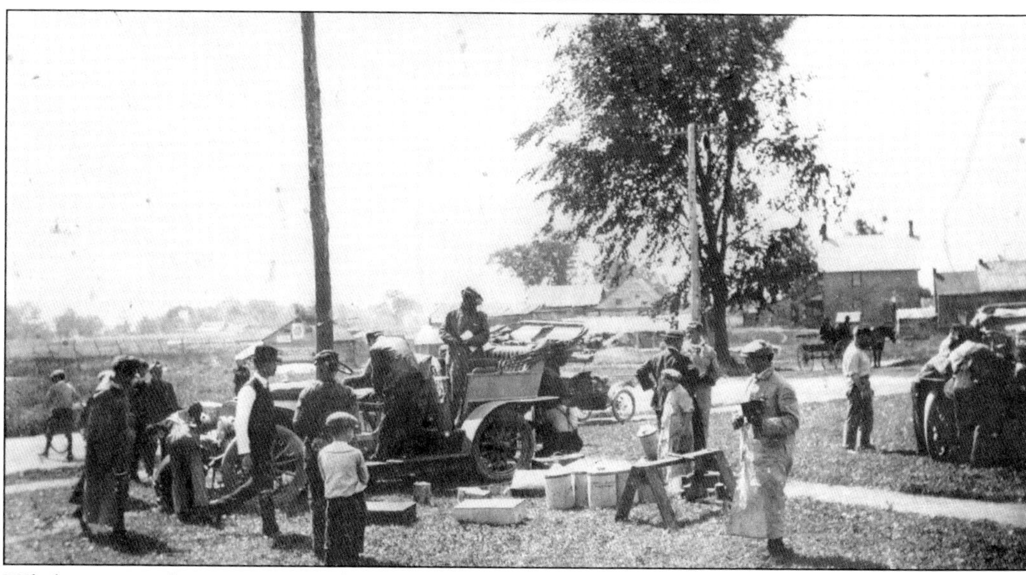

While car accidents can never be considered leisure activities, automobile traffic continued to increase throughout the 20th century in Clinton County. This photograph shows an accident in Chazy during the early years of car travel. Notice the horse-drawn wagon in the background.

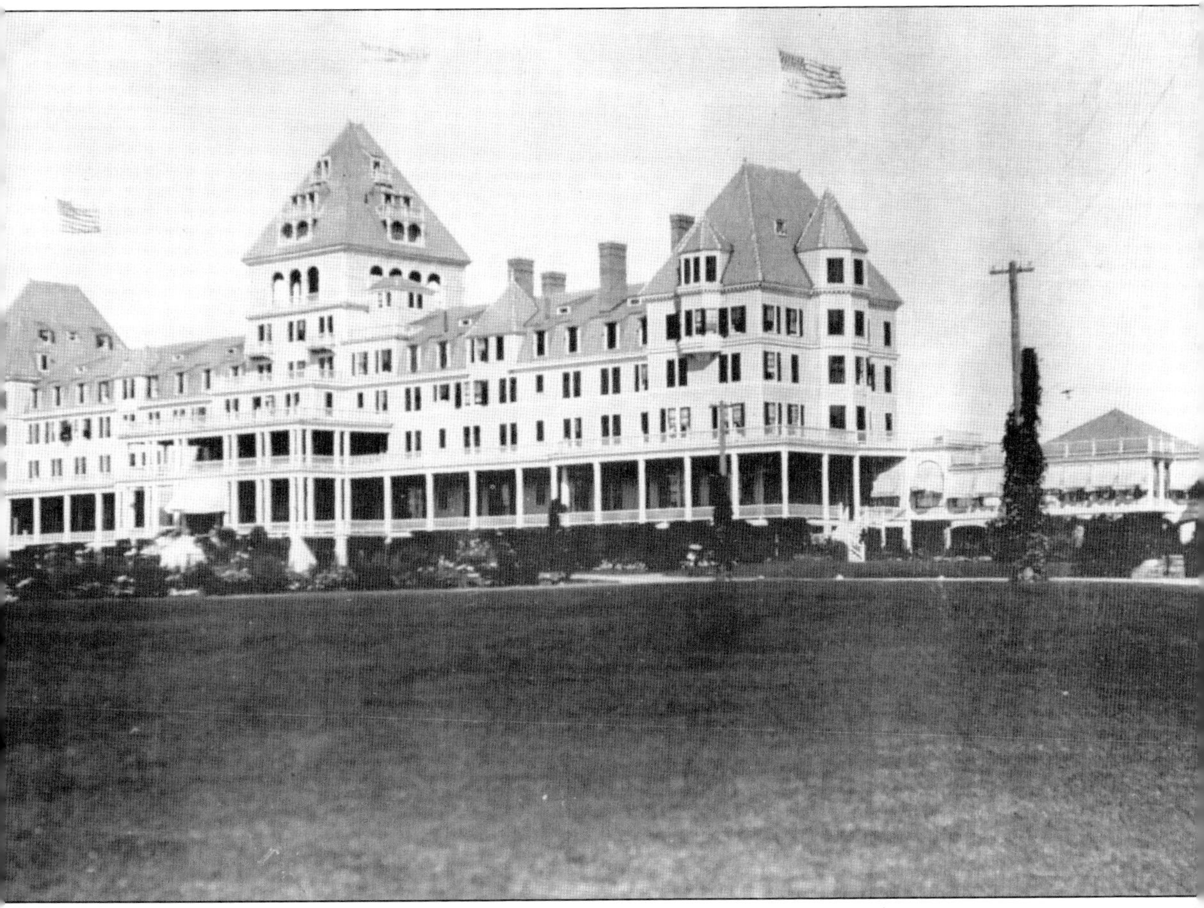

The Hotel Champlain opened in 1890. With its 500 rooms, the hotel offered guests a scenic view of Lake Champlain and the Green Mountains of Vermont. Owned by the Delaware and Hudson Railroad Company, the hotel attracted guests who rode a special train to Bluff Point and then proceeded by horse and carriage car to the hotel, perched atop a steep hill. Before its closure in 1951, the hotel boasted guests like presidents William McKinley, William Howard Taft, Theodore Roosevelt, Franklin Delano Roosevelt, and Warren Harding. Other notables included George Herman "Babe" Ruth, several New York State governors, and members of the British aristocracy. The hotel building was converted to Bellarmine College (a Jesuit institution), which left in 1967. Clinton Community College began operating on the site in 1969.

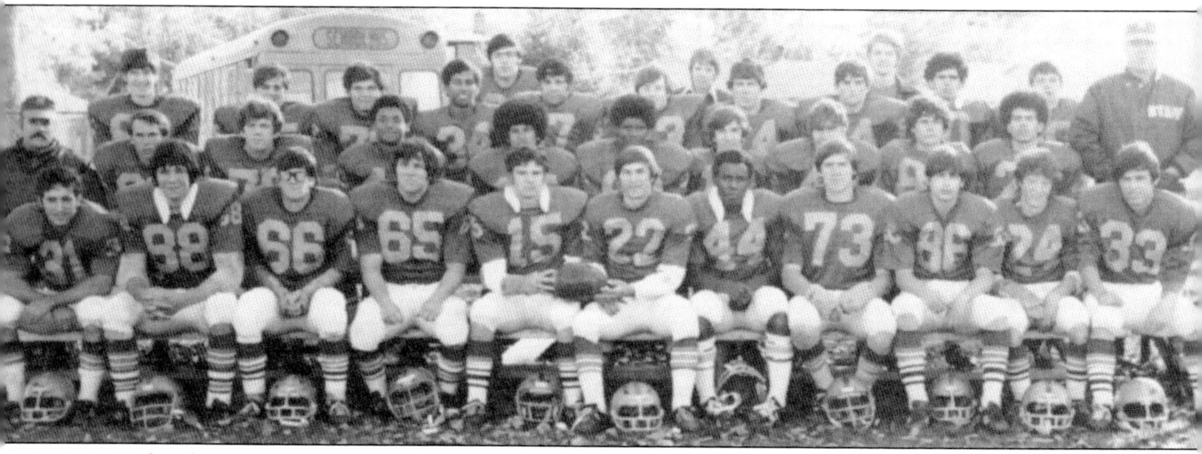

High school sports are among Clinton County's most popular and enduring pastimes. This 1975 photograph shows the Mount Assumption Institute football team. From left to right are (first row) A. Esposito, R. Boissy, K. Polhemus, B. Anderson, M. Bourdeau, M. Frechette, C. Piquant, W. Schaber, C. Gagnier, K. Everleth, and P. Drollette; (second row) James King (assistant), P. Huru, P. Polhemus, S. Young, R. Hernandez, A. Conwell, J. Lesage, J. Landry, T. Church, M. Dume, Robert Allen (head coach); (third row) D. Puckett, J. Breen, K. Hassam, J. Puello, S. Keaty, R. Miller, B. Frechette, V. Jameson (manager), K. Rock, D. Richardson, W. Gould (manager), G. Suddaby, and H. Savoy.

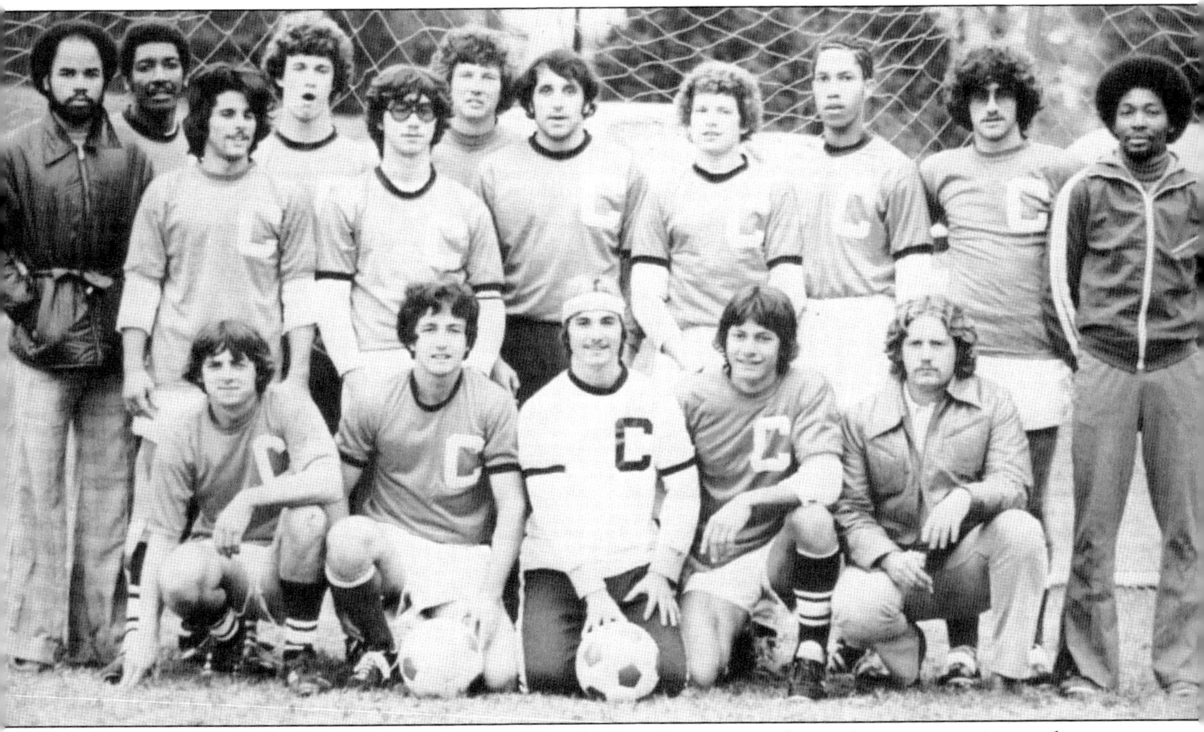

College sports, like high school athletics, offer Clinton County residents the opportunity to cheer for the hometown team. This 1978 photograph shows the Clinton Community College soccer team. From left to right are (first row) Jerry Irish, Bob Wood, Michael Gibson, Sam Dunnivant, and Vince McGoe (score-keeper); (second row) ? Lionel, Jean Claude Bernadette, Ralph Colicchio, Mitchell Case, Bob Bridge, Kevin Bielat, Randy Brown, David Timmons, Eddy Bartinez, Bruce Banker, and ? Yvon. Not pictured with this group are Alan Mowery, Robert Mowery, Frank McKenna, Peter Wasilawski, and Jim Lafauve.

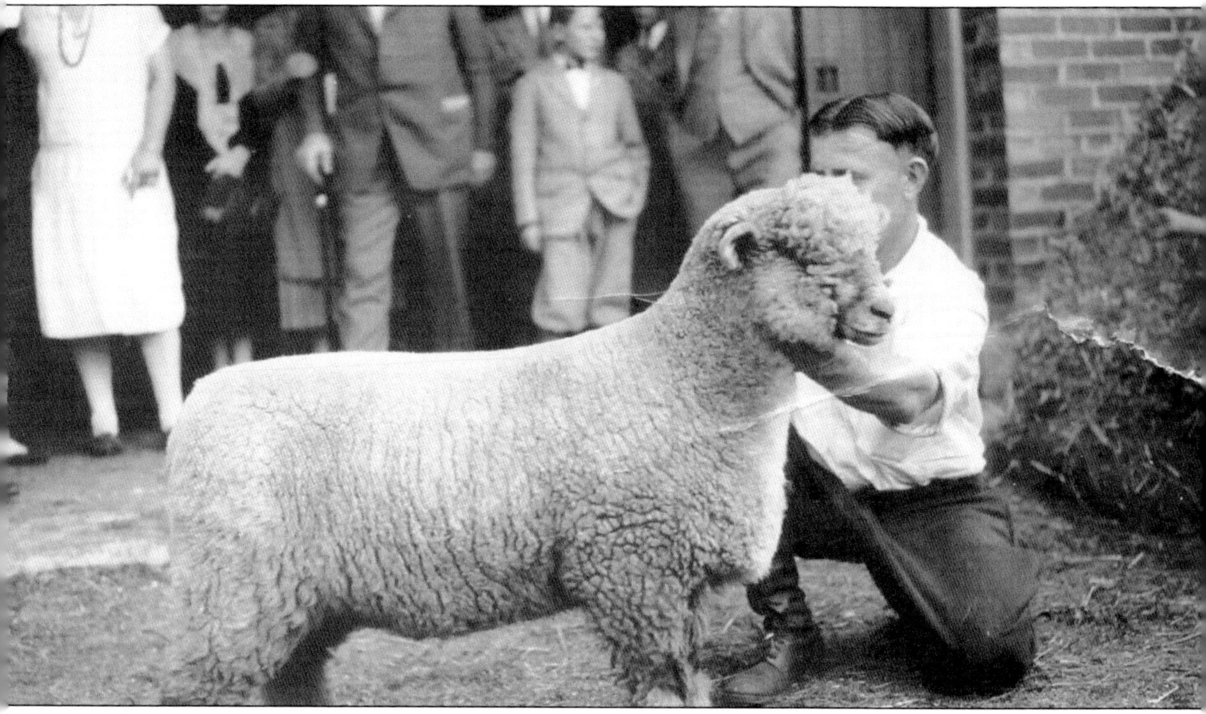

Showing animals at local, state, and national fairs is another longtime Clinton County activity. During the competition shown here, Marshall Cheeseman kneels with a ewe that won first place. The Agricultural Society, which had been around in one form or another since 1819, sponsored an annual fair beginning in 1860. Held on what is now Sanborn Avenue, the fair included a racetrack. After the Society was reorganized in 1886, the fair moved to Boynton Avenue, at the north end of Oak Street. In addition to showing animals, the fair included prizes for fruits and vegetables, homemade baked goods, and other foods. Horse racing, car racing, and amusement park rides were added over the years. Eventually the fair moved to its present location on Route 3.

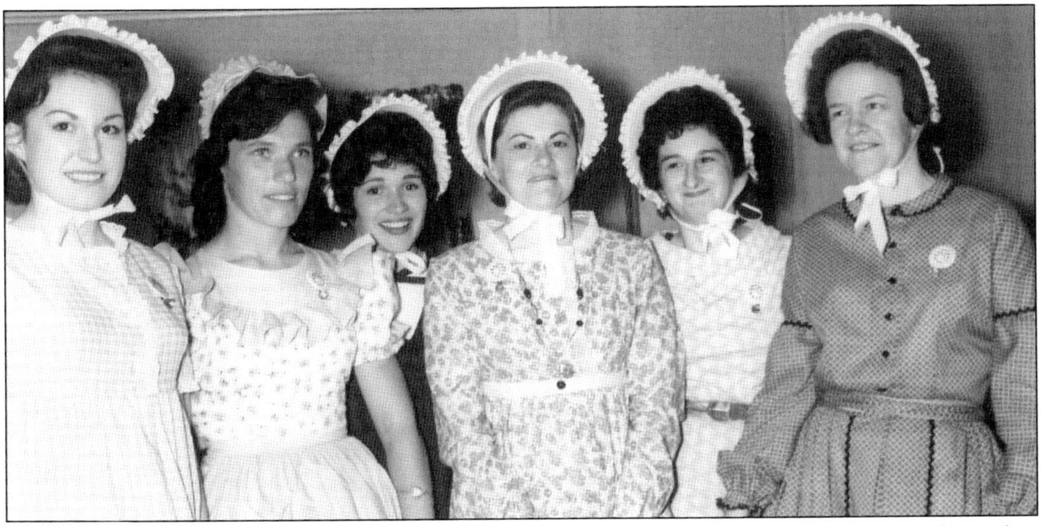

Known as the Celebration Belles, these women of the Ladies Auxiliary of Fuzzy Foxes dressed to celebrate the 150th anniversary of the Battle of Plattsburgh. During April 1964, they began to make old-fashioned clothes, which they then used to travel around the city to collect donations. In addition, the women spoke to local societies, researched the Battle of Plattsburgh, and agreed to fine members "caught downtown without their bonnets and Belle dresses."

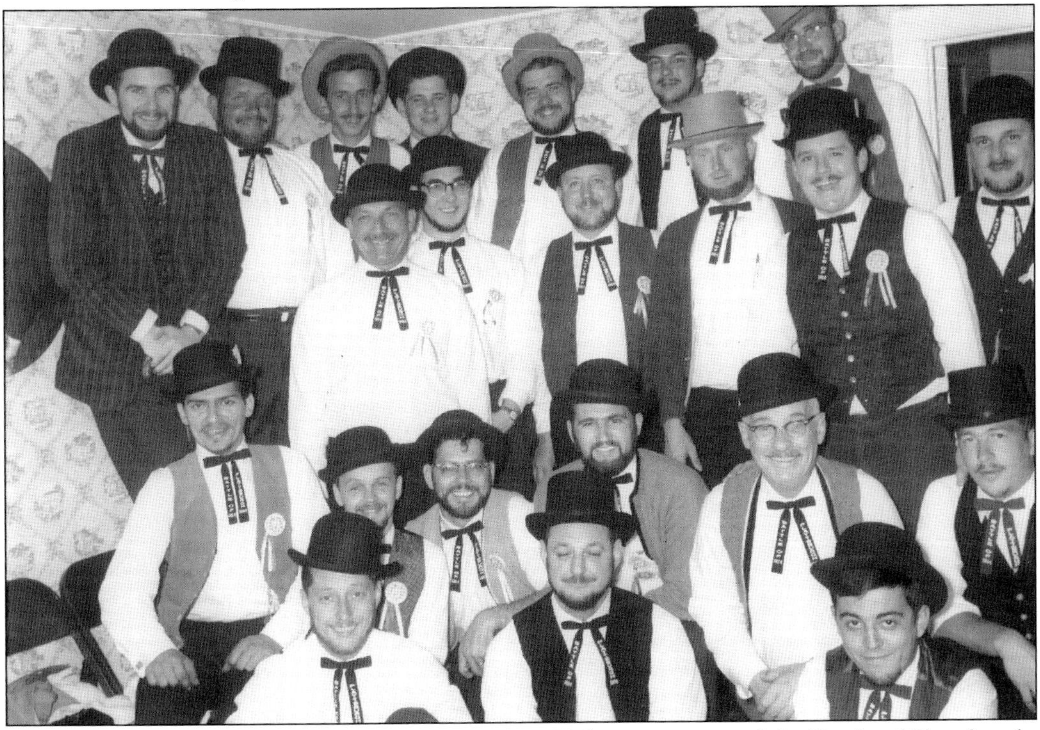

The Fuzzy Foxes each grew beards to support the 150th anniversary of the Battle of Plattsburgh. These men, affiliated with the Celebration Belles, organized a Battle of the Bands dance at St. John's Academy and participated in a charity baseball game at Our Lady of Victory. That game, known as the "battle of the beards," was designed to promote the Battle of Plattsburgh celebration and to draw attention to the various local chapters of the Brothers of the Brush.

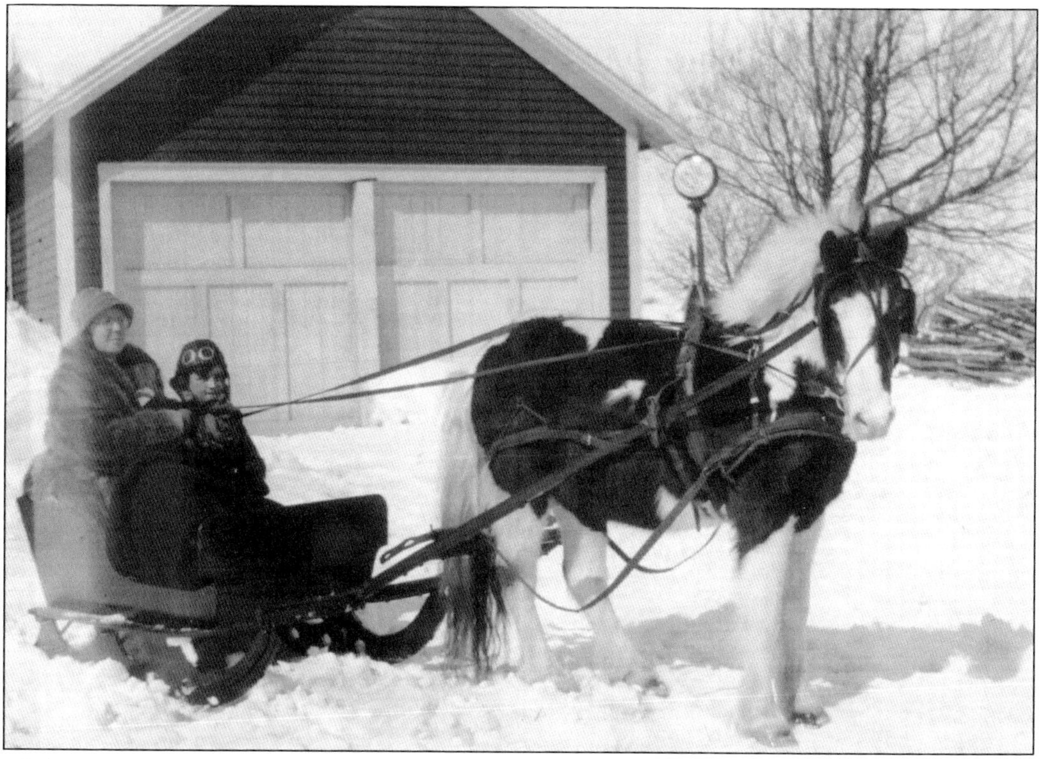

With long winters a norm in Clinton County, children and adults like Maddie and Winford Cheeseman rode in a horse-drawn sled. Other winter activities include sledding, building forts and snowmen, and waging snowball fights.

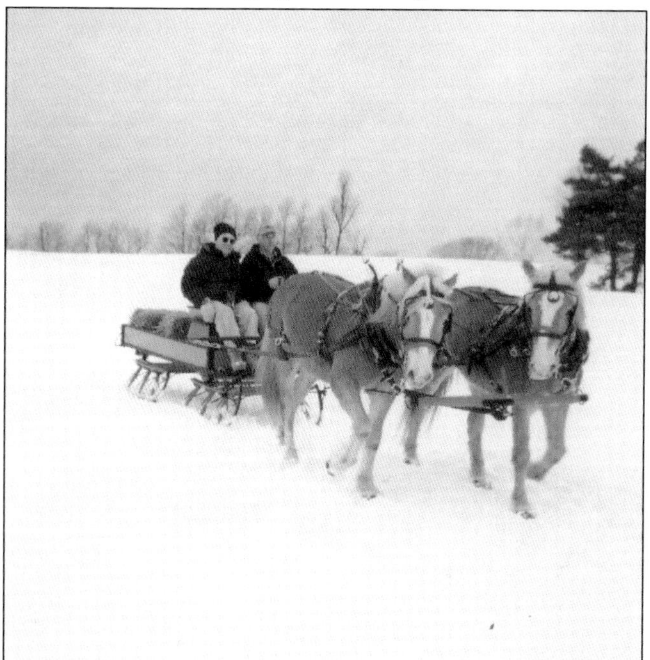

Long winters give rise to a variety of snow- and ice-related activities. Besides sculpture contests—generally held at Plattsburgh State University—county residents snowshoe, ski, snowmobile, and sled. They also go for winter sleigh rides, as Leeward Babbie and his companion are doing in this photograph. Babbie, the longtime owner of a farm in Peru, recently opened a museum dedicated to rural and farm life.

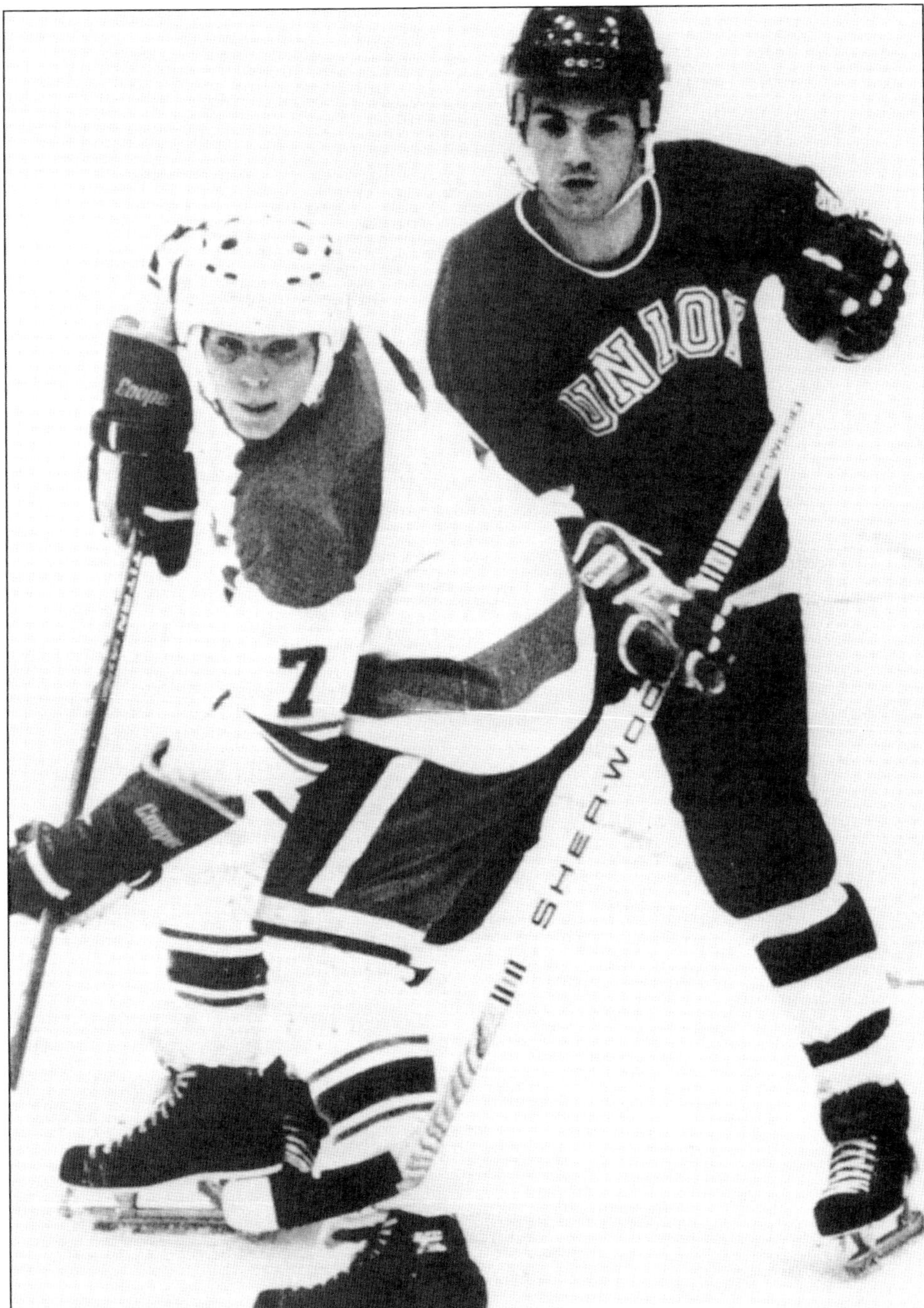

Though it did not come to Plattsburgh State University until the field house was built to host the 1971 World University Games (FISU), hockey has reigned as a leading pastime throughout the county, with both the men's and women's teams skating to national championships more than once. The 1981 creation of Burghy, the cardinal mascot, brought a spirit of fun to the games, which are widely attended by students, faculty, and community members. The ice arena in the field house was named in honor of Sen. Ronald Stafford, who strongly supported Plattsburgh State and the State University of New York system.

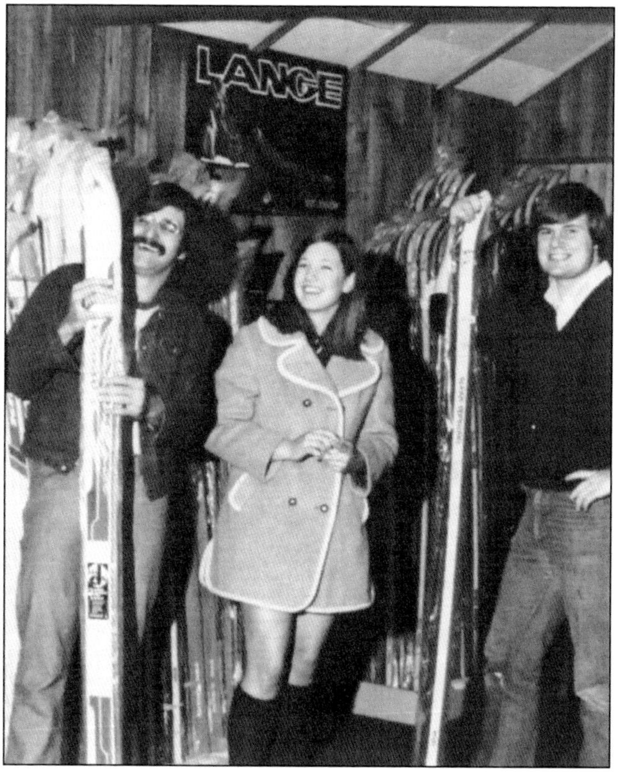

Miller's Ski Shop in Morrisonville, shown here in the late 1970s, was one of many county businesses that capitalized on the winter weather. Cross-country skiing and snowshoeing, which can occur throughout the county, have long been popular activities. Downhill skiing is popular as well, though the best skiing locations are outside of the county.

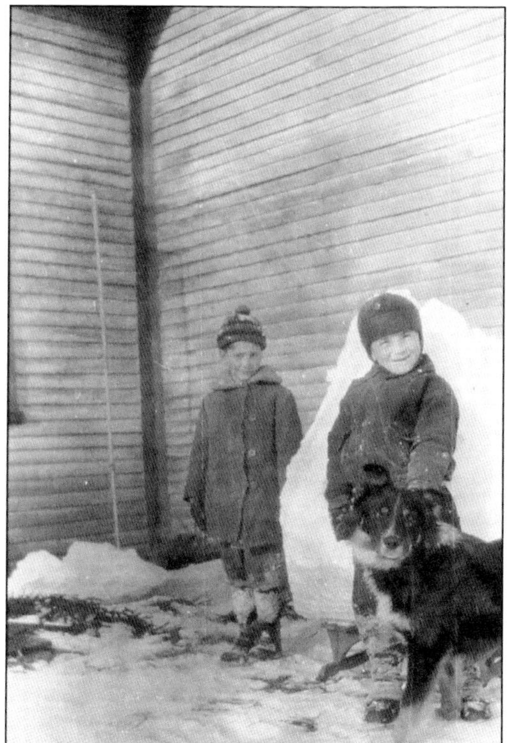

Winter play involves many layers of clothes. Here two boys—including Winford Cheeseman on the right—and a dog play in the snow near Cheeseman's Ellenburg home. Both boys wear thick winter jackets, hats, mittens, and leggings as protection against the cold, windy weather.

Children on Clinton County's farms have long raised animals through the 4-H club, Future Farmers of America, and other groups. Early 20th-century movements promoted the hands-on learning that became the trademark of the 4-H, which officially started with the 1914 creation of the Cooperative Extension Service at the USDA. Winford Cheeseman, shown here with two of his sheep, definitely participated in this organization.

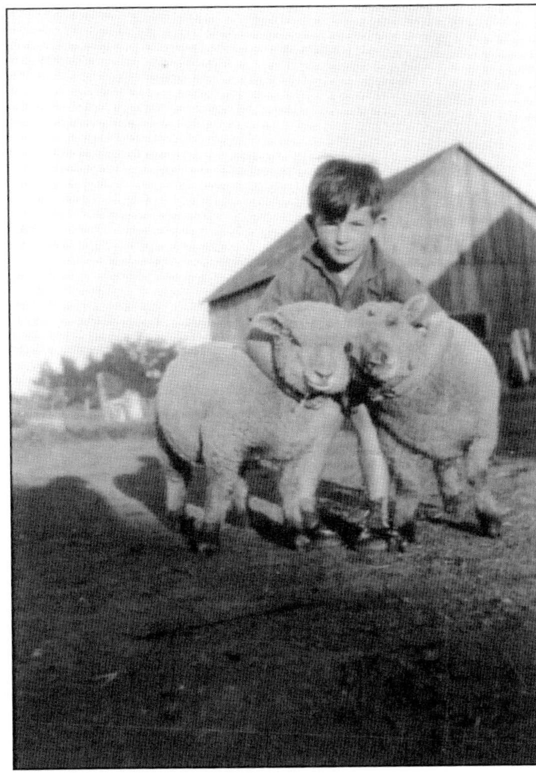

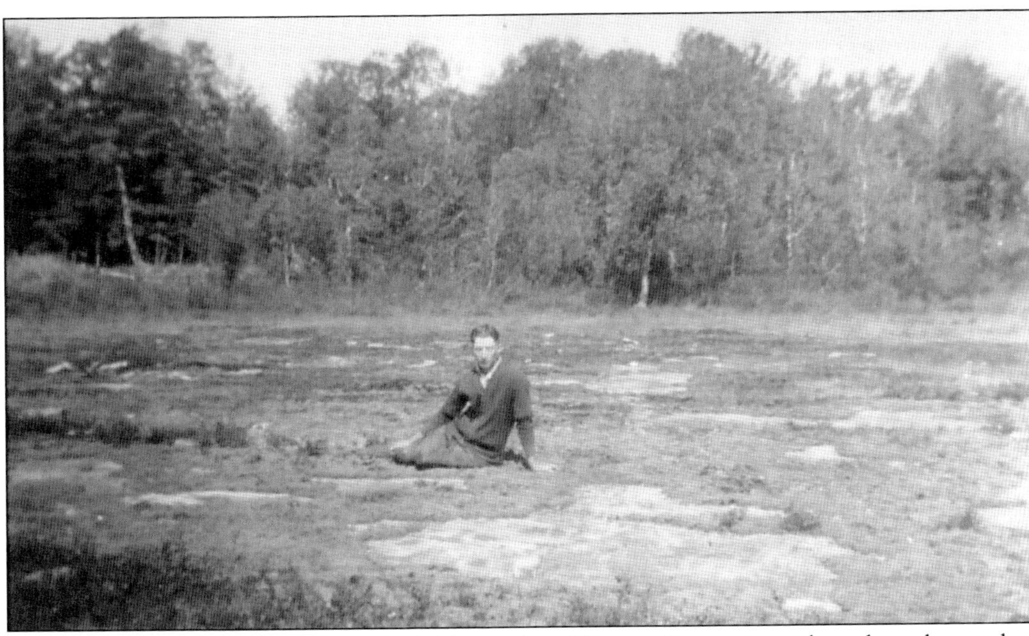

Situated just north of the Adirondack Mountains, Clinton County's residents have long taken to the woods to hike, as Arthur Watson did in this 1931 photograph. In 1922, the Adirondack Mountain Club (ADK) formed. Dedicated to protecting and responsibly using the land and waters of the Adirondack Park, the organization includes some 35,000 members. The Adirondack Park, which encompasses 6.1 million acres, includes the southern portions of Clinton County.

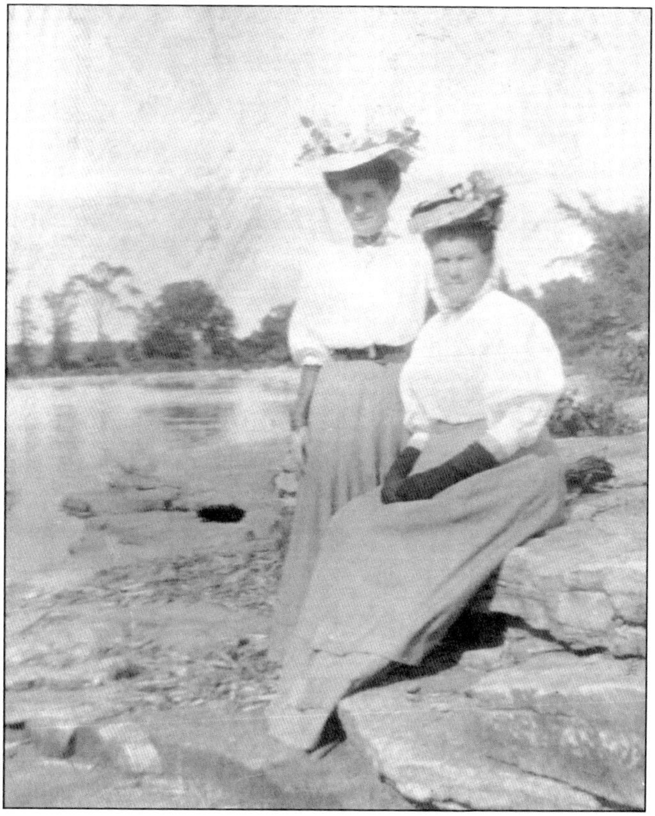

Leisure activities on Lake Champlain were not limited to fishing, boating, and swimming. Many Clinton County residents simply walked along the shores, taking time to enjoy the beauty of the shoreline and the Green Mountains in the distance. Others packed picnics and used the rocks along the shore as seats. In the most popular spots, beaches and parks were developed.

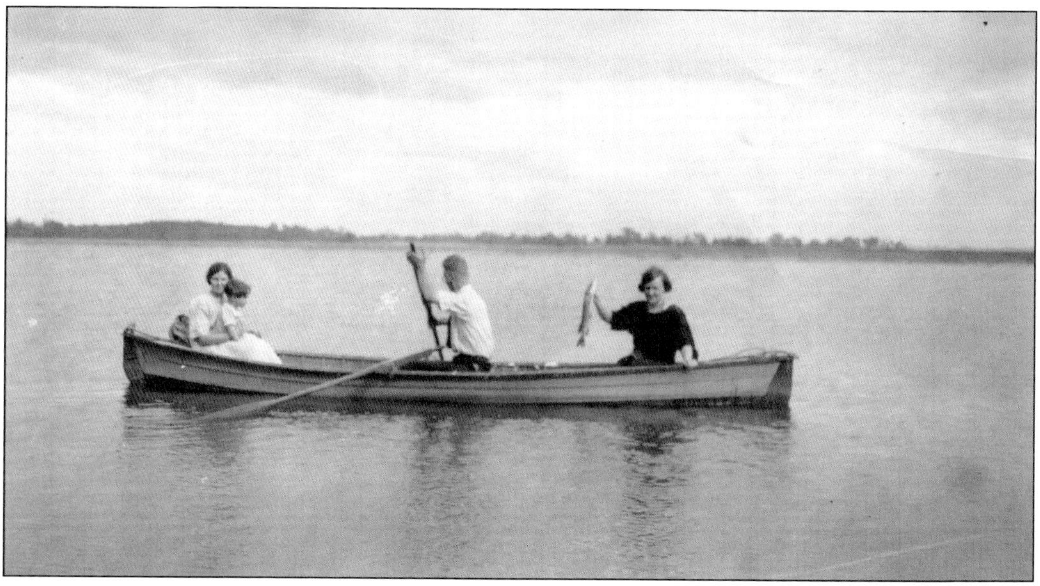

Ethel Spencer holds her catch while Don Spencer paddles the boat and Maddie Cheeseman sits with Lucy Spencer. Fishing on Chazy Lake (shown here), Lake Champlain, and Clinton County's various rivers and ponds is popular in the region. Various fishing competitions, including the FLW Tour and Bassmasters Elite, are held annually on Lake Champlain. Other, more local fishing derbies are annual events as well.

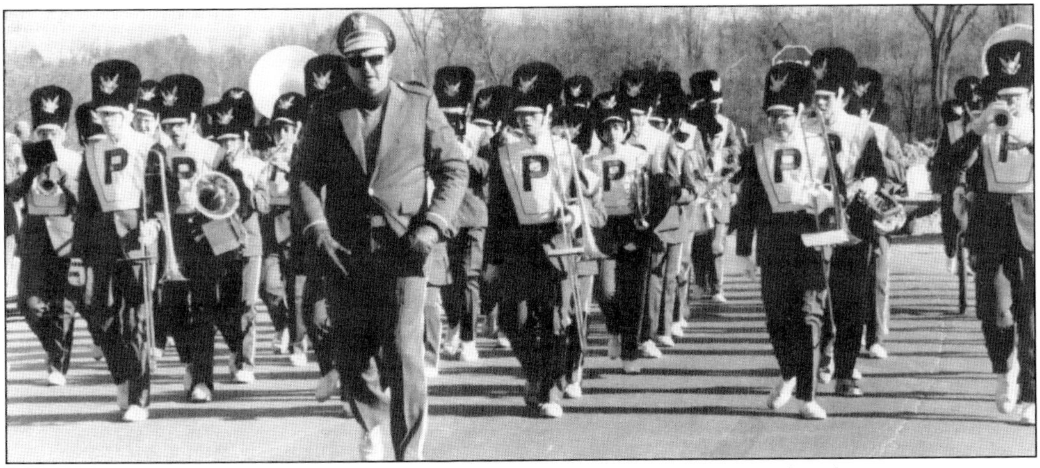

Local groups offered Clinton County's musicians many opportunities to play their instruments or to sing. This photograph shows the 1974 Peru Central School marching band, led by music teacher Lynn Wilke, practicing. Other groups at Peru included the school orchestra, concert band, and chorus. Throughout the county, bands and choral groups were attached to high schools and colleges. In addition, community orchestras and bands have periodically existed in Clinton County.

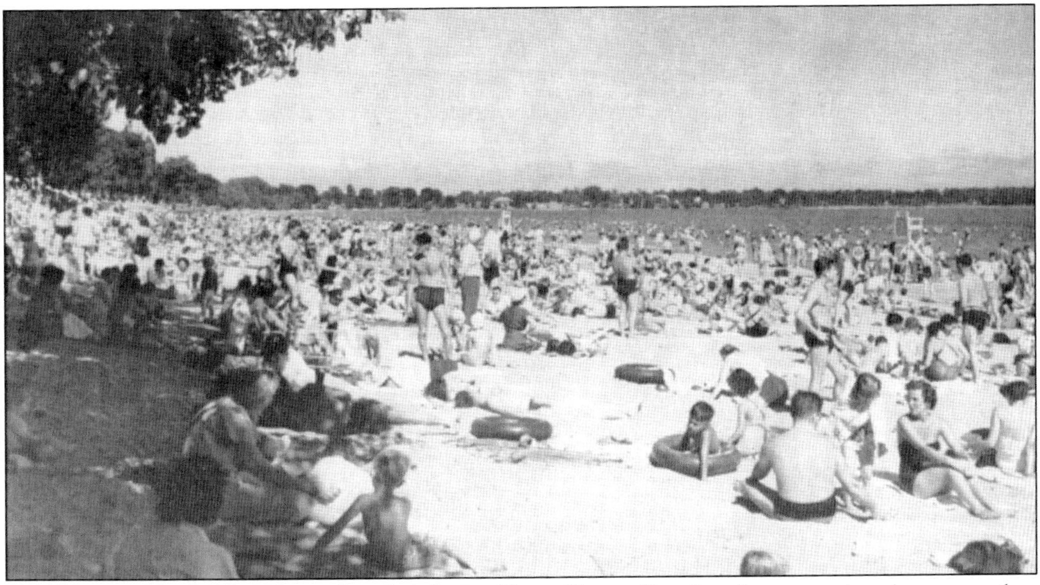

Shown in 1961, the beach at Plattsburgh Air Force Base offered a place to enjoy the sun and to swim under the observation of a lifeguard. Other supervised beaches existed at Cumberland Head, Point au Roche, and Au Sable Point.

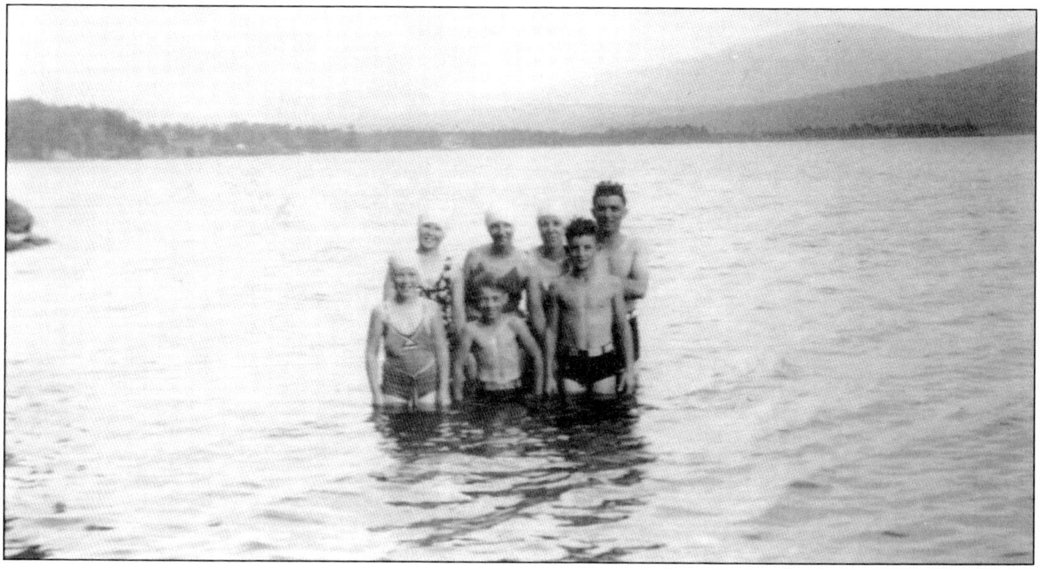

Winford Cheeseman (first row, far right) stands with an unidentified group in the waters of Chazy Lake. Presumably an image of the visitors' trip to the region—the photograph was developed in LaCrosse, Wisconsin, and sent back to the Cheeseman family in Ellenburg—this picture shows the importance of tourism to Clinton County's economy. Since 1998, Canadian tourism alone has accounted for several million dollars of annual revenue in Clinton County.

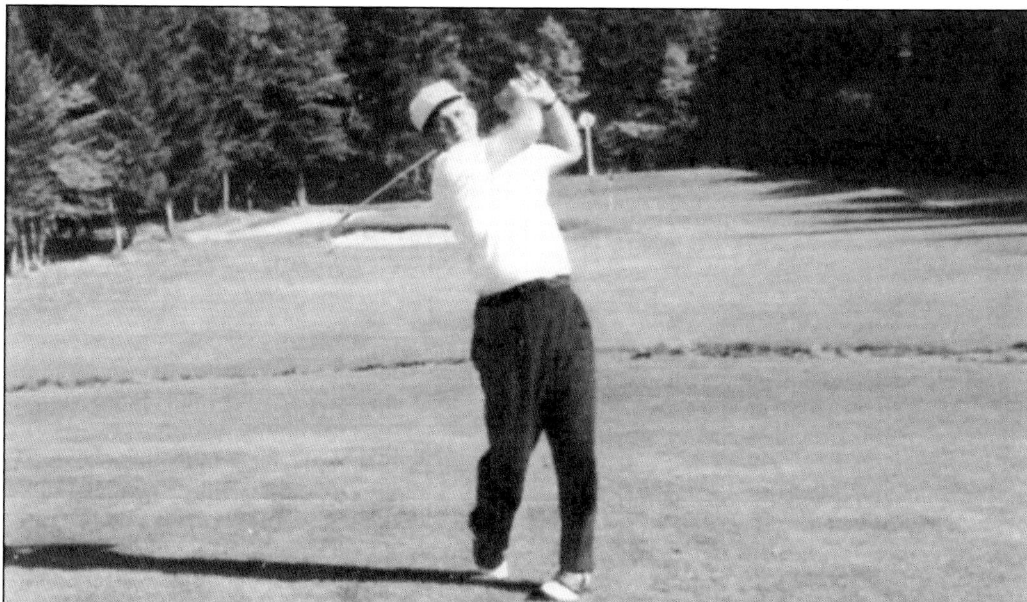

Clinton County is home to several golf courses. The most famous of these is the Bluff-Point Golf Club, which was established in 1870. The third oldest golf course in North America, Bluff Point attracted many Hotel Champlain guests. Still in operation, the course is currently under development; plans indicate that several green-side condominiums will be built along the course. Other golf courses in the county include the Adirondack Golf and Country Club, the Barracks Golf Course, and the North Country Golf Club. This photograph shows John J. Doctor, a member of the Class "A" PGA tour, on the Bluff Point course.

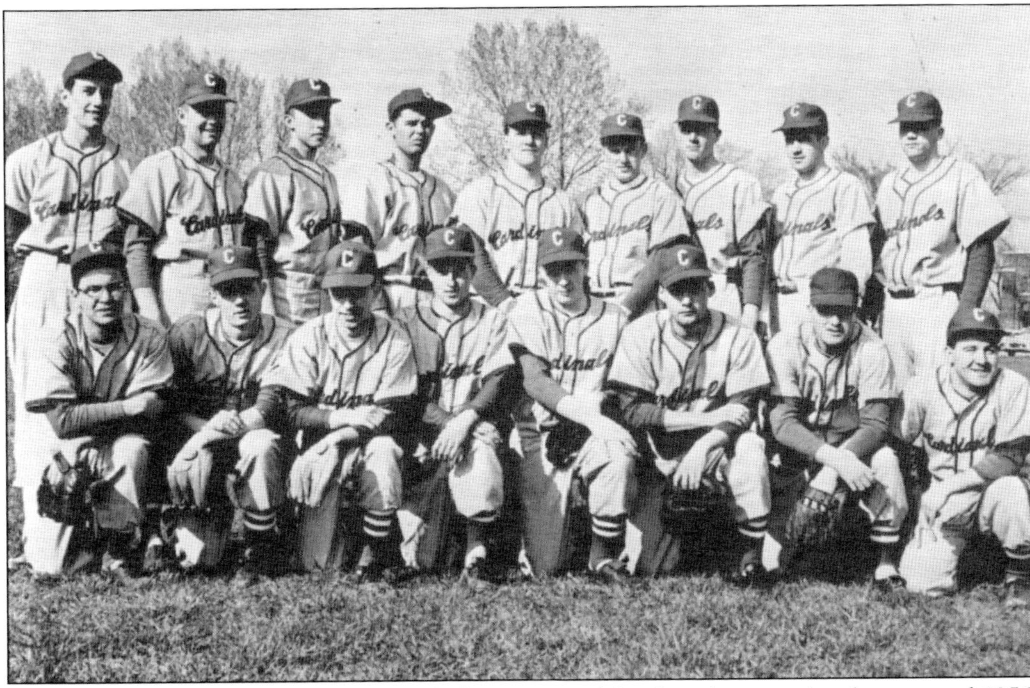

The Plattsburgh State University baseball team posed for this photograph taken around 1956. Pictured are (first row) R. Marcotte, J. Humistron, C. Jabaut, T. Cummings, E. Arthur, W. Marcotte, J. Donnely, and D. Gregoire; (second row) G. Burnell, A. Momot, J. Bird, N. Yakey, J. Ryan, R. McCormick, J. Luke, D. Shambo, and R. Merrill. From 1976 to 2001, baseball was not played at the college. However, in 2002, varsity baseball returned to Plattsburgh State.

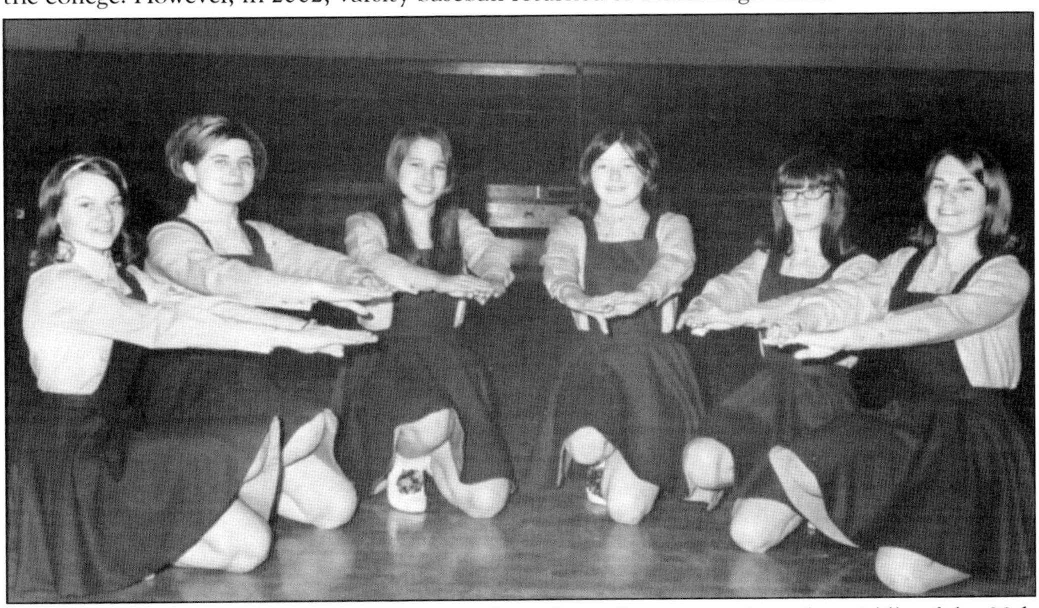

Cheerleading has accompanied team sports throughout the county since the middle of the 20th century. This 1969 photograph shows, from left to right, Mary Trombley (captain), Julie Mooney, Rose Babbie, Pam Staves, Patti Brown (cocaptain), and Pinky Bushy, the Our Lady of Victory Academy cheerleaders.

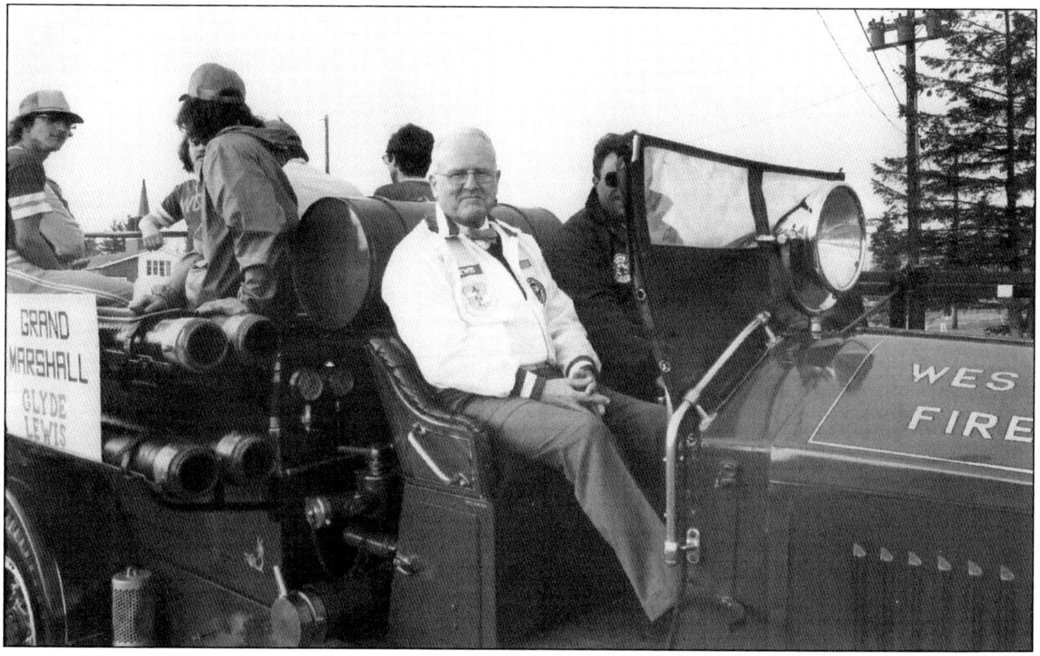

One of 1984's Firemen's Field Day parades featured Clyde Lewis as grand marshal. Firemen's Field Days, held throughout the county, were designed to raise money and awareness for local rescue squads. Timed to occur throughout the summer and fall, the Firemen's Field Days included games, food, concerts, and dances.

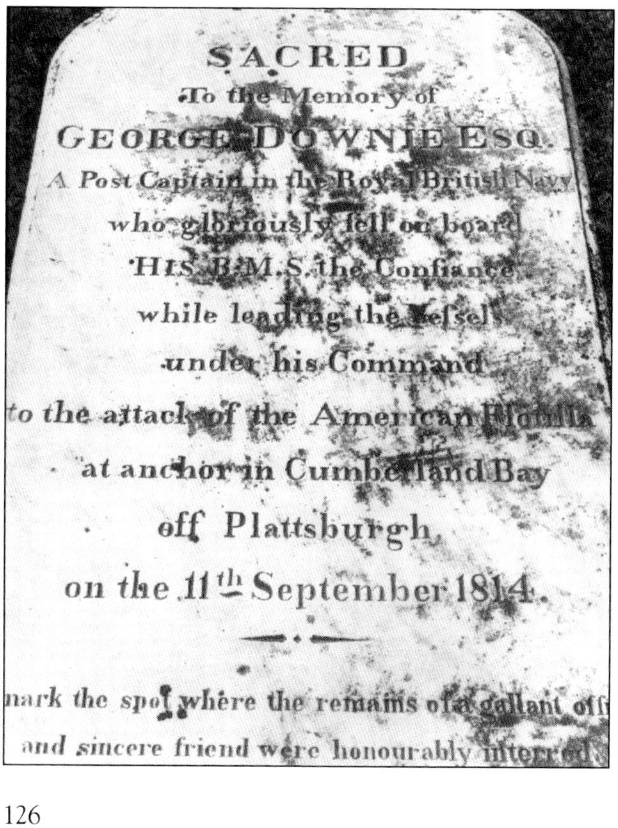

Capt. George Downie, commander of the British frigate *Confiance*, died during the Battle of Plattsburgh. He, along with all of the fallen American and British soldiers of that battle, are remembered every year during the Battle of Plattsburgh commemorations. In addition to memorial services, other activities held the week of September 11th include parades, concerts, reenactments, and dances.

Bibliography

Allan, Helen W., Carol G. Bedore, Allan S. Everest, and Mary G. Leggett. *Clinton County: A Pictorial History*. Norfolk; Virginia Beach, VA: The Donning Company, 1988.

Everest, Allan S. *Briefly Told: Plattsburgh, New York, 1784–1984*. Plattsburgh, NY: Clinton County Historical Association, 1984.

Fire departments of Clinton County and the Clinton County Historical Association. *FIRE! The History of Firefighting in Clinton County*. Plattsburgh, NY: Clinton County Historical Association, 1991.

Frost, Richard B. *Plattsburgh, New York: A City's First Century*. Norfolk; Virginia Beach, VA: The Donning Company, 2002.

Hill, Henry Rayland. *The Champlain Tercentenary: Report of the New York Lake Champlain Tercentenary Commission*. Albany, NY: J. B. Lyon, 1911.

Hogue, Roswell A. *Centennial, 1853–1953: St. Peter's Roman Catholic Church, Plattsburgh, N.Y.* Plattsburgh, NY: St. Peter's Church, 1953.

Hurd, Duane Hamilton. *History of Clinton & Franklin Counties, New York*. Reprint, Plattsburgh, NY: County American Revolution Bicentennial Commission, 1978.

Kellogg, David S. *A Doctor at All Hours: The Private Journal of a Small-Town Doctor's Varied Life 1886–1909*. Edited by Allan S. Everest. Brattleboro, VT: The Stephen Greene Press, 1970.

Skopp, Douglas R. *Bright With Promise: From the Normal and Training School to SUNY Plattsburgh, 1889–1989, A Pictorial History*. Norfolk; Virginia Beach, VA: The Donning Company, 1989.

State University of New York. Office of University Affairs and Development. *Sixty-four Campuses: The State University of New York to 1985*. Albany, NY: State University of New York, 1985.

Winans, Maggie, ed. *Clinton County: I Remember When*. Elizabethtown, NY: Denton Publications, 1983.